and he assisted my climb to engage with the group. It was a simple gesture of decency that instantly signified the human connection that Jonathan, the student protest leader, and I, the university president, had forged as we worked to define key social justice commitments to end a multi-day encampment on our Saint Louis campus. *With My People* reflects the care I've witnessed from him and documents his path to social activist and protest leader, and the lessons he learned along the way."

—**Fred P. Pestello**, PhD, president, Saint Louis University

"This book is a powerful, unfiltered account of the Ferguson Uprising, told by someone who lived it. Every page captures the raw truth of our resistance—our unity, our struggle, and our unwavering demand for justice. If you want to understand what really happened, read this."

—**Malik Rhasaan**, founder of Occupy the Hood

Praise for With My People

"This book presents a beautiful first-person perspective on pivotal moments of change in the racial history of Saint Louis and Saint Louis University, interweaving the personal and political while explaining both the trees and the forest of complex social justice issues. Jonathan Pulphus is a gifted writer: He places the reader in the middle of events, while providing insight that fosters understanding about what is happening all around. His is a thoughtful, caring voice that speaks to the time and provides mentorship and love to future activists."

—**Scott Berman**, PhD, associate professor of philosophy and academic program coordinator for the Prison Education Program at Saint Louis University; and **Ilene Berman**, MFA, sculptor and assistant professor in the Visual and Performing Arts Department of Saint Louis University

"This provocative book is a powerful personal narrative bridging grassroots activism and serious academic inquiries. Drawing on lived experience as a student organizer during the Ferguson Uprising, Pulphus offers unflinching assessments of systemic white racism, Black community resistance, and meaningful collective action. He uses poignant storytelling, incisive racism analysis, and calls to action challenging readers to rethink the intersections of education, justice, and activism. A vital contribution to the Black freedom-struggles literature and a testament to the enduring power of youth-led change movements."

—**Dr. Joe Feagin**, University Distinguished Professor emeritus at Texas A&M University, and author of dozens of books, including *Racist America: Roots, Current Realities, and Future Reparations, 5th ed.*

"A lot has been written about Ferguson, but far too few words have come from the courageous people who were actually there on the streets every night. Forging a new path in the tradition of student-activists who came before him, Jonathan Pulphus was there—facing down militarized police, reactionary politicians, and movement contradictions. It's refreshing to finally read and hear the voice of a Ferguson activist, who was A-1 from day one!"

—**Dr. Jonathan Fenderson** and **Dr. Bukky Gbadegesin**, Black Studies scholars in Saint Louis

"Jonathan Pulphus's *With My People* is an insightful, incisive, and moving examination of the Ferguson Uprising and its broader implications. It recounts the events of late summer and fall 2014, but also pushes beyond them by interrogating the complexities of social movements, the complicity of white institutions, and the challenges of formal and informal education in an unjust and imperfect world. Part memoir, part meditation, part call to action, *With My People* is brimming with insights and lessons garnered from the author's participation in those events, and his reflections—now a decade later—on their lessons and meanings."

—**Dr. Colin Gordon**, professor of history, University of Iowa, and author of *Mapping Decline*, *Citizen Brown*, and *Patchwork Apartheid*

"Part war memoir, part movement history, part organizing handbook, *With My People* is an insider's account of the crucial role of Tribe X in the fight for justice in Ferguson and beyond. Jonathan Pulphus writes with warmth, wit, love, and humility and yet delivers a wake-up punch to anyone who may have underestimated the significance of the moment and the movement. Tribe X isn't just an organization. It is a generation born of struggle and committed to changing this world. A decade later and Jonathan and his people are still at it."

—**Robin D. G. Kelley**, author of *Freedom Dreams: The Black Radical Imagination*

"Jonathan Pulphus was already on a justice-seeking trajectory before the Ferguson Uprising. In fact, that would be the very arc that planted him on West Florissant Avenue. He was not a youthful participant wearing rose-colored glasses. JP deeply understood then as he understands now, and that is "getting wins for the local Black community" goes far beyond militant chants. *With My People* is a must read for those interested in hearing the next generation's views on the struggle for human liberation."

—**Jamala Rogers**, long time community organizer, political strategist, and author of *Ferguson is America: Roots of Rebellion*

"As I approached the protesters, social justice activist Jonathan Pulphus saw me struggle to begin ascending the amphitheater. He sprang from the upper steps and moved down to me. His extended hand met mine,

WITH MY PEOPLE

WITH MY PEOPLE

LIFE, JUSTICE, AND ACTIVISM BEYOND THE UNIVERSITY

JONATHAN PULPHUS

FOREWORDS BY DR. STEFAN M. BRADLEY AND REV. OSAGYEFO SEKOU

BROADLEAF BOOKS
Minneapolis

WITH MY PEOPLE

Life, Justice, and Activism Beyond the University

Copyright © 2025 Jonathan Pulphus. Published by Broadleaf Books. All rights reserved. Except for brief quotations in critical articles or reviews, no part of this book may be reproduced in any manner without prior written permission from the publisher. Email copyright@broadleafbooks.com or write to Permissions, Broadleaf Books, PO Box 1209, Minneapolis, MN 55440–1209.

30 29 28 27 26 25 1 2 3 4 5 6 7 8 9

Library of Congress Control Number: 2025930371 (print)

Cover photograph by Ahshea1 Media on pexels

Cover design: Broadleaf Books

Print ISBN: 979-8-8898-3562-2

eBook ISBN: 979-8-8898-3706-0

For those who laid the foundation:
Grammy Roberta Zasaretti, Grampy Paulino Zasaretti Sr.,
Ganny Naomi Pulphus, and Grandpa Willie Pulphus

For those who placed the cornerstone:
Mama Loletta Zasaretti
and Poppie Jonathan Pulphus

For those who built the pyramid:
Ti Pulphus, David Pulphus,
Christopher Pulphus, T'Mya Pulphus

CONTENTS

FOREWORD BY DR. STEFAN M. BRADLEY

Of the thousands of students I have taught, Jonathan Pulphus has given me the biggest headache. Upon meeting and working with him, I found that he was equal parts Dwayne Wayne from the 1990s sitcom *A Different World*, rapper/poet Tupac Shakur, and human rights organizer Kwame Ture. Jonathan wielded charm liberally, slaying all he encountered. Yet he was consciously and unapologetically centered in his identity as a young Black man from the City of Saint Louis.

Simply put, Jonathan is a natural-born leader who earns the respect of everyone who knows him. As his new book *With My People* reveals, Jonathan, with a love of justice in his heart, has sacrificed his student status, freedom, and sanity to create coalitions of people from disparate backgrounds to risk it all for righteous causes. He was in the vanguard of liberation campaigns on campus and in the street before, during, and after the Ferguson Uprising of 2014–2015. In this moment, as the nation careens off the cliff of civic sanity, we desperately need organizers like Jonathan to rescue democracy. Thankfully, *With My People* is a model of modern resistance that young people, and those who work with youth, can use to navigate these perilous times.

I was lucky enough to be Jonathan's assigned mentor at Saint Louis University (SLU) when he participated in the African American Males Scholars Initiative. He also enrolled in my "Introduction to African American Studies" course in his first year. This all worked out well because as I was the new director of the African American Studies Program. I was on a mission to recruit the brightest students to major in the discipline. Unlike many other students, who found their way to the program after their first year, Jonathan knew right away that he intended to become a major. To be sure, he was one of the best representatives of the discipline that I ever encountered. This was not because he scored the highest on examinations and papers or because he gave the most refined presentations (although his work was among the best I have graded); it was that he embodied the essence of Black Studies.

Unique to higher education, Black Studies came to life because students in the 1960s protested for the option to explore the contributions, problems, and existence of people of African descent in a systemic way. In their curricula, predominantly white institutions consciously or unconsciously bolstered white supremacy by ignoring the role that Black people played in the world. So, necessarily, the discipline started with a chip on its shoulder and with something to prove. Young people, like Jonathan, wanted to show that they could use formal education and the resources of white institutions to advance the goals of the Black Freedom Struggle and improve the life chances of those in the community. Those agitators from a half century before and Jonathan in 2010s manifested what I call *Black Student Power*, the ability of those enrolled in school to use their student status a tool in building solutions for those Black people who, because of their circumstances, could likely never enroll in college.

For as bright and talented as Jonathan was when I first met him, he was also mischievous. For class, he read everything I assigned and even more from the library. During our discussions, I regularly heard, "But Dr. B., what about this?" Of course, as an instructor, I loved the curiosity and close reads, but I remember having to prepare particularly for Jonathan. He had the uncanny ability to remember exactly what one said and then remind one of one's own words when arguing a point. That talent proved annoying in his relationship with an extremely intelligent and witty SLU student, Alisha Sonnier, who like Jonathan had a wonderfully endearing personality. They, hilariously, acted like an old married couple, always fussing. They were funny and fun to observe, but they were also impressively effective when they worked together.

Jonathan, to the best of his ability, tried to use his influence to resolve racial issues on campus. He helped relaunch a campus chapter of the National Association for the Advancement of Colored People (NAACP) and became an officer in the Black Student Alliance (BSA) as well as a residential advisor in a dormitory. When he found a racist and antisemitic message left on a public screen, he, along with fellow students, pulled together a rally that the university interim president, provost, campus minister, dean of students, and general counsel attended. After one administrator spoke, Jonathan, in his typical charming style, wished the administrator happy birthday, bringing a smile to the administrator's face. Not more than three minutes later, however, Jonathan and the student-agitators issued a set of demands to the university. The administrator stopped smiling.

Jonathan's charm and daring were on full display on a night in October 2014, when Tribe X, the community organization he and Alisha helped found, collaborated with other organizations for "Ferguson October." After Saint Louis City police officer Jason Flanery killed a young Black man, VonDerrit Myers Jr., who was the son of a SLU employee, leaders of OBS, Hands Up United, Millennial Activists United, Tribe X, and organizers from elsewhere invited sympathizers from all over the nation to travel to Saint Louis and Ferguson to be in solidarity with the movement. For context, it was similar to Martin Luther King Jr.'s call for good-hearted people to come to Selma in 1965. Hundreds answered the call and showed up, including figures like scholar Cornel West and rappers like Talib Kweli. After marching in the streets of Saint Louis, organizers led demonstrators to the edge of SLU's campus. In perfect Pulphus fashion, Jonathan stepped between campus security and the demonstrators. Holding up his student identification card, he smiled and told security his name and that the members of the crowd were his guests, then led them triumphantly to the center of campus, where they gathered near the Clock Tower.

The demonstration turned into a week-long occupation, featuring a negotiation between various factions from the campus and the community. They included the university's administration with relatively new President Fred Pestello at the helm, Tribe X, representatives of the Metro Saint Louis Coalition for Inclusion and Equity (M-SLICE), and the campus BSA. Jonathan and his fellow protesters were the cause of great controversy that led to cameras being installed in public areas, heightened campus security, and countless meetings. I facilitated a junta of the factions in the president's office and worked as a liaison to help bring what was called #OccupySLU to peaceful end. Jonathan and Alisha, who were in a precarious position as students and demonstration leaders, handled themselves with aplomb. Amid threats and constant internet trolling, the young people negotiated what the university refers to as the Clock Tower Accords, which promised resources to incoming and enrolled Black students, university-sponsored community space, artwork commemorating the moment, and a more productive relationship with the neighborhoods surrounding SLU. The community-campus coalition that Jonathan and his peers put together advanced the local Black Freedom Movement and became an inspiration for college students elsewhere, including the University of Missouri (Mizzou).

It was a major point of pride for me and so many others when Jonathan finally graduated from SLU. It marked the completion of a goal. By the time he graduated I had taken a job in Loyola Marymount University in Los Angeles. I was sure to invite him, Alisha, and two other youth organizers to share their experiences on campus. They shared their experiences and taught students, faculty, staff, and community members how they believed we could "get free."

As a historian, I think it essential that A-1 Day-1 activists, organizers, and leaders publicly remember the movement from their perspectives before those outside of the community create errant or false narratives. For posterity's sake, I hope that other young participants of the Ferguson Uprising share their experiences widely in written form. As the nation speedily careens toward anti-intellectualism and authoritarianism, there should live a record of what is possible when young people commit themselves to actualizing democracy. In this book, Jonathan shows that it did not take fame or money but rather the recognition of injustice and the willingness to be "with my people," to create viable and necessary change. More of that, please.

Dr. Stefan M. Bradley,
Charles Hamilton Houston '15 Professor of Black Studies and History, Amherst College; author of *If We Don't Get It: A People's History of Ferguson* (2025)

FOREWORD BY REV. OSAGYEFO SEKOU

"Each generation must, out of relative obscurity, discover its mission, fulfill it, or betray it."

—Franz Fanon

JONATHAN PULPHUS LAYS bare the intent and emotions of thousands of protestors who gathered night after night—answering the call of Michael Brown's blood. His leadership reflected a deep commitment to the struggle in solidarity and community. The boundary between the university and the city divided, evaporated in an instant when he used his privileges as a student to escort hundreds on to campus and claim the space for a greater good. He was, indeed, with his people.

While the memoir elucidates the necessity of training, discipline, education, and demands in social movements, the power of the narrative rests in Pulphus witness to history. The connection between community activists and students shifted the political landscape of universities around the country. The resulting Clock Tower Accords was one of the few successes of the hundreds of protests that shook the nation. The Ferguson Event shook the foundations of American democracy and initiated a global solidarity movement. This memoir is a testament to the yet-to-be fully comprehended impact of the Ferguson Uprising.

The Ferguson Uprising was formed by the Great Depression of 2008, inspired by Occupy Wall Street, and the Arab Spring, prompted by social media, articulated the class divisions and generational differences and highlighted the limitations of Obama's election. It launched worldwide protest and international solidarity and midwifed the modern civil rights movement. Like Occupy Wall Street and the Arab Spring, Ferguson was an event. Noted French philosopher Alain Badiou characterized the activity of occupation: "In the midst of an event, the people is made up of those who know how to solve the problems that the event imposes on them. It goes the same for the occupation of a square: food, sleeping arrangements, protection, banderols, prayers, defence fight, all so that the place where everything is happening, the place that has become a symbol, may stay with its people at all costs."

This event produced different if not new kinds of social beings. Pulphus, Tribe X, and community folks were not simply objects of their material conditions but subjects who resisted. The international character of the uprising was evident in the chief form of social disruption, which was the occupation of public space.

We were Zuccotti Park and Tahrir Square. The January 25 Egyptian Revolution was called by youth groups and supported by labor unions to protest against police brutality at the annual Egyptian Police Holiday. In the United States Occupy Wall Street transformed Zuccotti Park into a site of resistance. The Saint Louis University action was part of an international phenomenon that repurposed public and private space for the common good.

The Ferguson Uprising was many things converging at once. The murder of Michael Brown was the convergence of *white supremacy* and class. Stop and frisk, poverty, and other previous diagnosed social ills illustrate the historical and contemporary role of racism in Black life. The Operation Ghetto Storm Report found that 66 percent of young Black people killed were under 32 years old—with 40 percent of the 313 being between the ages of 22 and 31. Brown's is just a part of a legacy of Black people killed by the police or vigilantes with little to no recourse. Equally, each interview without hesitation asserted that racism was key in Brown's murder and a function of a historic system.

Though we are separated by a generation, both Jonathan and I know all too well the machination of a police force's incentive to demonize our humanity. Dorian Johnson—Michael Brown's companion on that fateful day—recalled a life of harassment in his community during his grand jury testimony: "Every day I hear different stories about people's different encounters with Ferguson Police." Canfield residents regularly warned each other to be wary of the Ferguson police—letting folks know that 12 (slang for the police) were in the vicinity. "People are always giving you a warning, be very mindful of whenever you're coming outside. . . . They are down the street or something in that manner basically keeping you aware of Ferguson Police." To this end, Ferguson residents are needlessly harassed by police—Officer Darren Wilson was no different.

During my younger years, my sister, Linda would not allow me to drive through Ferguson. In their 2014 Missouri Municipal Court White Paper, the legal services nonprofit The Arch City Defenders confirmed what Linda and Dorian already knew. In Ferguson, "86% of vehicle stops involved a black motorist, although blacks make up just 67% of the population. . . . After being stopped in Ferguson, blacks are almost twice as likely as whites to be searched (12.1% vs. 6.9%) and precisely two times more likely to be arrested (10.4% vs. 5.2%)." The *Washington Post* and NPR also reported on this reality: "In 2013, the municipal court in Ferguson—a city of 21,135 people—issued 32,975 arrest warrants for nonviolent offenses, mostly driving violations.

This was and is not a people who can afford the trouble. Again, Ferguson is one of 91 municipalities in the Saint Louis County. These suburbs have poor public transportation, and very few grocery stores. Corner stores like the Ferguson Market, where Michael Brown had his confrontation with the clerk, are where residents' shop for basic needs. If these stores carry meat, fruits, and vegetables, they are low quality. Blunt rolling utensils, cigarettes, and Red Hot Ripples potato chips, a local favorite, are in abundant supply. These food deserts, which are designed and a form of apartheid, fund their city budgets by ticketing the poor because neoliberalism mobilizes state institutional resources and enforcement to promote market-based regulatory arrangements.

In 2014, one in four Ferguson residents lived below the poverty line, and the African American unemployment was at 13 percent. Devastated by the subprime mortgage fiasco, 50 percent of Ferguson homeowners were underwater. To add insult to injury, Ferguson was a predominately Black community subject to predominately white rule. In addition to a white mayor, five of the six city council members were white. Although the school district was 70 percent Black, six of the seven school board members were white. The police force had only two Black officers. Such a disproportionate representation of the white minority in the most critical aspects of community governing made Ferguson apartheid-like.

The Ferguson Uprising sits within a histography of resistance inside the highly militarized American Empire. To overcome the death-dealing empire, the people responded with a tragicomic sense of hope. They called on the nonmaterial resources in the face of material. The protest that ensued after Michael Brown's murder had a religious quality. When folks gathered to protest state violence against the most vulnerable, there emerges what sociologist Emile Durkheim calls "collective effervescence"—a spirit of joyful yet mournful resistance saturated the night air. "Michael Brown saved my life," declared Alex Templeton, a young queer Black woman who was home contemplating suicide on the day Michael Brown was killed. His death gave her meaning. That is existential.

To this end, culture, particularly music, was a critical feature of the protest in Ferguson. For instance, the popular song "Fuck the Police" often felt like the liturgical mantra of the street protest. Many elders and religious folks found the profanity to be disconcerting and offensive. The spirit at the Clock Tower was church. It was spiritual and reviving. Ferguson was political. The Ferguson Uprising undermined a postracial discourse that was ushered in by the election of the first Black president of the United States. Pulphus and his comrades would impact the culture of protest by using die-ins as collective symbol or resistance that would be repeated the world over. Their unique chants reverberated throughout city large and small all over the world.

There were over 250 Ferguson solidarity protests worldwide, and foreign governments roundly issued rebukes of racism in the United States. Ferguson gave birth to a twenty-first-century civil rights movement in the United States that thrived online and in the streets. There is no Black Lives Matter movement without the Ferguson Uprising. Young people led the longest protest in United States since the Montgomery Bus Boycott.

Jonathan Pulphus's work offers us a front-row seat to his generation's odds-defying work of calling a university with a $1 billion endowment to account. Armed with nothing more than their dogged strength and desire to redeem the blood of Michael Brown, they moved history and heaven. They heard Franz Fanon's admonishment and seized their times.

Jonathan Pulphus is one of the most important leaders of his generation, and I am honored to have marched alongside him and those who struggled with us. His witness helps us to understand that when we stand with those who do not matter, history will bend to our will and heaven will bear witness to our faithfulness. Read it and be changed.

Rev. Osagyefo Sekou, pastor,
Valley and Mountain Fellowship,
Seattle, Washington

PROLOGUE

The Lou Blues

1764, the Lou was founded.
Roll past Laclede and Chouteau astounded.
Pigeonholed, stoled, then shackled and bounded.
Lost Souls built this town while being hounded.

That sounded like an exaggeration.
Scott and McCintosh were our situations.
Blood Clots, Knots, Shots, by administration.
Sumner, thought spots sought for information.

Disorganization before the Arch.
Nation, No, World's Fair, stationing research.
Laugh Saturday, on Sunday at their church.
Frustrated, a Fairground riot, we marched.

Of course we had moments of resistance.
Delaney forced mad change with persistence.
Percy scorched earth, high for our existence.
Scourges of Racism call for distance.

Insistence, major key to what we need.
We can't take seats and watch our people bleed.
Want us pleading on knees, hanging from trees.
Remember our past, study victories.

The story that I write is a love song. It is also a pain song. The joys of being a part of something larger than myself. The thrill of meeting brilliant and talented individuals from different walks of life. The excitement behind walking in my purpose. However, it is also about anger. The tragedy of writing something that I should never have had to write. The anger of recognizing that Michael Brown, VonDerrit Myers, and many others should be alive. The trauma of knowing that while I write my story, some who demonstrated aren't alive or able to tell theirs. Soldiers have fallen such as Darren Seals, Edward Crawford, Bassem Masri, and more. My Ferguson song was about more than forcing this country to live up to its principles and ideals. I wrote this to process what happened to and around me. Since Mike was murdered, I learned many things on my journey. One that stands out is that as we struggle to leave this world better than how we found it, we cannot do it alone.

When the governments in both Ferguson and America failed in their duties around the murder of Michael Brown Jr., I and many others committed to being in the streets, battling for justice. This story is about nine months of journeying toward justice and making extraordinary strides toward transforming the community. Many people aspire to fight for something larger than themselves and to make an impact; few people have the courage, character, and teachability to accomplish that.

I hope to dispel myths about the Ferguson uprising and activists. I know that Mike did not get murdered because of a pack of cigarillos. He was killed because there was and continues to be a racist and dangerous imbalance of power in our society. Activists and protesters in Ferguson did not demonstrate for personal gain. Many demonstrators, higher-profile and otherwise, have been killed, injured, targeted, or traumatized following their involvement. Many have caught cases, myself included, for their rebelliousness. We acted because we believed that through our resistance and sacrifices, justice would come.

As a mentee under the leadership of the executive director of the Metro Saint Louis Coalition for Inclusion and Equity, Queen Mother Ms. Romona, in concert with Mama Lola, my mother, I was able to learn the necessity of grassroots organizing by participating in community-based projects in the 21st ward of North Saint Louis. A lot of hot days, gardening, and snacks from Bro. Zhudi's shop, which was an anchor business in the ward. I had moments when I couldn't stand being outdoors all day, in soil and mulch. However, Queen Mother Romona and my mom would soothe the experience with cold beverages and delicious food from Zhudi's while reminding me of the purpose of advocacy. This included addressing issues ranging from public health to bank accessibility. Using lessons from Queen Mother Romona, I was able to help cofound an activist group named Tribe X, which responded to the Ferguson, Missouri, uprisings following the murder of Michael O. D. Brown Jr.

As a member of Tribe X, I helped conduct more than ten peaceful direct actions and events featured in *Ebony*, *St. Louis American*, *St. Louis Post-Dispatch*, *St. Louis Public Radio*, *Washington Times*, and the *New York Times*. One critical highlight of this experience was garnering a substantial agreement for equity between Tribe X and Saint Louis University (SLU). As a result of my activism in the Ferguson uprising, I was awarded the 2014 Jamala Rogers Young Visionary Award, named in the honor of a well-respected Kansas City activist affectionately referred to as Mama Jamala.

Through my African American studies major, advocacy on behalf of Black people, and professional skill sets in various capacities, I have developed this story and song. As an undergraduate student at SLU, I was published in the *Western Journal for Black Studies* as a coauthor with my adviser, Dr. Stefan Bradley, alongside Joshua Jones. This included accumulated academic experience around qualitative storytelling and several research papers as part of the rigorous African American studies curriculum. As a leader in the SLU's Black Student Alliance, I aided in the retention of Black students, from coplanning study halls to securing new affinity space. Working with SLU's Residence Life under the Leadership and Social Change learning community, I was able to practice storytelling while developing my narrative. This specific experience played a major function in growing my vocabulary to articulate my passions.

This text is divided into two parts, each signifying a different phase in my life. The first captures my experiences as a college sophomore wrestling with the Ferguson uprising. Here, I write about my journey from August 2014 until the end of my sophomore year in May 2015. The second is a glimpse into the near present. I explore some of my early moments with my first full-time job with the Quaker organization American Friends Service Committee. Each of these sections offers something different to the reader.

I argue there must be more written about the Ferguson uprising through the lens of those who were on the front line to counter stereotypes and misrepresentations characterizing the moment. Each Ferguson uprising demonstrator must represent themselves. The slogan Black Lives Matter became a household name and a rallying cry for Black freedom at a cost that is often glossed over. Coined by Dr. Marcus Anthony Hunter on Twitter, the hashtag #BlackLivesMatter is known around the world. Patrisse Cullors, who alongside Alicia Garza and Opal Tometi who self-identify with founding the #BlackLivesMatter hashtag through Facebook, once wrote, "#BlackLivesMatter would not be recognized worldwide if it weren't for the folks in St. Louis and Ferguson," with which I agree. This acknowledgment cannot be overstated.

In the summer of 2014, I joined the early phases of a larger organic protest movement referred to as the *Ferguson movement* (or *Ferguson uprising*). This became a wave of antipolice-brutality demonstrations that responded to and were in the spirit of addressing the murder of a teenage boy named Michael Brown Jr. by Officer Darren Wilson on Saturday, August 9, 2014. While many of the demonstrations were decentralized, without one leader or tactic, many of those involved formed a collective identity. This is sometimes referred to as the *protest family* stemming from the collective memory of literally seeing Brown's lifeless body or facing state violence early on West Florissant in pursuit of lifting Brown's name. We broke bread together. We bumped heads together. We endured together. We looked out for each other. Many of us remain locked in.

I remember seeing many Black women and young people who were on the front line in early protest groups like Millennial Activists United, Lost Voices, and Freedom Fighters.

On Saturday, August 9, I remember hearing about Brown's death when my mother called me. On Sunday, August 10, I remember being rescued by Alisha, my partner at the time. She aided me after I had been ferociously pepper-sprayed for refusing to allow police to violently disperse children. On Saturday, August 16, I remember standing beside my mother and other Ferguson protesters, some clad in blue and red gear. Together, they were protecting a younger folk at a Family Dollar store when they were about to take their appropriate anger out on predominantly noncommunity-owned property. On Sunday, August 17, I remember running onto West Florissant to help rescue and nurse a demonstrator back to health after the police's tear gas nearly choked her to death. In September 2014, I, like many, helped form an organization within this organic protest family with a group of brothers, sisters, and mentors, later to be called Tribe X to help distinguish our goals. Themes of my story as a demonstrator during the Ferguson uprising are not an anomaly.

While the police tried to suppress the Ferguson movement with tear gas canisters, five-second rules, detainments, rubber bullets, free speech zones, and curfews, we would not be subdued. Demonstrators sustained the movement by responding to law enforcement with various respectable and unrespectable tactics including returning tear gas canisters, growing protest organizations, burning down businesses, looting businesses, protecting businesses, rescuing each other, performing a direct action by encamping on West Florissant, impeding traffic, taunting law enforcement with chants, and engaging in other forms of civil disobedience that helped to lift the names of Brown and Ferguson into national and international consciousness. After bearing the cost of refusing to go home or be silent, some Ferguson protesters and allies suffered job loss, homelessness, pauses in their schooling, injuries, jail sentences, penalties in their profession, mental health struggles, and death.

The limited number of published books on Ferguson calls for more production to acknowledge the lessons to be learned from the true diversity of the people involved in the work, particularly those less visible yet fundamental to sustaining the Ferguson uprising, which, in turn, helped spark the larger Black Lives Matter movement. Naming participants from the Ferguson protest movement like Queen Mother Romona, Mama Mix, Mama Lola, EJ, Rockit, Alisha, Darius, HJ, Talal, and Dhoruba of Tribe X, who helped organize the encampment of SLU, is critical. Lifting up Mama Cat of Potbangerz, who organized dinners for protesters; celebrating Damon (formerly known as Diamond) Latchison, Shermale Humphreys, JaNina Jenkins, and Autumn Mae of Freedom Fighters, who worked hard to organize movie nights and many actions. These are merely a few names and organizations. Their stories and many others should be told, documented, and learned from.

Throughout my involvement with the Ferguson rebellion, I often wrestled with this tough question: *Does protesting work?* After centuries of Black resistance, racism and systemic injustice are still very much alive. While the hashtag #BlackLivesMatter existed before Ferguson, it exists as it does today due to the bloody and traumatic sacrifices, organization, and energy of Ferguson. The phrase is now often used to reference a broad protest and social justice movement. Until more authorship is produced—much is forthcoming—the significance of the lessons to be gained from the Ferguson protest movement concerning the larger

Black freedom struggle is minimized in literature. Mainstream media often presented the organic protest movement as a ragtag and uncivilized crowd of animals to appeal to respectable sensibility. We never cared. We were outside. I hope this song and story will contribute to a larger holistic literary narrative for all.

This project could be described as a labor of love. I started writing while an undergrad at Saint Louis University. The audience for this book is those who identify as or with youth activists, student activists, Saint Louisans, progressives, leftists, the working class, policymakers, teachers, Americans with a passion for social justice, and Black freedom demonstrators abroad. I hope that after looking through this, the reader feels the emotions of joy, hope, resilience, love, faith, and relief.

The acknowledgments lift up those who either inspired these emotions or challenged me to remember the value of these feelings in times of doubt, stagnation, fear, and disorganization. Additionally, the acknowledgment section includes from memory those who have been integral to the manuscript process. The text includes names relevant to navigating the moment between 2014 and 2015; those listed are used for the purpose of telling my narrative based on my knowledge. The poetry included in the text was my way of reflecting on direct actions, organizing in that moment, and arriving at the stated primary emotions above. It will read like a series of reflections because it is me piecing together details from memory. These are my best recollections.

While I wrestled a lot, I don't look like what I've been through. Not everything in this work may read perfectly. Nevertheless, I write anyway. I write this to speak to the young Black soldiers sick of the conditions they find themselves in, facing hell and feeling alone. I write this to encourage and promote justice in a world with centuries of old issues that persist. I write this to encourage Ferguson uprising demonstrators and soldiers on the side of justice to share their stories in literature. I write this to make fading memories solid so that they can be revisited. I write this because if I were to disappear, die mysteriously, face untreated health issues, be jailed, or suffer retaliation, it wasn't random. Whether at gunpoint or no point, you will know where I stand: with my people.

ACKNOWLEDGMENTS

I'd love to thank God! I'd like to show gratitude to my creator for guiding my pen in materializing this text.

My baby sibling, T'Mya Patience Christiane Pulphus, is my inspiration for this book. She was born shortly after I entered second grade. For my school show and tell, students were invited to bring a gift. This would be an item that young people valued enough to share out about with the class. Some of my peers brought new toys and others talked about their new shoes. With full smiles and visible excitement, each student took turns storytelling. Students described who they got their gift from, when they received it, and how excited they were about it. When my turn came, I gently pulled out a small glossy picture of this carefree Black baby. I began my story with pride sharing: "This is my baby sister, T'Mya." My Ganny ("grandmother") Naomi Pulphus and Grammy Roberta Zasaretti would cradle T'Mya in their arms. With tender smiles, you could read their minds. My grandmothers were thinking: *This baby has been here before.* T'Mya has grown into an activist, small-business owner, scholar, artist, and determined young woman. In a world that too often values the fleeting, her being constantly reminds me to fight for the timeless. I love her dearly. You have this story because of her.

I'd love to emphasize and thank the following supporters for investing in my writing and art during this process through my journey with Broadleaf Books, Patreon, and beyond: Dr. Ilene Berman (deeply appreciative of all the love), Dr. Stefan Bradley (The Doc, Ribsey Hussel), Justine Collum, Elle Dowd (My Bridge to Broadleaf Books, "Baptized in Tear Gas" Author), Jason Ebinger, Nia Hampton (Formidable Developmental Editor), Lisa Kloskin (my connection to Jarrod at Broadleaf), Jarrod Harrison (Stellar Broadleaf Books Acquisitions Editor), Marissa Wold Uhrina (Phenomenal Broadleaf Books Production Editor), the entire Broadleaf staff for your bringing this book to life, DeMario Jones (First Reader), DeRay McKesson ("On The Other Side of Freedom" Author), David Pulphus (Illustration Concepts), Dr. Tandra Taylor, Trevor Woolfolk (my brother), Dr. Amber Johnson (introduced Ethnography and I), and Loletta Zasaretti.

I'd love to thank my family for their love, adoration, and care for me during the ups and downs of navigating this writing process. Between the raw yet warm feedback and instilling in me values that guide my best efforts at being a principled grandson, son, brother, nephew, cousin, and more. You all remind me of my why: Ganny Naomi Pulphus, Grandpa Willie Pulphus, Grampy Paulino Zasaretti, Grammy Roberta Zasaretti, Mama Loletta Zasaretti (Mama Lola), Papa Jonathan Pulphus Sr., Christopher Pulphus, David Pulphus (Captain Blacc), T'Mya Pulphus, Ti Pulphus (Tianay), Etefia Umana (Mr. E), Uncle Paul Zasaretti, Aunt Janel Zasaretti, Uncle David, Uncle and Cousin Mondis, Randy Jones, DeMario Jones, Jalen and Jayla Jones, Elijah Bivins (YK Da Don), Amara Bivins, Dr. Tandra Taylor, Grace Griffin, Yosiyah Griffin, Alisha Sonnier, Izaya Alexander, Felicia Bunting, TT Brienne Holmes, and Enrique Bronner.

I'd love to thank advisors and teachers for being a blueprint and roadmap for how to navigate the hurdles and successes that come grounded in your own journeys. From demonstrating excellence in terms of being people in service to others while pursuing your own personal and professional aspirations, you've been stellar role models and confidants. You all remind me of what's to come: Dr. Stefan M. Bradley, Queen Mother Dr. LaTanya N. Buck, Aleidra Allen, Dr. Ashley Gray, Dr. Ilene Berman, Dr. Scott Berman, Rev. Dr. Starsky Wilson, Dr. Olubukola Gbadegesin, Dr. Jonathan Fenderson, Ms. Gail Owens (from Patrick Henry circa 2006), Osagyefo Sekou, Mama Jamala Rogers, Tony Boykin-King, Dr. Katrina Thompson-Moore, Joshua Jones, Justin Hansford, Dr. Jonathan Smith, Ms. Dana Guyton, Bro. Joshua Saleem, and Dr. Norman White.

I'd love to thank mentors and members of two of the most consequential groups that have existed to date in the history of the Saint Louis grassroots organizing scene. Metro Saint Louis Coalition for Inclusion and Equity fostered in me a sense of purpose in organizing and Tribe X forced me to have a crash course in materializing this amid crises. To this day, I use the Tribe handshake and will for years to come. You all remind me of the thrust of educate, empower, and organize: Queen Mother Romona Taylor Williams, Mama Alisa Mixon, Mama Loletta Zasaretti (Mama Lola), SOS Ransom (or Tony White, formerly known as Talal Ahmed), Brandon Ali (Rockit), Alisha Sonnier (Ms. President and Alderwoman), Darius Ali, Dhoruba Shakur (Jeffrey Hill), Emmanuel Jones (EJ), HJ Rogers (Huey Jahki), Christopher Pulphus, and Trey Mixon (Kid X).

I'd love to thank my #23rdFamily for giving me a sense of grounding and a home base. In many ways, you and many others have seen me in all forms yet have always given me a reason to center realness in the everyday in the moves that I make. From the ups and downs, I've always seen the levels of beauty and soul. You all remind me of a beloved community: Uncle Rodney Holt, Tracy Wheeler, Dave Crawford, Andrew Crawford (Drew Buckz), Lilmonties (Lil Tez), Deonta Ervin (Black), Jabbor Pernal (Unc, Jigga Jay, Beer Can), Jarell Pernal (Neeno), Dorian Scott (Doro), Shakia Pernal (Law and Med School), TT Troyetta Patton, TT Shakmia Pernal (Twin), Davon Weathers (Lil Tee), and Nykeia Pierra (Fat Lady).

I'd love to thank my fellow #BlackBillikens, #BlackCurrents, and Allies for helping a younger me wrestle with tough questions, reminding me to stay true to myself, and being unapologetically critical of a campus out of love for its possibilities. You all remind me of learning to make change over learning for learning's sake: Larry Saddler (L-Boogie), Chris Walter Jr., Eric Moody Jr., Benjamin Hayes, Jaden Janak (formerly Noelle), Gold Gladney, Brittany Kendrick, Briana Moody, Deionna and Dewonna Ferguson, Trevor Woolfolk, Brendan Underwood, Taelon Smith (TK), Ashaki Jackson, Stanford Cooper, Paul Watkins, Mia Watkins, Brittany Conners, Sam Jones, Nia Sumpter, Marcus Wolff, Brinia (Robin's heart), Ryan McKinley, Sarah Nash, and Jason Ebinger.

I'd love to thank those involved in Ferguson Uprising and movements beyond for putting your bodies, souls, minds, and hearts on the line for change. You and many others inspired me to fight and continue to wrestle with systemic injustices inspiring young people to make strides to make this world a better place. You all remind me of the power of collective action: Michael Brown Sr., Lezley McSpadden, VonDerrit Myers Sr., Syreeta Myers, Kofi Ansa, Rasheen Aldridge, Bruce Franks Jr., Daniel and Yasmine Aguilar, David C. Turner III, Kareem Jackson (Tef Poe), Mama Julia Davis, Elizabeth Vega, Destiny Crockett, Storm

Ervin, Ayanna Poole, Reuben Riggs, Danielle Blocker, Jelani Brown, Derek Laney, Anthony Shahid, Kenan Morrison, Sarah Rose, Rachael Ibrahim, Marcellus Buckley, Julia Ho, John Costello (Mo, and the Costello family), Charles Smith (Churc), Barbara Stanford, Jessica Seratti, Angee Serwin, Arissa Marniece, Renita Green, Jessica Hollie (Bella), Nabeehah Azeez, Jae Shepherd, Kristian Davis Bailey, Derk Brown, Ohun Ashe (LaShell Eikerenkoetter), Alex Templeton (formerly Alexis), Brittany Ferrell, Malik Rhasaan (Che Butter Jonez, OccupytheHood), Chad Jackson, Ebony Williams, Ashley Yates, Devante Jackson (Low-Key), Tara Thompson, Michael Hassell (Mike Mike), Mike Avery, Cheyenne Green, Clifton Kinnie, Alicia Street, Auriel Brown (Cookie), Angel Carter, Rika Tyler, Antoine White (T-Dubb-O), Calvin Kennedy (Cap), Fran Griffin, Camron Rhodes, Farrakhan Shegog, Amir Brandy, Tory Russell, DeRay Mckesson, Johnetta Elzie, Brittany Packnett, Jessie Sandavol, Montague Simmons, Melissa McKinnies, Anthony Cage, James Meinert, Kayla Reed, Aaron and Kira Banks, Ned Alexander, Charles Hatley (Big C), Michael Johnson (Spud), LaRhonda Brown (Nuccy Nucc), Jarel Williams, Hassan Shariff (400 years), Rod Colvin, Velma Bailey, Darrick Smith, Cathy Daniels (Mama Cat), Carlos Ball, Toni Taylor, Kristian Blackmon, Joshua Williams (Kid Ferguson), Edward Crawford, Danye' Dion Jones, MarShawn McCarrel, Oluwatoyin Salau, Bassem Masri, and Darren Seals (King D-Seals).

CHAPTER 1

Does Protesting Work?

I MAKE THE claim that protests continue to have worthwhile value that, in addition to various forms of agitation, contributes to making significant advancements grounded in the tradition of the Black freedom movement. There have been achievements, accomplishments, and celebrations. These range from the battles to make America live up to its values in myriad ways to the fights to counter kidnappings from Africa and survive the inhumane conditions of enslavement. In addition, there are struggles to address unjust laws and ongoing disparities across systems. Each of these periods and times lends itself to a revelation of the ways that Black people have sought to express their dignity. One way that has been done is through *protest*. The lens that often comes to mind for me is that of nonviolent demonstration.

There have been a variety of methods used to affirm dignity, self-respect, and freedom that are beyond the scope of this book, yet these activities yielded significant advancements in terms of policy. The fights against enslavement helped lead to the Thirteenth Amendment. The battles against Jim Crow helped lead to anti-segregation laws. The struggles around civil rights helped lead to *Brown vs. Board of Education*. The post-civil rights activities helped lead to fair housing practice laws. The near-present-day efforts have helped lead to antipolice-brutality practices, abolitionist-oriented policies, and the addressing of systemic disparities. Each of these moments involved *protest* as a means. However, despite all of these efforts, there continue to be activities aimed to revert and maintain the status quo. If protest works, why do injustices persist?

The effectiveness of this tactic is well documented within the development of the United States. Despite the evidence, successes, and watershed moments stemming from protest, social ills persist. There continues to be segregated schooling decades after *Brown vs. Board of Education*, redlining goes on despite *Shelly vs. Kramer*, and access to basic needs continues to be stifled. The Slave Codes were put in place to make it impossible for enslaved people to read, write, and stand flat-footed while talking without the possibility of cruelty, suffering, and retaliation. Centuries later, there continue to be disparities in academic access and achievement. The overruled verdict of *Plessy vs. Ferguson* stated that Black people have "no rights which the white man was bound to respect." However, constitutional rights are still violated following the dismantling of the ruling. Each of these moments was responded to with the risky, bold, and courageous activities of people who disobeyed or expressed dismay toward unjust laws, policies, and practices. Black people employed protest as an activity to face obstacles in their journey to achieve dignity. However, ongoing issues demand that we ask the question: Does protest work?

The purpose behind protest is to create meaningful and lasting differences. This translates to protest not simply being performative. It is a vehicle for ushering in substantive developments that address societal ills. There are different manners in which targeting unfairness with the intention of gaining progress has emerged and continues to be present. This includes street demonstrations, voting at the poll, and joining advocacy groups to build capacity. In addition, there's raising awareness around issues and appealing to lawmakers around new policy. People can lift up the voices of those most proximate to an issue or write opinion editorials on problems. Individuals can serve populations most impacted by their cause, and the list goes on in terms of methods of agitating for justice. Street demonstrations look like Anne Moody sitting in at a Woolworth's counter, fighting for integration and employment. Voting at the poll presents James Chaney fighting to register residents in the 1960s South. Joining advocacy groups looks like Fred Hampton launching a Black Panther Party chapter in 1970s Chicago to address medical, child-care, and defense causes. Raising awareness is reflected in Sojourner Truth's "Ain't I a Woman," wherein she names Black women's rights. Appealing to lawmakers shows the activities of Dred and Harriet Scott toward shifting the nation's mindset on systems of enslavement. Lifting up the voices of those closest to the issues exemplifies Fannie Lou Hamer sharing her experiences at the Democratic National Convention. Naming or writing op-eds about problems includes Ida B. Wells's research and findings on lynchings in the South. Serving populations most impacted by one's cause includes Marian Wright Edelman's working with youths and families for the Children's Defense Fund.

Throughout the development of this "Christian" nation, there have been efforts in various forms to force the country to live up to its core values of life, liberty, and the pursuit of happiness. No matter the tactic, the aim has been to shift the needle forward. The vision has consisted of observing what is dysfunctional and moving toward what is acceptable. The mission has included enduring costs to ensure that the nation lives up to its truth. In 1968, Rev. Dr. Martin Luther King Jr. demanded that America "be true to what you said on paper." There are lies, hypocrisies, and shortfalls in the manifesting of the principles that the country claims to honor. Protest has been a vehicle to hold the nation accountable for its shortcomings.

Part of why the question of whether protest works is critical ties into the strategy behind energies toward advancing the project of the nation. *First, if protest works, what results reflect that?* There are challenges made following every major achievement as a result of advocacy. While the signing of the Voting Rights Act was tremendous, legislators still seek to diminish the capacity of certain social classes of residents to vote. After the codifying of antidiscriminatory practices in employment, the market denies Black job seekers access. Following the Civil Rights Acts, prisons continue to mass incarcerate Black people.

Second, if protest works, which methods reflect the best approach in gaining desirable outcomes? As a result of sit-ins across the nation, public establishments integrate in both hiring and patronage. However, protest as a singular action does not create laws and policies that manifest the intended result. As a consequence of speeches such as those delivered at the March on Washington, acts of legislation are addressed. Still, raising awareness by itself does not lead to problems being addressed. Researching injustices, such as what the *Kerner Report* does, helps generate recommendations about Black issues. The *Kerner Report* is an example of research on injustices in the United States that helped to make suggestions for improving social conditions. Nevertheless, the findings alone do not address the cause that led to the need for recommendations to begin with.

Third, if protest works, why do social injustices continue to impact the lives of people following centuries of protest? There has been decades' worth of efforts to incorporate reform and transform systems of safety. Why are there still cases of police brutality? There have been years' worth of efforts to address poverty in urban and rural communities. Why are there still food deserts, unhoused populations, bombed-out buildings, and a lack of services to better communities? There have been years of fighting for access to the polls. Why are there still efforts made to deny people their right to exercise their voice or vote?

The resources invested in realizing change demand a return. Time, money, labor, bodies, and location are all tied to actualizing desirable outcomes. These are often not free and take a toll on those who invest them toward change. If the return on one's cost is meager, are these investments wasted? The institution of slavery, which centered free labor, ended following a war and representations of protest symbolized by the Thirteenth Amendment. Given the return that was codified into law, was it wasted if free labor persists in prisons, as elaborated in author Michelle Alexander's *The New Jim Crow*? The institution of Jim Crow "ended" following several protests and was "dismantled" after several Supreme Court cases. Given the return, was the investment wasted if loopholes are used to deny basic rights? The expense is paid mainly by low-income communities of color (Black, Indigenous, Latinx, etc.). The outcomes desired from protest are not sought to be temporal or Band-Aids for the nation's ills. Yet with every cost endured and every needle that is moved forward, the nation's core values are tested. The country's promises are shown to be empty as systemic injustices eliminate the steps forward. As critical race theorists such as Derrick Bell have argued with *interest convergence*, the returns from America seem to be concessionary and contingent on decision-makers negotiating its principles.

The mindset of protesters must be that of *courage, character, and teachability*. Lighting a fire on a fall night starts with initiative. While the conditions motivating one to create heat may be cold, taking any steps toward warmth starts with imagination. Passersby may say you are foolish for trying to start one due to the wind. It takes *courage* to gather logs, fuel, and the additional tools you need with naysayers discouraging your task. After several attempts of lighting the fire, the wind may leave you with small embers of possibility. It takes *character* to follow your heart and be persistent by trying to succeed at a set goal. As you navigate sustaining the fire, you may encounter individuals giving you feedback. They may speak to how the logs are positioned, where to put the lighter fluid, and which place to best light the flame. It takes *teachability* to listen to the right counsel on your way toward keeping your fire lit. Before you realize it, you are the creator of a source of heat against the brisk weather conditions. The flames will flicker as gusts of wind seek to extinguish them. However, if you never grabbed the tools needed to begin a fire, you would have been sidetracked by the naysayer. If you gave up at the sight of embers, you'd only have the possibility of a fire. If you did not accept feedback on how to start the fire, the wind would have no flame to try to put out.

Just as starting a fire requires strategy and organizing to be effective, so, too, does protest. The flames of protest alone are not going to eliminate the coldest of times, where injustice looms. Yet the fire of change must start somewhere. Let it start with you.

Cursory Analysis of Black Protest in the United States

The struggle for human dignity and self-worth for Blacks has been a long, protracted, varied, and complex struggle, which is manifested in a multiplicity of resistance mechanisms ranging from direct actions, political action, and organization to day-to-day nuanced applications of resistance. The primary conflict has arisen as a result of the legal status afforded Black people in this country alongside the mechanism and process by which we arrived at this place. When this book refers to "this place," it is referring to the geographic designation of Africans in America as well as the social, economic, political, and human dignity marginalization. Thus, the struggle for human dignity and civil rights has been with us for over a millennium.

The legal and social status of African Americans has been that of chattel. This designation of servitude was among the harshest and most inhumane treatments. Chattel slavery is propertied slavery. Thus, a human being cannot exercise any fundamental rights, and any transgression against their dignity is not regarded as a crime or transgression. For example, during the period of enslavement, if an enslaved Black woman was brutally raped by a neighboring plantation owner or worker, there was no recourse. The only thing that could happen to the perpetrator of the crime was that the slaveowner could sue them—not for anything criminal but only for the offense of trespass to property. Again, human worth and dignity were compromised or nonexistent. The individual was looked at as their function or utility of being a disposable asset that needed work extracted from them for the perpetuation of a social and economic system that operated to their personal detriment and to the unjust enrichment of those who owned and exploited the labor.

Historically, this has manifested into several forms of protest to assert human worth and dignity. This could come in the form of quasi-strikes during the institution of enslavement. It could also manifest as work slowdowns, art, the destruction of work instruments, and other methods of sabotage that are passive-aggressive in nature but were the only ways those oppressed could exercise some form of micro-protest. For example, the art of dance during slavery may seem like a functionless activity, but Dr. Katrina Thompson, Saint Louis University associate professor of history, reminds us that "for Blacks, performing constituted a way to gain agency, cope, entertain within their own community, and rebel."

In addition, there have been several direct revolutionary protests that occurred throughout Black history to gain rights, respect, and dignity, from the revolts of Nat Turner and Denmark Vessey to the revolution spurred by François-Dominique Toussaint Louverture in Haiti. The spectrum of protest as a mechanism to gain human dignity and rights has always been fundamental to the African in America and in the colonial era. The civil rights movement was a continuum of protest.

In the era of the civil rights and Black power movements, there was a great struggle primarily for Black women to assert their rights over their bodies. Little-known facts about some of the luminaries in the civil rights movement have been covered up as a result of bias and misogyny. For example, Rosa Parks is often looked at as someone who was "just tired" and decided not to give up her bus seat for a white man. The truth of the matter is that Ms. Parks was an extremely well-trained, hardened, and brilliant investigator whose sole focus was advocacy for Black women who had been brutally raped with impunity throughout the South. As a result of this multigenerational horror, the modern civil rights movement was organized and executed.

Contemporarily, there have been several iterations of the Black freedom struggle expressed since the widely accepted ending of the civil rights movement. Following every tragedy, there are several tactics of action that revolve around a show of struggle. For example, many may see the Jena Six as simply a series of 2006–2007 court battles between six Black students and one white student. The truth of the matter is that the Jena Six became widely known, in part, after the uproar and uprisings of more than 10,000 people within and outside communities in Jena, Louisiana, determined to assert their human worth and dignity. The same can be said of the responses from the freedom fighters of Sanford, Florida, after the police's reaction to the stalking and then shooting of Trayvon Martin by George Zimmerman; revolts in Ferguson, Missouri, after the police's killing of Michael Brown and their handling of his body after Officer Darren Wilson's bullet; and the Staten Island uprisings after Officer Daniel Pantaleo's chokehold on Eric Garner for suspicion of selling loosies without a tax stamp. It is important to note that during every protest of these tragedies, the struggles stretch across cities and inspire action directed at a larger system beyond state violence. Issues of education, municipal court reform, jobs, prisons, health, and more arise, answered with various measures of success reaching across borders, geography, government, and institution. In contemporary cases, we still see the Black freedom movement engaging in methods of protest from day-to-day, nuanced practices of resistance to direct action and the forming of organizations.

While it has been over ten years since the murder of Michael Brown and the ensuing Ferguson, Missouri, rebellions, it is important to remember the racist context in which this iteration of the Black freedom struggle arose. In other words, there are many examples of race-related incidents that make up the straw that later breaks the camel's back. We must remember the suspicious 2013–2014 firing of Art McCoy, a Black superintendent from Florissant, Missouri, without appreciable cause. The Department of Justice's probe into the Ferguson Police Department also shows findings of several racist horrors faced by Black residents, including but not limited to the following: (1) the 67 percent of Blacks in Ferguson account for 93 percent of arrests made in 2012–2014; (2) the disproportionate number of arrests and tickets, as well as the amount of force used, stemmed from unlawful bias rather than Black people committing more crime; and (3) from October 2012 to October 2014 in Ferguson, Missouri, every person arrested for "resisting arrest" was Black. It is in this racist context that momentum for the present Black freedom fighters campaigning for Michael Brown in Ferguson, Missouri, becomes more vibrant. However, this racist context has always existed.

Today's Black freedom struggle as a continuum carries a variety of tactics and strategies, perceived victories, and fresh perspectives. Similar to how the Sanford protests for Trayvon Martin catalyzed national protests, showing that their cause was less about the victim and more about the system, the Ferguson protests are catalyzing events (like the Twin Towers blowing up, but it wasn't about them in its totality) that deal with the whole system, reaching the nation's highest office. It is this political home that also plays a critical role in the emergence of the Black Lives Matter protest movement. So it is with little wonder that scholar Keeanga Taylor and activist Angela Davis characterize Ferguson as a "catalyst" and "symbol" of resistance. The small town of Ferguson is now understood as a rallying point for change, gains, and wins for the entire Black community. However, the Ferguson community itself continues to face repression.

CHAPTER 2

We Outside

Duty
When duty knocks on your door your whole house shakes.
The floor beneath your feet quakes.
Fast heartbeats accompanied by deep breaths you take.
There's no grey; just do or die, are you authentic or fake?

Saturday, August 9, 2014

"Did you hear about the young brother who got shot by police?" my mom asked. My mother, with fawn, yellow-brown arms had a silvery voice that calmed thunderstorms.

Earlier that day, I was in my feelings. I was at my dorm window, looking at the manicured lawns and thinking about another year on a white campus. The lawn was trimmed like the head of a son whose father is a talented barber. I was thinking of the hands that were cutting the lawn: hands that looked like my dad's.

A couple of people walked over the blades of grass toward a hammock to lie down, relax, converse, and enjoy the sun. The net was wide enough for them to lie on it together. They didn't look up from their rest to give attention to the group of people jogging on the pavement for exercise—a gang of white Billikens resembling Greg Smithey: Asics shoes, thigh-high shorts, and sweatbands.

The pack of runners made me think of my grandparents, who used to keep workout VHS tapes in their exercise room. At the bustling age of twelve; I was more into enjoying Dragon Ball Z: Goku, the heroic character, competed with Vegeta, the antihero.

I stepped outside my grandparents' home. For safety reasons, I wasn't supposed to unlock their screen door and go outdoors without their supervision, and they'd get angry with me for violating their rule. Defiant, I did it anyway because I figured they wouldn't know if I was sneaky quiet and did not stay out long. I was a hard-headed child. As I stood outside, my head was in the clouds, thinking about the workout trainer. I felt like Mr. Smithey was somebody because he could be found on the cover of the VHS sleeves. My emotions complemented my young, impressionable, and innocent eyes.

At my youthful age, I'd be ready to fight at the suggestion that my grandparents didn't know everybody there was to know in Saint Louis (the Lou). My Grampy Paulino, who could talk your ear off in a cheerful tone from morning to evening, knew the whole town. None of those stars on the cover of the VHS collection looked like the people he'd introduced me to. My grandparents rarely invited me to meet somebody white. Instead, I met their hardworking mechanic friends, Devout Kingdom Hall members, and the neighbor with sons across the street. They introduced me to the flashy man next door who drove the '98 Camaro and the elderly woman whose grandson, Trent, ended up going to Patrick Henry for middle school. None of them were on any VHS tapes. They were Black in all the richness of its shades. They all looked like me. My grandfather let me know they were somebody.

Jogging quickly past the hammock, perhaps the group was running from something just as much as they were traveling toward. A trio of people was walking in the opposite direction of the runners. I was amused looking at all the different bodies, shapes, garments, and styles. My Pops, who had an eagle eye for the land, would've described what I was doing as *people watching*. Studying the land and its inhabitants. Studying life in motion. Studying like my Pops would as he gripped clippers, staring at my head to ensure my at-home haircut was symmetrical.

While this was my second year on the white campus, it still bothered me that I couldn't see myself in any of these people on the yard. I was familiar with the environment yet never saw myself here. Feeling isolated is something you make peace with but never feel okay about. I didn't have to wonder where the people who looked like me were. They were on my grandparents' street on the quarter, 25th Street. It was my choice to enroll here. I knew damn well the reason I had rarely seen someone with hands, arms, legs, a face, or a body like mine. I hustled throughout my freshmen year, intentionally seeking out Black thinkers, writers, researchers, dancers, athletes, and poets. *Affinity groups* are what some campus employees called us. *Affinity*, a label stamped on us no different than a Food, Drug, and Administration sticker on milk.

I shifted my attention from the dorm window to my bed. The thick comforters and pillows looked like a pair of heavy arms open and ready to hug me. I felt tired. The brother working the lawn had hands like my father. He came from a family, had a hustle, and worked to meet his responsibilities. He was like a pianist, and the green spaces were the keys. Like the residents I grew up with across town in North Saint Louis, he probably wasn't on a VHS tape either. He was still special.

I was always happy to hear my mother's voice because despite how I felt, she wanted me to know that I belonged. Here in this supposedly white campus, city, nation, and world.

Just as my mother had a voice that could soothe, it could also startle. By nineteen, I was used to hearing my mom keeping me up to date on community affairs. Ever since I can recall being able to recall, she'd turn on National Public Radio during commutes to school. This was the case throughout middle and high school. Information from a stereo became a thread connecting my educational journey. If it wasn't NPR, it was HOT 104.1 or 100.3, *The Beat,* which featured hip-hop, RnB, and Saint Louis local news. I loved Hot 104.1 because it was less jargon and more hip-hop. My mom would harmonize to all kinds of RnB: Amy Winehouse, Robin Thicke, Nina Simone, Donny Hathaway, and Miki Howard. Regardless, community news was guaranteed to fill her black SUV's cabin, booming from its stereos. Long stretches from my grandparents' tall brick home to school were colored with songs about love or reports. Hearing news commentary from the stereo felt like tasting cough syrup from my mother's bathroom cabinet. I knew it was good for me, but it didn't feel pleasurable.

It was the fall of 2009, and I was fourteen years old. Crisp autumn leaves decorated the streets, flipping like cartwheels in the light breeze. This was my kind of weather: hoodie weather. I felt good knowing I'd be able to dress comfortably in stylish ways that only Black youths I grew up with would know. The hoodies and jumpsuits were in my closet waiting for me, and I was thrilled to rock them out. While in the car on the way to my ninth-grade classes, I was playing my cherished video game: a Sony PlayStation Portable (PSP). I was trying to enjoy myself as much as I could. I had to be attentive during a day of lectures from teachers who did not look like me—well-meaning people whose kindness rarely translated beyond the realm of their classrooms and into a world that could be frightful. A world that often attempted to terrorize Black youth.

I didn't understand my mom's fascination, curiosity, and attention around being tied to hearing folks talk all day about other people's problems. At that age, the PSP was my escape from all the noise from the stereo—until it wasn't.

"You hear that?" my mom asked to see if my siblings and I were paying attention. Pop quizzes are not just the tools of teachers but also temperature checks of Black parents. Annoyed by the interruption of my game, I quickly replied, "No."

"No?" my mom shouted with anger at both *how* I answered her and what I said. She bellowed in a soulful yet authoritative cadence unique to Black mamas, "Who the fuck you think you talking to?" Cussing was sometimes second nature to adults in my family, like eating.

I swallowed my pride. I had known better than to answer any adults in my family without putting a *ma'am* or *sir* before the period. Preferring to correct myself rather than wreck myself, I quickly updated my response to a humble "no, ma'am." As I continued punching the buttons on my plastic entertainment device, she stated, "You need to put that damn game down and listen up!"

Begrudgingly, I complied with her direct command to hear the stereo. The quickest way to the grave in my family, like most Black families I grew up around, was disrespect. I was regularly reminded that even as her first son, I wasn't above being the first child to meet my maker.

Being my parents' first son made me feel important. My dad, who has a little brother, Uncle David, always explained to me, "Your younger siblings are always watching you." I have a gang of them. One of my siblings is my senior, Ti (Tianay), and there are three who are my junior: David, Chris, and T'Mya. Walking with my younger siblings was my first step in understanding what it meant to lead or be in charge. When I was left home alone with them, my voice regulated when my folks went to bed. If an argument happened, my arms separated my warriors. If hunger unsettled our stomachs, my culinary creativity came to fruition in the kitchen to make sure we all ate. With that obligation came a bunch of pops across the mouth, whooping on my behind, and privileges taken away when I failed to honor the values instilled in me. Abusing power came at its costs. I got the most spankings out of all my siblings growing up, which is probably why I became the tallest.

Listening to the radio, I heard the booming and smooth delivery of Barack Obama. I paused to appreciate the nation's first Black president talk. He had a distinguishable cadence. I never really listened to the content of his conversation as much as I paid attention to how he spoke. He was a formidable orator. Anybody who knows me will tell you that my favorite ballplayer has been LeBron James since I knew the sport. I loved how he dominated the game and put Cleveland on his back despite not yet having a championship ring. Whatever LeBron James's dunk was on the court, that's what Obama's voice was at the podium. Obama's delivery was smooth, well-rehearsed, and dynamic.

The hair on my mom's skin raised as she was listening to Obama, signaling that she was growing agitated. She repeatedly rolled her eyes from the road to the radio and had this look of disappointment on her full face. Eventually, she shut off the radio as he was speaking. My mom pursed her full lips, mumbled some words under her breath, and repeatedly pointed her slender finger at the radio. She always had this still-waters-run-deep demeanor, where she gave a heavy sigh if ever she was upset. I wondered why she had just cut off the nation's first Black president. More importantly, why did she have me put down my PSP to listen to the man if she was going to shut him off?

After we cruised for a moment in silence, my mom rolled her brown eyes in a final act of annoyance before finally letting whatever she was feeling all out. She opened her mouth and said, "Just like a nigga! We did all that pushing for him, and now white folks got him *scared* to fight for his own people!"

Scared? I struggled with that adjective being applied to the nation's first Black president. What did he say or do that reflected fear? I felt like his election was a courageous and huge win for Black people. I grew up with elders who were unwaveringly confident that "it'd be a cold day in hell before we get one in the white *man's* house." America would never have Black people in 1600 Pennsylvania Avenue unless they were mowing the lawn. They were wise. They taught me a lot. Nevertheless, it meant everything to me as a young Black boy to see somebody who looked like me in the highest position of authority in the nation. My understanding was that everybody, including white folk, had to answer to Obama. He did his job by winning against all the odds. As a young Black boy at the tender age of fourteen, I thought Obama could do no wrong.

My mom slowly pulled the van over to my high school, located across town from our neighborhood, in the "prestigious" Central West

End. Before letting me out, she stated, "Kids, listen, if you aren't angry with how our people are living, you aren't *paying attention.*" The seriousness in her voice was her way of letting us know she commanded attention. She demanded that I pay attention.

I was engaged but felt cheated out of my game time prior to Obama and NPR pissing off my mama. Sitting in the SUV, I was hot—heated and frustrated. I had a deep want to yell, "Fuck the news" from my bottom of my stomach, at my diaphragm, to the top of my lungs. I knew better than to satisfy that risky desire with actual action. I was born at night but not last night. My mom didn't play, and I wanted to at least live to see another day of video games. I swallowed my ego.

What did Obama say that indicated to my mom that he was afraid to fight for Black people? He was so well-spoken. His attire was regularly sharp and dressed up. He honored his family. He was a presidential kind of somebody. My mom explained that she did not want me to be in love with appearances. She articulated her criticism confidently as if she knew what it was like loving something or somebody that looked more than what they turned out to be. Disappointment like a prom king who leaves with the queen instead of the date he brought. She emphasized that love does not mean without accountability. Love does not mean without critics or scrutiny. It wasn't until about a couple of years later, the spring before my seventeenth birthday, that I began to grasp what my mom meant.

Later, I started to understand why my mom cussed out the nation's first Black president. On February 26th, 2012, a boy was murdered by a coward in Miami Gardens, Florida. The teenager happened to be only a few months older than me and seemed to share my love for hoodies. His name was Trayvon Martin.

At the time Martin was murdered, Mama Lola had worked with a social justice organization called Metro Saint Louis Coalition for Inclusion and Equity (M-SLICE), with the director, Romona. Queen Mother Romona, which I affectionately call her, was a powerful organizer. When her russet, reddish-brown arms hugged you, it was heartfelt and full. Her hands could make a deliciously moist and mouthwatering chocolate cake. The way words flowed when she opened her mouth came with a breathy cadence. Together, they helped expose the racial, economic, and environmental injustices happening in North Saint Louis. This part of town was not just a community but a location my grandparents let me know was filled with somebodies. Examples of their work included tackling the racist Delmar Divide (in partnership with the brilliant Dr. Ilene Berman) and gun violence, such as the Eye on the Sparrow Peace Project. Dr. Ilene, a warm yet sharp-spoken white Jewish woman, whom I met through Mama Lola while she was married to her husband. Dr. Ilene and Scott Berman, a snazzy and laid-back white Jewish man, who kept a smile and often dressed classy, would call out the Delmar Divide. They were some of the first white people I felt I could be myself around.

I was born in the hands of a doctor that happened to be a white woman. I was taken in like a family member by my mom's white coworker, Ms. Debbie at Cardinal Glennon. However, Dr. Berman's organized resistance gave me hope for white people on questions of justice. Anyone driving from South Grand going north to where my family stayed will pass a street that makes them feel like they've gone through a portal into a world of haves and have-nots. This street is called Delmar. Traveling across the boulevard is like entering an imaginary gate that's very real. On the south side of the entrance are luxuries such as the Fox Theater, the Best Steak House, Grand Arts Center, and the Gothic architecture of Saint Louis University. On the north side of the entrance, there are Check-N-Cash locations, Church's Chicken, and vacant buildings. I loved the crisp drumsticks that my Ganny Naomi Pulphus purchased after services at Azariah Baptist Church. The south side of Delmar was majorly where the white somebodies stayed. The north side of Delmar was where the Black somebodies lived.

To expose this, using nine pieces of illuminated signage and a group of volunteers, Dr. Ilene and M-SLICE set up shop one night near the boulevard. As cars crossed the imaginary gate, the light bulbs on the signs would read I-N-V-I-S-I-B-L-E. On one side of the portal was substantive investment, while there was little to none toward where my family lived. I'd later learn from Mama Lola that this was tied to a slick plan called the Team Four Plan. This was a devious plot by white developers that advocated resources in areas populated along racial lines.

This village that my mom connected my siblings and me to gave youth like us a platform to express ourselves and realize our own power. My mother took my younger sibling T'Mya to see Common in 2013 at Saint Louis University, which ended in a photo of which I was proud. Common was one of the few "conscious" hip-hop artists my mom would play in her black SUV when Hot 104.1 offered age-inappropriate options. He was a socially conscious celebrity who openly critiqued systems and institutions. At my mom's three-story brick home around the corner from my grandparents, she kept a library of books on social issues and justice. This included works such as Herb Boyd's *We Shall Overcome*. In addition, there was Doris Wesley's *Lift Every Voice and Sing: St. Louis African Americans in the Twentieth Century*. She even had Ellen Levine's *Freedom Children*. This is just to name a few.

Just as my mom blasted music in the van, she'd regularly play songs in the house. Examples included Billie Holiday's "Strange Fruit," Sam Cooke's "A Change Is Gonna Come," and Aretha Franklin's "Respect." There'd also be Nina Simone's "Mississippi Goddam." You'd listen to Jill Scott, Lauryn Hill, India Arie, and Erykah Badu too. Almost every January for Martin Luther King Jr. Day, my mom took us to participate in the Saint Louis City–sponsored march in his memory for the values he was killed for so soon.

My rearing and experiences shaped my understanding of justice for my people. My mom and dad grew up near each other on the north side. My dad stayed near 23rd and Bremen, while my mom stayed on 25th and Bremen. I've lived all over Saint Louis, but I feel like I became who and what I am today growing up on this side of Delmar. It is because of my mom's story and lessons I've heard from my father, Jonathan Sr., that I have always felt grounded. My father, who was always a husky, strong guy, picked up books after weights following football practices. Since my Ganny Naomi was a piano player, he naturally learned how to dance on the instrument. Somewhere along the line, my mom and dad got together, and boom: my older sibling, Ti, was eventually born. My folks were salt-of-the-earth servant leaders who didn't walk over pennies on the ground. They wanted us to know that the little was the first step of something major. The glossed over and overlooked was often gold.

Having courage is not synonymous with popularity, but at the time, I mistakenly believed it to be so. Tied to this, I believed that rocking the boat too hard or making a mistake was the end all, be all. Life is about learning from missteps. Everybody didn't agree with, break bread with, or want to be around the radical Dr. Rev. Martin Luther King Jr. According to a 1966 Gallup Poll, most Americans did not approve of King. Despite the naysayers and devil's advocates, King's stance did not falter. King didn't mince words when it came to his people, and he refused to back down when the rubber hit the road. It was what it was, and it was going to be what it was going to be. At the same time, King's courage required a level of responsibility and a temperature check with reality. He had to dot his Is and cross his Ts: be on top of the clock and keep track of what was in his backpack.

It is critical to be unashamed of rocking the boat, pushing yourself, and making mistakes during your journey as an activist. While I was at Fairview Elementary School, my father, Jonathan Pulphus Sr., taught me a poem by Quincy Jones called "Once a Task Has Begun." In college, he was into poetry and learned a whole host of gems that he could spit at any minute. I feel that he taught me the Jones poem because when I was challenged, I'd go the easy route. I was heavy on video games and Konami Yu-Gi-Oh cards growing up yet light on school work. My parents wouldn't allow Konami Yu-Gi-Oh cards in the house because my mom had sensibilities from being raised as a Jehovah's Witness. She barely tolerated my siblings watching the show because her parents deemed all the references to Egyptian gods (characters on the show) as demonic. My dad went along with it to keep peace with my mom. Since my parents would never buy them, I'd sneakily steal decks of the cards from the store. One time, I got caught, and my parents made me walk the cards back into the store past security. I felt deeply embarrassed.

The first game I can remember my dad buying my siblings was a Sega Dreamcast around 2000, which came with fun discs like Crazy Taxi, Tony Hawk, and Sonic. While I found joy playing the Sega game, I always had to share and wanted my own. I had three siblings at the time—that was a nice amount of sharing. While in the fourth grade, I asked my dad to purchase a Nintendo Gameboy Advance SP. It was a portable game that came with a backlight, so I figured I could play all night when I was supposed to be in bed. When he refused to purchase the game because I wasn't doing my homework and underperforming in school, I felt overwhelmed. I took it on myself to steal again. I took a game from the son of my mother's childhood friend. I ended up getting caught by my mom; my dad ended up whooping everything but the Black off my ass. After he cooled down and the punishment was over, he sat me down and asked why I *ever* felt the need to steal, notwithstanding taking something that my family could provide. I complained about how badly I wanted a game of my own. My dad recited to me the Quincy Jones poem and made me memorize it. He emphasized that shortcuts lead to short results. The end of the poem states, "Whether the task be great or small / do it right or not at all."

She was born on Monday, November 22. This is the same birth year as Tupac, the hip-hop trailblazer and nephew of legendary Assata Shakur. Neither of her parents' families was from Saint Louis. Her dad, my Grampy Paulino, had a family from the South, while her mom Grammy Roberta's family came from Kansas City. My mom's parents were not very politically involved. She had a very religious upbringing raised as a Jehovah's Witness, and politics were frowned on. Her parents believed in a theocratic system. They felt like their particular branch of Christianity should not be involved in politics. They thought the best way to change society was by being better people. As Witnesses, they didn't vote, so there was no political involvement in a traditional sense at all.

Because my mom was brought up as a Jehovah's Witness, she was able to get out and see more of the world than what was in her immediate surroundings. Her family didn't celebrate holidays or the Pledge of Allegiance. She learned at an early age that Jehovah's Witnesses were ostracized for the kind of work they do, going from door to door spreading what they called the *gospel*, or *good news*. Sharing the *WatchTower Magazine* with people made it easier for her to learn how to talk to people in the community. She was able to observe the levels of poverty, what people do to exist, and how people cope. This experience was on an intimate level because she got invited into people's homes and saw how they lived. From these visits, she realized that the majority of people in authority with power seemed to not be doing anything to help except putting Band-Aids on problems. Wraparound services were not reaching families wrestling with high levels of stress and trauma. Social services were grossly and pathetically underfunded. The city was giving them a little bit of soothing, some hope. But to my mom, it felt like receiving the crumbs of empty hope.

As Witnesses, my mom and her family were discouraged from participating in anything that could be construed as rebellion or activism. However, at home, my grandparents would talk about events going on in the world. My mom said she had a conversation with my grandmother where she asked, "Why is it that you all are not standing up on certain issues?" My grandmother stated, "If my faith wasn't as strong, I would be out in the streets right now. But I believe that, basically, God will take care of things in time and that this is a sinking ship." My mom was puzzled by my grandmother's description of the world as a "sinking ship." Why put all your effort into building or seeking change when the world is going down the drain anyway? My mom would equate that to other religions where people would say, "Well, I don't have anything to do with this. I'm just looking to go to heaven." My mom was frustrated with that because it suggested that our existence here doesn't matter.

Despite this hands-off mentality, my mom's parents would talk about corruption in Saint Louis and how certain elected figures such as aldermen, mayors, or other individuals were engaged in affairs that were counter to transforming the community. At the end of the day, there was no action plan to counter the nonsense due to the family's background. The religion did not address or hold decision-makers accountable.

My mom went to a K-8 school called Waring A. B. I. school. According to her, there were a lot of Black teachers, primarily women. The teachers instilled a sense of pride in their students. She spoke about how they made sure she and her peers felt proud to be Black. Teachers would tell students to "stand up tall" and give affirmations that made them feel good about who they were. Unapologetically, the staff would tell the young people that their lives would be different from those led by white kids.

By high school, my mom was involved in a lot of activities. Both my parents were a part of the desegregation program. In the mid- to late 1980s, they went to a high school down in South County, Saint Louis, called Mehlville. There was a lot of anger from the white community about Black youth being in the schools. My mom told me it was to the point where she'd hear stories of how some whites would drive down the road and "play frogger" with Black students. In other words, it was open season, and kids would be targeted for hit and runs. She had heard many stories from my grandparents about what was happening between white and Black folks back in the day, giving her a sense of how ugly things were. As a result, my mom committed herself to trying to make a difference and seeing that her kids would be prepared. Their kids were going to face the realities of the world, including racism, and always be in service to their people.

Beyond the retaliation from the white community, many students did not want Black classmates attending Mehlville. White students would deface Black students' lockers. During my mom's geometry class, after her name was called for attendance, white students questioned her Blackness. They asked, "Well, you're not Black, are you?" My grampy's father was Mexican, and his wife was Black. My mom said it was so bad that she helped start an anti-racist student organization called the Bi-Racial Committee. Through this organization, anti-racist students started complaining to the administration about these racist incidents.

My mom talked about how she had a counselor who was racist. She recalled going to him for college counseling and wanted to take some university-level courses while in high school. This made sense because it'd give you a head start for college, and white students were taking advantage of this opportunity. The counselor told her that "college isn't for everybody." Instead of helping her prepare for a postsecondary opportunity, he made her take the Armed Services Vocational Aptitude Battery test. At the time, my mom wanted to be a nurse, not a member of the military. This further upset her.

After graduating, my mom decided to go to community college. She got pregnant with my older sibling, Ti, and enrolled the next fall. While at school, she connected with the United African Peoples on campus organization, which was focused on empowering Black students. They'd invite dynamic speakers and host resource events. Through this experience, she learned a lot about the struggle across the African Diaspora around the world.

After gaining credits, my mom transferred to the adult program at Saint Louis University. The fields of study she was interested in include organizational psychology, community, and real estate development. Years later, she ended up connecting with her sister-friend Queen Mother Romona. Conversations with my mom about her hurdles and growth helped me better understand courage, character, and teachability. Nothing was simple or easy for her, yet these principles guided her toward transforming the community despite the challenges.

I hopped off the porch in Jennings, which is less than ten minutes from Ferguson. My family stayed on Dawson Street until the summer before my sixth-grade year in 2006. I attended Fairview in Jennings and transferred across town to a city school named Patrick Henry. I had the privilege of going to Crossroads for high school and then finished up at SLU in 2017.

Henry was a school near the Cochran neighborhood, and a lot of my peers were from the north side. Living on the north side was all about survival. The trauma my peers faced in the community was often brought to class. Our school lacked resources and funding to treat the unique needs of its students. Regularly, there were challenging moments.

The encouragement I had from my peer and brother Enrique Bronner helped me stay focused. Enrique had tawny, orange-brown hands that he'd use to draw designs for architecture and video games.

Many of my classmates had run-ins with the law in different forms. Being exposed to life on the north side gave me a reality check that educational and justice systems in Saint Louis were not designed for the betterment of Black families.

I had my first fights and physical altercations at Patrick Henry. I remember my first scuffle and loss. During outdoor recess, my peers were playing basketball, passing footballs, double dutching, and more. Beyond the regular recess activities, kids being kids meant sometimes doing ignorant shit that can lead to harm. An example of this is a trick wherein a quarterback would lob a spiral in the air with no intention of the ball being caught. As the receiver was unsuspectingly preparing for the catch, the quarterback would bullet pass another ball at the receiver's chest or head. I had the misfortune of being the receiver in this instance and got hit in the face hard. In retaliation, I threw the ball back at my aggressor and ran. Hella funny. In Saint Louis, if you get hit, you hit back, but I wasn't staying around for the retaliation. After all, dude was going to have to catch me for that lick back. Another youth witnessed my brisk escape and called me a *bitch* for running. Being called that word out loud by somebody was the ultimate level of disrespect and shame. Ashamed of feeling cowardly, I stopped in my tracks and stood my ground. The quarterback rushed me to the ground, and all I could remember was his shoe turning my head into a trampoline. Staff immediately broke up the fight and disciplined the other youth. They never sat us down together to unpack what healing could look like. There were no programs for mediating conflict, which meant students were kicked out of class or school.

I had my first experience seeing students hustle to support themselves and those they cared about. There were no efforts to assist with the economic injustices students faced, so the black market became attractive. I had my first time seeing students cuss teachers out. There were no counseling services to scale in place for healing. There were few boundaries for the expression of trauma. I journeyed through my first time losing a peer, James, to gun violence. We never had any schoolwide campaigns to address violence plaguing our neighborhoods. It takes nine months to give birth, but a life can be taken in less than nine seconds.

I studied far outdated textbooks and witnessed my peers being told they'd never amount to anything. I learned to stand up for myself, focus on my responsibilities, and be humble.

Having Enrique at Patrick Henry made the tougher times seem bearable. He was a solid brother and always kept his head up despite the instability. Many a day in class, we'd talk about our aspirations beyond the brick and mortar we studied in. He wanted to be an architect, given his artistic ability, and I wanted to be a lawyer. I'd bring a suitcase to class, while everyone else had book bags. My peers used to chuckle about me to each other and ask, "Who this nigga think he is?" Enrique always used to carry around his drawing pad to design different concepts. When either of us lost a fight or failed an assignment, we'd encourage and defend each other. Our dreams were worth more than the hell that tried to take them away. It ain't about who won but that you stood yours, demanding respect. When we had assignments, we compared notes to sharpen ourselves. This was our brotherhood.

While at Patrick Henry, my siblings and I were enrolled in the Freedom School afterschool program. I used to get picked up, typically by Brother Ted Gaitlin, and taken to Jamison Memorial Church on Washington and Leffingwell. From after school till pick up, we were immersed in enrichment lessons that nurtured our self-esteem, public speaking, education, health, and artistry. I remember the hot meals, loving staff, field trips, friends, and chants. We'd sing "Something inside So Strong" by Afro-British singer Claudius Afolabi "Labi" Siffre to kick off every day. After that start to our late afternoon, the rest of the evening was just filled with engaging activities.

My life was transformed when I walked into Crossroads. I listened to privileged kids complain about not having parking spaces, while I pinched together money for the metro bus. This immediately taught me it's not how you get there but the journey and destination that teach the most valuable lessons. I saw people complain about not being able to go off campus to buy food for lunch while trying to decide how I could find nourishment in the snack machine. This immediately taught me to feed my soul and nourish my mind because that was invaluable. Many of my peers loved visual diversity but didn't like putting in work to serve diverse communities. When Meek Mill dropped *Dreams and Nightmares* in October 2012, many white students knew every word. When Trayvon Martin was murdered in February 2012, many white students were silent. The nation's first Black president played both sides. First, he got on the news and said, "This could have been my son." Then, in the same sentence, he stated, "Law enforcement has got a very tough job." I felt rage at George Zimmerman but was upset that Obama seemed to be sending mixed signals. I felt either you are with your people, or you are for yourself. Clearly the racist attitude of law enforcement enabled the neighborhood watchmen to pursue and murder Trayvon. In addition, I was upset that no space was available in school to process the tragedy. Crossroads was located off Delmar and DeBaliviere. As a Black student, I gained the value of being cordial or learning how to pretend to like a lot of people.

I learned the dangers of neoliberalism—the free market. Saint Louis City is a place where the disparities are systemic, its terror felt in communities bearing both failing and succeeding schools. At the end of the day, getting accepted into and even succeeding in a school like Crossroads doesn't mean you'll be retained and graduate. Deep poverty, a triplet to racism and sexism, is the root of our issues. Entering Crossroads, I dealt with more than simply culture shock or academic struggles but also access issues. While Crossroads offered a wonderful curriculum with academic support, its best available financial aid package could only do so much concerning access. I was only able to attend and graduate from Crossroads because of gracious support that helped me in addressing some of these structural issues.

Throughout my experience, I constantly got introduced to the insidious nature of institutional injustice that can emerge as neoliberal tokenism. One significant highlight was my eighth- to twelfth-grade guidance counselor, Ms. Gina Watkins (affectionately called Ms. G.). While the school touted diversity, Black students regularly complained that the school ostensibly served as a nesting ground for white student leadership by default. This was evidenced by the abysmal representation of Black students. Naturally, this expressed itself in several areas of organized student life. Through storytelling about injustices within a culturally relevant space, Ms. G. encouraged us to think about and respond critically to our conditions and resources. By doing so, we intentionally began to compete in student body elections and partake in various activities. Black students' involvement increased, making us better prospects for college rather than simply numbers on a diversity chart. As students, we were encouraged to be honest and taken seriously about our experiences with injustice. We felt empowered to use our agency to gain skill sets and experiences we needed to prepare for college. We forged space within a neoliberal tokenizing educational system and grew aware of the ways in which we had the wherewithal to resist our conditions.

One of my Crossroads brothers, Stanford Cooper, was with me in this literature class when he reminded me to always stand your truth. We were reading Mark Twain's *Huckleberry Finn*, and the teacher said it was all right for white students to say the word *nigger*. This was to be done in quoting a passage when responding to a prompt. Stanford and I looked at each other, befuddled and angry. We knew white people should never be given a license or a pass to say that slur. Stanford ended up writing an entire paper to the teacher expressing his discontent with the Finn reading policy. I am grateful for Stanford's standing unapologetically and with integrity.

When I entered Saint Louis University in 2013, all of the lessons I faced growing up as a Black student in Saint Louis became imperative. I remember feeling self-doubt about who I was in comparison to my white counterparts at the institution. To be myself, I had to remember to stand on principle. Fortunately, I met a host of Black students and staff at the campus who also wrestled with the environment. I benefited from building with the constituents and leaders of the Black Student Alliance. Students like Christopher Walter, Gold Gladney (who also attended Crossroads with me), Brittany Kendricks, Jaden Janak, and Trevor Woolfolk all reminded me to unapologetically be myself. They understood the pressures of being the only Black scholar and told stories about the advantages of togetherness. I also got to build relationships with faculty and staff that proved critical to my development. Members in and outside of the African American studies program, such as Ms. Dana Guyton, Dr. Stefan Bradley, Dr. Olubukola Gbadegesin, and Professor Justin Hansford, held me to a standard of excellence despite the racism permeating the institution. Staff throughout campus such as Queen Mother LaTanya Buck, Mr. Terrance Hubbard (#23rdFam), Ms. Aleidra Allen, Mr. Steve Wong, Mr. VonDerrit Myers Sr., and Ms. Mae Cox all encouraged me to persist when times were bleak. There were many non-Black staff members and students who lifted me in my process. Students like Ryan McKinley, Sarah Nash, Matt Heskamp, Emma Cunningham, and Jason Ebinger kept it real about privilege and power. Staff like Dr. Ilene and Scott Berman, Martha Allen, Bryan

Sokol, and Dr. Lauri Glover all poured into me. It was these and many more people on campus, combined with my grounding off campus, that gave me strength.

Not feeling lonely because my village of support helped me overcome many trying times during my first year at SLU, I still struggled to live in a dorm with a majority of white students, despite select Black students being around such as my resident adviser, Tasso Pettigrew. Establishing interracial relationships was a task because certain students were just outrageously ignorant. It was impossible to build friendships with them due to their racist dispositions. They would make racist assumptions, and I wasn't in the business of faking along to get along. I remember in my first year, pictures leaked of several members of a white sorority donning brown face. The disrespect was off the chain. Some say, "If you don't want to experience racism, why not go to a historical Black college and university?" You shouldn't have to go to Morehouse or Spelman to be in an environment that doesn't challenge your humanity because of your skin. My professors were mostly all white, while the maintenance crew and cafeteria staff were mainly Black. This made me feel all kinds of ways about how SLU could recruit and retain Black staff for hard labor but not academic labor. Then they hardly offered job security, quality pay, or benefits to Black staff on either side. My first year had its hurdles, but I was far from isolated due to the community of support around me.

When I got the earlier question from my mom about Mike Brown Jr., asking "Did you hear about the young brother who got shot by police?," I was in the middle of decorating my residential hall. I held down several jobs in undergrad at SLU, including as resident adviser and student worker / circulation clerk at Pius XII Memorial Library. In addition, I served as the youth outreach specialist with Williams and Associates. As a resident adviser, I felt like I had a special call to encourage my residents to respond to Mike Brown's murder from a perspective of mentorship and activism. There was no better way to exemplify guidance than by setting the example. The theme for our floor was leadership for social change. That phone call from my mom sharpened the trajectory of my undergraduate experience.

"No, ma'am, I haven't" was my response to my mom's question.

"Well, it's all over social media. It looks like a young man has been killed by police."

I scrolled through my Facebook (I didn't get Twitter until later, on August 21, 2014) and saw a photo of Lezley McSpadden's, Michael Brown's mother, boyfriend, Louis Head, holding signage. On cardboard, marked in big, bold letters, it stated, "Ferguson Police Just Executed My Unarmed Son." All I could think about was Trayvon Martin. I was infuriated.

Overcoming Challenges as a Black Student in a White School

One of the worst activities or attitudes that a white school can partake in is to believe and behave like race is not a factor in its dwellings. After and around the election of the first Black president, a major news outlet promoted a mentality that we were in a multi- *but* post-racial society. Being a multiracial nation means that white schools will always have multiracial issues, while there is an imbalance in power in this country.

Eight days after the swearing in of the first Black US president, the late Daniel Schorr, a journalist for National Public Radio, unpacked the term *post-racial*. Schorr explained that since Barack Obama won the election, American politics now transcended race. He explained that citizens should "begin to make race-free judgments on who should lead them." His use of *post-racial* may have been well-meaning in terms of naming the unseating of a racial monopoly of the nation's highest office, illustrated by 232 years of 43 white presidents from 1776 to 2008. The National Education Association, the biggest labor union in the United States for educators, defined *post-racial* to provide language to aid in topics on race: it is "used to describe a time in which racial prejudice and discrimination no longer exist." Thus, Schorr's employment of *post-racial* to describe the political moment is dangerously untrue. No system in America, politics or otherwise, operates with race-free judgment. The same is true of education.

The punishment of Black youths in schools counters notions of a post-racial society. Dr. April Duncan, a racial trauma expert and counselor, cites data from the Office of Civil Rights, pointing to the disproportionate ills Black students face in their school matriculation. Looking at the 2017–2018 school year for public schools nationally, Dr. Duncan shared how "Black students accounting for 15% of enrollment . . . made up 38% of expulsions . . . 33% of students with one or more out-of-school suspension." The US Department of Education Office for Civil Rights published a more recent report assessing the 2020–2021 calendar year, indicating that "Black boys were nearly two times more likely than White boys to receive an out-of-school suspension or expulsion in K-12 public schools." These figures, which allude to the phenomenon known as the *school-to-prison pipeline*, is only one way to illustrate the national crisis of race and education.

Decades after the civil rights movement, being a multiracial school should be a standard less than a celebratory outcome. White schools that celebrate themselves for being "diverse" environments may unintentionally look at Black students as a number on a demographic count. Just because a white school has increased its number of Black students from 5 to 10 percent does not mean those students are valued and protected. Issues include a range of challenges that Black students face in white schools, from attacks on self-esteem to violence; Black students having to sit at lunch tables by themselves or being the last approached by their white peers for collaborative study when it's time to do group assignments; and Black students being treated by white students as the exception to or spokesperson for their race when questions about Blackness arise. Race is implicated on all levels of white schooling except where it matters, such as significantly increased resources for Black student recruitment, retention, and graduation.

Microaggressions and biases abound. In white colleges, some whites assume that Black students are the immediate beneficiaries of affirmative action and race-based scholarships that were actually tailored toward white women. In addition, white schools lack services and resources that allow Black students to build connections with each other, such as Black student organizations; refuse to challenge white students to wrestle with the implications of their identity (white privilege, power); and do not offer culturally relevant curricula that emphasize teachings about Black experience and contributions (Black art, STEM, history, literature, politics). Schools have core values and mission statements claiming to value diversity but no robust plan and investment tied to increasing their Black student count or faculty numbers. Since race intersects with class, many Black students can benefit from fruitful relationships between their schools and community resources such as wraparound services to help assist them beyond the walls of the school buildings. Connections to organizations that offer support tied to housing, transportation, health (physical and mental), food, and other basic necessities go a long way, but white schools rarely make the trip.

Dr. Jasmine Harris, an associate professor of African American studies at the University of Texas, speaks to the persistence of racism in education despite civil rights legislation. Pointing to historically white-serving colleges and universities (HWSCU), Harris explains that "*Brown v. Board of Education* was meant to be a turning point . . . but race-based hardships persist." There were high hopes and dreams following the codification of anti-racist educational legislation; however, it failed to outpace the nightmares and horrors endured by Black students. Schools that tout diversity or emphasize meritocratic notions to Black students still fall short of actual inclusion. In Harris's words, "Willpower and grit may improve achievement for Black people in school, but it doesn't guarantee our belonging." No matter what Black students academically accomplish, buoyed by their laborious determination, it does not mean their schools will offer a space that welcomes them.

The ubiquitous racial trauma endured by Black adolescents sheds light on the prevalence of racism in and beyond education. Citing various studies and research, Dr. April Duncan writes about the frequent experiences of racial discrimination that Black youths face: "Black youth experience an average of five incidents of discrimination a day." This means that in one calendar year, one Black youth faces over eighteen hundred racial incidents. Being bombarded like this day to day can make them numb to racial trauma; however, desensitization does not make this less of a problem. Educational institutions, as the spaces where Black youths spend a significant portion of their year, play a role in either perpetuating or reducing the trauma that Black young people experience.

Schools taking steps to embrace Black students by implementing policies and practices that develop a culture that's psychologically safe is one way to counter such challenges. Marcene Robinson, a former staff writer at the University of Buffalo, wrote recommendations for creating school environments conducive to Black students' well-being. Robinson features research by Dr. Kamontá Heidelburg on schools employing Afrocentric approaches to creating inclusive and fulfilling learning environments. Heidelberg, an assistant professor of counseling and psychology at the University of Buffalo, presents thoughtful insights in his publication titled *Reconceptualizing School Safety for Black Students*, emphasizing the need for shifts in curriculum, school rules, discipline, and mentorship for Black students. Robinson also shares Heidelberg's critique of schools' treatment of Black students: "Culturally incongruent curricula, discipline disparities and bias from school staff are all part of the schooling experience for Black students." Moreover, the classes Black students take are Eurocentric, security responses to Black students are brutal, and internalized prejudices of school staff abound. Countering these ills "could have a positive impact on the educational experiences of Black youth," Heidelberg emphasizes.

When it comes to multiracial politics in white schools, it's like bringing people together who normally would not interact with each other, live by each other, pray in the same religious spaces, eat at the same table, or shop in the same businesses. The differences in experiences and stories create space for needed racial conversations. Unfortunately, some schools do not even offer spaces for students to dialogue with each other about identity, challenges, and joys that stem from their backgrounds. Students are expected to navigate at least four years of classroom time and build relationships without genuine and intentional spaces that shed light on racial analysis in a country that was built on the damning racial assessment that Black people are subhuman.

There are ways white schools can implement practices that make their environments anti-racist and welcoming for Black students. Edith Lewis, a senior lecturer in social work at Canterbury Christ Church University, provides micro- and macro-suggestions on creating school settings conducive to Black students. In an article published by *Times Higher Education*, Lewis shares that on a microlevel, teachers should "discuss White fragility, race and racism with all students and take time to be knowledgeable on these issues." Faculty should unpack how conversations about racism create defensiveness or discomfort in some whites. They should also explore the ways in which systems of injustice based on race have existed to the present day. This helps address the elephant in the (class)room in white school environments.

For schools that allow students to converse about these relationships, it is not to be applauded if it is not backed by systemic shifts within white schools themselves to address inequities and exclusion. Schools are hypocritical to require that their own white students wrestle with bias and microaggressions when the institution itself does not address its own complicity or direct role in perpetuating problematic racial policies and practices; when white students commit acts of racial aggression, and there's no restorative accountability measures in place; when all the cafeteria, maintenance, and manual labor staff members are Black, but the teachers, board, and administration are white; and when the only outlet Black students have to talk about Black history and accomplishments is during the month of February.

The schoolwide attention of campus administrators placing a priority on the hopes and grievances experienced by Black students can help create a stronger sense of belonging. Lewis asks on a meso-level, "How actively does your university seek the voice of black students on a regular basis?" Are Black students actually included in the decision-making processes surrounding campus affairs? If not, an adjustment that centers their experience at various levels of the school structure can help create a more inclusive learning environment.

The challenge Black students face in white schools is not only to their detriment but also to white students' and professionals' despair. White schools can create bubbles where students matriculate believing race is a nonissue or an issue for just Black students or people of color to wrestle with. White students then live with a false reality and shortsighted understanding of the human experience and consequences of systems that diminish human potential. In that way, white schools produce future politicians, lawyers, doctors, journalists, police, teachers, blue- and white-collar professionals who buy into the lies of meritocracy, neoliberalism, and post-racial mindsets. How can the inequities in policy, legislation, health, education, media, criminal justice, and the workplace be resolved when the one place charged with educating people about power imbalances refuses to do so? It's impossible to transform society when white schools do not address the fact that social ills endured by Black communities due to past and present white-centered policies must change.

Racism diminishes the quality of life for Black students and their families while enriching the experiences of white students and their families. White unearned benefits may not always be reflected as material gain or impunity tied to expressions of bigotry. They can simply manifest in whiteness as primacy. *Internalized racial superiority* (IRS) is a concept introduced by the People's Institute for Survival and Beyond, a national collective of anti-racist organizers and educators. This group introduced the term to articulate that racism impacts how white people perceive themselves as dominant. Mary Pender Greene, a social worker who works with executives on developing anti-racist leadership styles, copublished an article unpacking IRS, defining it "as the unconscious assumption of the inherently superior qualities of White people and White culture." Many White students suffer from inflated senses of self-importance, value, and voice, or a superiority complex. Greene further explains that "IRS, however, is absorbed through cultural transmission and shows up subtly." The superiority complex manifests in a delicate manner but stems from perceived dominance in societal norms, religion, architecture, art, language, food, and values.

Many white students and families may struggle with understanding the power of racism as an extension of internalized racial superiority. Dr. Joe Feagin is a sociologist and professor at Texas A&M University who writes about whiteness and its implications in America. In one of his works, Dr. Feagin shares, "Today, most whites greatly underestimate the degree to which the United States remains a very racist society." This mentality is the mother of post-racialism in that it is the idea that race is not relevant because America has come so far. In addition, Dr. Feagin writes that whites "underestimate the extent of white racial privileges and resources and the degree to which these . . . have been passed down." Whiteness makes it challenging to comprehend privilege and the ways in which it manifests in America.

Dr. Robin DiAngelo, a professor of education at the University of Washington, echoes Greene regarding the cultural transmission of IRS and gives examples of how America centers white lives to the detriment of nonwhites. She writes, "Virtually any representation of human is based on white people's norms and images—'flesh-colored' makeup, standard emoji, depictions of Adam and Eve, Jesus and Mary, educational models of the human body with white skin and blue eyes." This can make it challenging for white students to comprehend the ways in which they are privileged due to racism, whether they consider themselves biased or not. One can only imagine how this dynamic manifests in schools.

It is not enough to embrace the cultural and enriching aspects of Black cultures within white schools. Having an enlarged Rev. Dr. Martin Luther King Jr. quote outside your central office is only decorative if his tenets are not followed. Having a schedule full of Black history programming in February is simply symbolic when there's nothing else in the other months of the school year. Recruiting Black students from impoverished communities is lazy if there's no financial safety net to support their transition and journey through to that cap and gown from white private institutions.

Self-determined Black students tend to advocate for themselves. Being in the throes of a white academy has necessitated that they speak up, challenge nonsense, and forge their own community on their path to self-sufficiency. Instead of ignoring and dismissing racial insults and microaggressions, they confront the perpetrators, calling out ignorance and arrogance. Rather than thinking their education starts and ends with a class, book, or test, they deepen their study with social practice, hoping to stabilize their environment and open doors for Black students coming after them. While others may be complacent or find no issues with their white schools' lack of investment in advancing racial analysis and outcomes, these students fight for their schools to embody the best of their humanistic mission statements. These Black students understand that white institutions of education cannot escape the call to engage societal issues in and beyond their walls by hiding as citadels located in an oasis.

Black students participate in organizing work as a vehicle to affirm their self-dignity. Greta Anderson, a journalist for *Inside Higher Ed*, which provides news on higher education, shares about activism as an outlet for Black students. Anderson quotes Sharon Mitchell, president of the Association of University and College Counseling Center Directors, to provide an illustration of activism as a coping mechanism for Black students: "If nothing else, they have found a sense of community . . . They have found like-minded individuals that are identifying some of the same issues or problems." When wrestling with racial tension on their campus, Black students are not on an island by themselves. Activism gives them a conduit toward other activists and students who are enduring the same experiences. Anderson quotes Annelle Primm, a psychiatrist and medical director, who emphasizes the healing aspect of student organizing in the face of the gross, grim gutters of the ivory tower. Primm writes that pushing to transform their campuses provides Black youths and students "a sense of agency and self and collective efficacy." Rather than feeling sentiments of helplessness and isolation, activism gives young people a sense of "hope that things can get better."

This sense of positive possibility buoys young people who are fighting for change to demand respect.

The methods by which self-determined Black students affirm their sense of dignity in white schools vary. Across the board, the struggle is in them and not on them. Truly, a myriad of events can activate these Black students, such as being called racial slurs, becoming sickened by off- and on-campus police brutality, or feeling tired of representing the race as the only Black student in their classes, to name a few. These students will find their people and form affinity relationships with Black teachers, peers, and allies as a vehicle for establishing a cultural-political familial community. They may follow the channels of the student handbook for issuing complaints when disrespected and violated for being themselves. Should this method not suffice or resolve racial issues with a sense of urgency, these students will take on alternative means of having their voices heard. This can translate to writing letters to their school or local papers, contacting community organizations, organizing rallies and protests, or finding other vehicles for affirming their self-worth.

There are various devices that Black youth organizers employ to demand just outcomes from their schools. Dr. Ty-Ron Douglas, associate athletic director for Diversity, Equity, Inclusion and Belonging at the University of California, Berkeley, wrote a book capturing various academics and voices on the question of student activists tackling racism. Douglas's work includes the lens of Dr. Stephanie Shonekan, chair of the Department of Black Studies at Mizzou. Shonekan describes the #ConcernedStudent1950 movement of 2014, following the murder of Michael Brown, where Black students pressured Mizzou to make advances toward addressing equity and anti-Black problems: "Outside our classrooms, students began organizing silent processions, peaceful marches, sit-ins and die-ins, all of which had historical roots in the Black experience." Tapping into a wealth of strategies and tactics, Black students at Mizzou put their bodies on the line to have their voices heard in service of change.

Dr. Erica Morales, who completed her doctorate at the University of California, Los Angeles, conducted a study for her dissertation on how Black students resist white students' racial ignorance. Black students employ defense mechanisms to address racial harm without being lost in the associated emotional trauma: "Black students employed 'equalization strategies,' such as 'beasting,' or debating classmates, 'being the best,' educating others, silence and humor to resist these microaggressions." The ways in which Black students employ activism are not limited to direct action but also include addressing myths through consciousness-raising.

Self-determined Black students have seen the pits and lows that come with navigating a white school, and this has emboldened them. The barriers outlined above are not shocking to them because they face them every day. While disappointed by the experiences they encounter, they refuse to be discouraged. They may feel academically betrayed by their white institutions of learning, but they are not bitter. Through the hateful and harmful tragedies they endure and witness, they are not hardened but hopeful.

There are Black students who are comfortable with what is happening at white schools, despite the ills that plague them. Frankly, these Black students accept the same myths that advocates are seeking to dismiss. Their desire to fit in, be down, or have a carefree and colorblind white educational experience causes them to have an aloof attitude. It makes them behave as if the challenges explored above are nonissues. These Black students believe that we as a nation have arrived and that their white school owes them nothing. Some will look the other way when racial insults occur, feel they are special to be at their white schools, or defend the status-quo politics of these white environments because of a belief that they are exceptional. It is a dangerous, self-serving mentality.

CHAPTER 3

Elbows, Fast Feet, and Butt Cheeks

Tears of Joy in Gas

Tear-Gas canisters bond us forever.
Passed to crash us, but brought us together.
Clashes, flashes, we dashed through war's weather.
Trashed a riot, our passion's rebellion.

How did who that is become family?
How did crews make peers in Academy?
How did we woo against brutality?
How did truth prevail after casualty?

Tragedy, who knew we'd fight like we fought.
Take flight above the bull they thought we'd bought.
Apply lessons, smart and bright, we were taught.
Despite the traps they built to get us caught.

Poisons hurled at kids we threw from hot thumbs.
Poisons whirled at women we milked till numb.
Poisons pearled at elderly, slashed to crumbs.
Poisons of a dark world, chewed through like gum.

Sunday, August 10, 2014

"You trying to go to this vigil?" my partner, Alisha Sonnier, asked.

We connected through my mentor and stepfather, Mr. Etefia Umana (whom my siblings and I affectionately call Mr. E). Mr. E was russet, reddish brown, and had an easygoing demeanor with a frame that stood about six feet tall and great wisdom that matched his unapologetic love for Black people. Mr. E and my mom were together, and he did what he could to take care of my family with love. I'd later learn he was an alumnus of SLU and SLU Law. He happened to be the first recipient of the African American studies bachelor's degree at the university.

Alisha was beautiful and smart. Her tawny brownish-orange skin, warm embrace, and fierce attitude won me over at eighteen. Alisha and I were dating at the time and did almost everything with each other. I first met her at a football game when I was a senior at Crossroads and she was a junior at Cardinal Ritter. In high school, I nicknamed her Ms. President because she knew right from wrong and which side to choose. Alisha wasn't just book smart, involved in the National Honor Society and a member of the theater club, but also held a moral compass. After I graduated from high school and began SLU, Alisha would later follow. She was a recipient of the Martin Luther King Jr. Scholarship, one of the few Black recipients of the scholarship at SLU. She was always solid in terms of looking out on my behalf, despite my recklessness during the Ferguson uprising. When the uprising began, we were two years into dating. She was preparing to enter her freshman year at SLU when news of Michael Brown's vigil rang out.

I'd been to vigils before. Attending M-SLICE's Eye on the Sparrow Peace Project, I learned the role of vigils in remembrance and hope. This event was hosted to honor the names and lives of Blacks killed due to inner-community violence. In collaboration with Rabbi Susan Talve, families submitted photos of their loved ones whose lives had been taken due to gun violence, and it was shared as a call for justice. These spaces were about more than just candles and balloons. It was about honoring those who have transitioned and alerting the community's attention to the need for togetherness. There were high levels of homicides, sex work, substance abuse, divestment, and unemployment in the community. When it came to public safety, there was overspending on policing instead of addressing stressors and trauma. A lack of investment in quality mental health care, counseling, day care, employment, transportation, and schooling feeds frustration, anger, and more funerals. Social service funding intended to stimulate just outcomes for residents was shoddy.

Alisha and I went to the vigil for Michael Brown Jr. with her homegirl Jami Cox and my homeboy Christopher Walter. Jami was umber, dark yellow brown, dressed relaxed, and had a purposeful demeanor. Christopher was umber, outfitted comfortably, and had a determined focus. Alisha and I shared a car, which we took together, while Chris and Jami rode together.

While I had never attended a vigil for someone I personally knew, places of mourning were not new to me. At the time, I had lost my Ganny Naomi and Grandpa Willie due to health causes. Everybody grieves differently in life. You can't tell someone how to feel when they've lost a loved one. All you can do is bear witness and hope they receive the care needed to support them in their grieving process.

When we arrived on West Florissant down from the Quick Trip, we parked at Chambers. When we got out, the scene was charged with energy. There was nothing but pro-Black everything on the streets—crowds of Black people with Black power fists in the air shutting down the street and blasting music from loudspeakers. There were groups of people who seemed to be discussing what had transpired and more. As we navigated up to West Florissant toward Nesbit Street, nearer to Canfield, the police presence intensified.

There were careless officers with vicious dogs directing traffic and mugging the demonstrators, which seemed to be done with the intention of intimidating the public. It made me forget that this was 2014 and not the 1960s. However, this sight didn't compare to the police presence on West Florissant Ave and Ferguson Street. As we walked toward Ferguson Street, where the McDonalds sits at the corner, we couldn't get through to that location. There was an entire platoon with hundreds of armed officers.

I later wrote about this experience in an opinion article for the *University News* campus newspaper at SLU in the spring of 2015. For the purposes of this book, I revisited the writing and made edits. However, I described the moment as follows:

> By late afternoon Sunday, my friends and partner had made our trip after finalizing our plans, coordinating our visit, and driving out to Ferguson. Along the way, I remember listening to songs, such as Bob Marley's "Redemption Song." More details of the post-shooting affairs were still isolated to our Facebook timelines, as local news struggled to pick up what was going on. As a generation of Twitter and Facebook users, we are used to sharing and retweeting everything instantly, like any other trending topic.
>
> My friends and partner had heard that Ferguson was alive with police, activity, and people our age. I was learning many

> different background stories. For example, I would hear that people our age were asking established leaders for satisfactory advice, swearing to take justice into their own hands. When established leaders were not in a position to give such mentorship, people our age responded.
>
> As my friends, partner, and I were arriving in Ferguson, we had passed up many entrances that were blocked by police cars signaling with their blinding lights. By the time we navigated around to West Florissant Ave, people were sitting on top of their cars. Vehicles were lined up and down business parking lots on West Florissant. Police presence was prevalent but disengaged. My friends, partner, and I could feel the spirit of the atmosphere, and the streets were riled up. The sound of stereos bumping to the likes of NWA and Lil Boosie's street anthems; the visual of red, black, and green-colored "Back to Africa" flags; and hordes of people our age filling the streets set an ambiance my friends and partner had never felt before.

As time flew by, different events developed. The Quick Trip was broken into. I wanted to explore it despite the warnings of my peers. Alisha reluctantly followed me into the Quick Trip. I walked through the front door, carefully watching out for glass, and then went outside through the side emergency exit. Afterward, my peers agreed that it was getting late, so we walked back to the car on Chambers and West Florissant Avenue.

I didn't want to leave. While we came there for a vigil, so much more was going on that I'd never seen before. As my peers were about to leave, I remember getting into an argument with Chris about my choice to stay. Concerned for me, he locked my backpack in his car and wouldn't let me get it out. In a guttural voice, Chris stated, "If you want to go back, you'll be without your stuff." While Chris and I were going back and forth about my belongings, I'd been updating my mother all along by phone on what I had seen. She said she was on her way to my location. She pulled up and ended up taking Alisha and me around the corner to Mr. E's house.

Mr. E just so happened to have lived nearby off of Nesbit near Ferguson Street. The minute we got to his house, I was ready to go back out into the streets to demonstrate. After a disagreement with Alisha, who was concerned about how reckless and uncalculated it seemed, we decided to go back out together anyway. We walked up to Nesbit, where we encountered police pepper-spraying youths in the neighborhood. I cannot emphasize how enraged I was to see these youths being mistreated. In response, I held up a sign that read, "Freedom ain't free, the price is sold separately."

My first job was in high school, serving with Better Family Life's (BFL) summer camp in 2012. I was referred to this opportunity through Mr. E. BFL held Afrocentric enrichment programs that put me in the mind of Freedom School and also provided wraparound support. It provided many Black families with services if they needed utility, legal, or housing support. I was working with them prior to entering my last year of high school that fall. The camp was hosted out of Saint Luke's Hospital on Delmar near DeBaliviere. While applying, I learned that the organization was based on community, youth empowerment, and holistic development. Participating in the youth program, I got to practice the necessary skill sets in real time, such as problem-solving, time management, and teamwork. The young people I supported were creative, energetic, and brilliant scholars across Saint Louis. The ages ranged from kindergarteners to high school students.

While with BFL, I met a lot of talented and caring adults who helped support me through my journey as a professional. In addition, the staff was overwhelmingly Black. There was Mr. Malik Ahmed, Ms. Deborah Ahmed, Ms. Miranda Jones, Mr. Jihad Khayyam, and many more. I was still attending Crossroads, so being under the wings of professionals who looked like me was encouraging. They held me to a standard of excellence while grooming me to be a professional who valued creativity and Black consciousness.

The young people I served reminded me of my younger self, and they made me embody patience and accountability. While this was my first job, I knew what it was like being a part of a family of young people. Working with BFL was not easy work, but it felt fulfilling. The youths were just being youths. I felt honored being a part of a summer program that allowed Black kids to be Black kids. Through many field trips, swimming lessons, dance classes, drumming instruction, and more, youths were immersed in a cultural and enriching journey. While they often had conflicts, our staff loved them through it all.

As I walked toward the police to address their misconduct with the young folks, I was met with hostility. In a raucous scream, one officer about my height said, "Get the fuck out of here!" Feeling disrespected, I decided to refuse the command. Suddenly, what looked like an M-16 rifle was raised to my face, and out came a string of oil. The substance drenched me from head to toe while soaking my clothes and skin. I felt bathed in whatever mist it was that felt like Lysol. I chuckled, thinking to myself, *Really? What is this? Water?* Moments later, I understood what I was dealing with: pepper spray. Throughout elementary school, I remember watching Batman as he worked with Detective James Gordon to fight criminals and leave a safer world for families. The way police attacked the Black youths made me wonder exactly which families *they* were fighting for.

The first pinch of pain from the pepper spray led me to the ground. If Alisha had not been there, I felt like I'd have to be waiting in an ambulance to be hospitalized due to the pain. I felt like I was dipped in hot sauce with nothing but raw open sores on my body. Alisha helped and carried me from the incident to the porch of the nearest home on the corner. The owner, with good intention, attempted to treat me by pouring water on me with his garden hose. That was a mistake because all that did was spread the oily substance. Alisha helped walk all six feet two and 180 pounds of me back to Mr. E's house, losing her wallet in the process. I was bawling like a baby in agony. I stripped and was helped into the shower. My clothes were drenched with pepper spray chemicals. As I looked down at my skin, I had red welts the size of continents all over where the pepper spray touched.

Alisha, a biology major, saw that magnesium, which is found in milk, would help treat the pain. There was no milk in Mr. E's house. Alisha and Mr. E's mother, Ms. Umana, left the house to go to neighbors nearby to ask for some milk. During their door-knocking efforts, neighbors with cars in their driveway wouldn't open their doors, and some shouted out, "We are not home!" Many were alarmed because their community was under siege by the police, and the news did not help. Much of the local news centered on the giant smoke cloud coming from the nearby Quick Trip that was set ablaze. Finally, one couple answered their door. The woman had a gun, and the man had a bat. They agreed to give us milk. Once Alisha and Mr. E's mom returned, Alisha poured milk over my welts. The fluid's icy and soothing touch worked wonders.

After my incident on Nesbit, I returned to campus for my resident adviser orientation and felt out of it. My skin was still sensitive from being blasted with that pepper spray, and I was dead tired from being unable to rest. Sitting during the training and trying to listen was hard. I was in my body, and my emotions were everywhere.

As an African American studies major, I'd be able to study trends that led to what I was living outside. Counting all my courses, I spent well over three hundred dollars on books that were required material for my fall classes. These works included Assata Shakur's *Assata*, Chinua Achebe's *Things Fall Apart*, Anne Moody's *Coming of Age in Mississippi*, and Clayborne Carson's *The Eyes on the Prize Civil Rights Reader*. While the last thing I had on my mind was reading, I could not dismiss the fact that a lot of these works would continue to build my Black consciousness.

After I had exited the shower, Mr. E let me know that I had a call from my undergrad mentor, Dr. Stefan Bradley. Dr. Bradley was a fawn, light yellow-brown, sharp-dressing, brilliant, and clean-cut man who never skipped a beat when it came to style. At this time, he was regularly pushing SLU to wrestle with the issues Ferguson raised. It was late, and I wasn't even thinking of the fact that I had resident adviser orientation at SLU that morning. This night was my introduction to the Ferguson uprising and the young brother I would come to know as Michael Brown Jr.

Supporting Students in the Face of Community Challenges

There's a saying do not let your studies get in the way of your education. There's a misconception that students must master hundreds of terms, concepts, dates, formulas, and theories in order to be successful. It is true that learning, memorization, and command of lesson outcomes will help youths score well on assignments, tests, and exams. Students spend hours, days, weeks, months, and years getting knowledge poured into their minds. However, they typically spend even more time in their lives outside of school. True schooling cannot happen without application of learning. Excellent academic performance without real-life practice is obsolete. Since schools are where young people develop critical thinking skills and spend a significant time of their development, it's critical that leadership, staff, and faculty of these institutions provide avenues for students to demonstrate their lessons in real time. Opportunities for adults to expose youths to, and place them in positions to execute, their lessons are ubiquitous in a society where community matters are ever-present. It is a disservice to students for them to matriculate in a setting that alienates, disconnects, and detaches them from the realities and responsibilities of community.

It is important for students to perform in the classroom, but it's also critical for youths to be able to exercise their lessons beyond school. Educators charged with teaching students are uniquely positioned to facilitate a process of instilling in students the ability to do more than think but also act. Paulo Freier, a world-renowned Brazilian professor and philosopher, critiques the traditional academic approach to students, treating them as objects rather than subjects with agency: "The more students work at storing the deposits entrusted to them, the less they develop the critical consciousness." This *critical consciousness* is necessary for them to be "transformers of that world." Having to receive information without any interrogating or challenging of the data teaches students to internalize knowledge one-sidedly. As a result, they "tend simply to adapt to the world as it is and to the fragmented view of reality deposited in them." They become robots who learn to follow commands and do not question anything, especially authority. The problems of community become an afterthought because youths are taught to not think critically about it.

The late and great Dr. bell hooks, a nationally known Distinguished Professor in Residence at Berea College, authored a text marrying teaching with affairs beyond the classroom. Dr. hooks quotes Parker Palmer, founder of and senior partner emeritus at the Center for Courage and Renewal, to name how communities of education and resistance are life enhancing and enlightening. Palmer states that "great teaching is about knowing that community, feeling that community, sensing that community, and then drawing your students into it." There's an inseparable relationship among great educators, the surrounding environment, and their students. Dr. hooks describes teaching as a practice of freedom that is ongoing beyond the classroom doors. Writing to deconstruct the myth that learning cannot happen in community, Dr. hooks explains, "Teachers who have a vision of democratic education assume that learning is never confined solely to an institutionalized classroom." The knowledge generated for students transcends the often sterile environment of academia in service of youths being ready to apply it in community.

Without the community, there'd be no students. Surprise! Without students, there'd be no schools. The basic unit of any community is the neighborhood and thereafter is the family. Naturally, what happens in society impacts young people. This chain of events influences the goings-on of the academy. Whether schools accept the call to be responsive to the need or not says more about the academic institution than anything. Schools do not exist in silos. They neighbor churches, businesses, organizations, and residential areas. Whether private, charter, or public schools, area legislation and policies implicate the lived experiences of the young people, their families, and adults in school buildings. When students graduate, they are expected to have the faculties needed to survive and thrive in society. Alumni are charged with being representatives of their alma mater as they take on adult responsibilities in the world. When schools do not prepare students for and expose them to the barriers that communities face, they give their graduates the mentality of individualism in a world with problems that demand collaborative and collective care. Schools owe it to the community to produce conscientious and community-centered alumni who will strive to leave the world better than how they found it.

There's an interplay between the academy and the society, wherein one accompanies the other toward advancing learning in service of change. Dr. Bertram Bruce, an educator and professor emeritus in information science at the University of Illinois, elaborates on the exchange between schools and society. When matriculating students to become alumni, "the community provides the foundation of the curriculum ... The academy side brings knowledge and tools for connecting to other communities, times, and places." It is the community, which provides the subjects for study, and the academy, which produces the skills to address the need, that shape student experience. When institutions of learning ignore the pressing needs apparent in community and selectively focus on narrow-minded visions, they produce alumni with short-sighted lenses on issues in society.

Dr. Kong Wah Cora Chan, who served as a vice principal at Christian Alliance P. C. Lau Memorial International School in Hong Kong, speaks to the need for adults to instill in youths a sensitivity to using education to advance community well-being: "Through adult guidance in the process of youth transformation and self-awareness . . . individuals can foster a desire for self-directed learning." By investing in the growth of students and their command of their thoughts, feelings, and actions, this opens up windows for their natural curiosity to be nurtured beyond themselves. Dr. Chan continues by sharing that this process helps students "develop an awareness of how they might change oppressive power structures, and build confidence and skills to work for collective change." As students better understand their own identities, they can engage in an educational process that gives them tools toward wrestling with systemic injustices. By the time they become alumni, properly trained graduates should have a strong grasp on how the academy prepared them to answer the calls of community.

Community injustices abound, and our educational institutions are uniquely designed to address them. There is an endless list of issues that happen in the community. Responses to these issues do not always have to be surrounding a crisis and actually should be hand in hand in addressing the point that it does not take an emergency for academic settings to be involved in making change happen. Some schools center community service as the mechanism for having students address issues in their backyard. Volunteer opportunities such as tutoring, working in soup kitchens, feeding the unhoused, and being involved in neighborhood cleanups are a few examples. While these are important methods for students to understand the value of service, the problems emanating in society call for advocacy. Students have the power to influence decision-makers, give youths a voice to legislation, and call out the difficulties that their communities endure daily. Instead of academies simply having days of service, there should be schoolwide efforts championing causes tied to progressive outcomes. The core values and principles of schools should reflect a responsibility for and accountability to their surrounding environments.

Teachers and staff at large institutions can leverage their status and position to help foster an environment where students feel supported in their pursuit to impact community change. It truly takes a village. These individuals spend a significant amount of time with students. There's a need for trusted adults to act as mentors providing advice, models that set examples for best practices of exercising voice, and instructors raising awareness about issues. When professionals in schools tap into their capacity to act as changemakers and support one another, it encourages young people to follow suit. There are traps and pitfalls in advocacy that these school representatives are aware of that can provide warnings and cautionary tales to help protect youths. The wisdom that school officials have gained based on their own experience and expertise can help enhance a student's efforts. School workers can use their networks and wherewithal to push for social change, setting an example for young people on tactics tailored toward making a difference. By demonstrating how to healthily juggle multiple hats while conducting activities around justice, they help students learn how to pace themselves and not burn out. Trusted adults can use their own voices to educate students about community challenges that help give youths exposure to and ways of thinking about complex societal issues. Staff conducting presentations, holding teach-ins, and recommending readings help reinforce the importance of research, study, and education for students. Professional development opportunities should be in place to deepen staff understanding. It is critical that all school representatives are on one page with regard to the setting they are fostering for youths to answer the call of community.

Impactful teachers and staff treat the needs of their pupils in service of preparing them to leverage the knowledge they've gained toward making a difference in society. Dr. Joe Nichols, a professor and chair of the Department of Educational Studies at Indiana University-Purdue University, points out the steps successful educators take in developing young people. Great teachers lead by example through the assistance they provide students. In his book, Dr. Nichols explains, "As a servant leader to students, the effective teacher supports the needs of students in a variety of ways where the focus is on aspects of cognitive, psychological, and socioemotional growth." Compelling educators move beyond simply providing information to students, as they also seek to develop young people's emotions and relationship to society. Dr. Nichols further explains, "As servant leaders in the teaching profession, we serve the needs of the children we teach while also understanding and serving, in a limited sense, the needs of their parents and families." Teachers who focus on the growth and needs of the whole student do not simply work to better their students but strive to reach the support systems in their pupils' lives. Reaching that which grounds the student includes their family and communities.

The leadership of academic institutions should support, defend, and stand beside staff striving to help youth pushing for change. Being the face of the school calls for more than approaching donors, participating in board member duties, and facilitating strategic planning. To be sure, the presidents and principals of academic institutions should be considering the ways in which they can leverage their power to best prepare their campuses and sites to answer societal questions. Without their direction, teachers and staff can feel like they're on an island in isolation, absent the backing of their institution. Because of their passion and sense of righteousness, some staff members choose to guide students toward activism with or without their colleagues' accompaniment. Similar to the students they shepherd, staff face risks and backlash for their advocacy. True leaders of schools lead from the front and embody a politics that challenge systems of inequity and exclusion. Acts that perpetuate and further antiquated thinking and outcomes do their campus a disservice. Strategic plans should incorporate short- to long-term goals aimed at addressing social ills through the doors opened up by education. Boards of trustees of schools should weigh how its members work as change agents in their own professional lives and to the benefit of their institution. A key selling point of fundraising must be marketing how the power of donor impact will permit academic institutions to transform students and the community. By supporting staff and taking on this attitude of being community-minded education houses, school leaders make an invaluable impact on students as they advocate themselves.

Leaders lead from the front by setting an example for others to take direction. Administrators and presidents of schools who have an attitude grounded in bettering the community serve as a lighthouse for staff and students to follow. If those who serve as the head of academic institutions embody a mindset that's simply self-serving, it sets a negative tone for the school. This reality is illustrated in a book by Dr. Mary Culver, professor at Northern Arizona University, who distinguishes characteristics of leadership. Citing Robert Greenleaf, founder of the servant leadership movement, Dr. Culver writes, "Greenleaf marked the difference between 'servant-first' and 'leader-first' leaders . . . The 'servant-first' leader seeks to ensure the needs of others are met, whereas the 'leader-first' leader strives for personal power and possessions." Effective administrators of schools embody a mentality of service as leaders rather than focusing on being simple authority figures.

Dr. Daniel Wheeler, professor emeritus of leadership studies at the University of Nebraska-Lincoln, further emphasizes the impact of *servant-first* leaders on school environments: "Servant leaders are not about quick fixes or activities to make a splash. Instead they want to build the foundation and culture for the organization to carry on the service ethic and to create more servant leaders." Creating more servant leaders by example and substantive leadership is a reflection of successful administrators. Dr. Wheeler also states that presidents and administrators who are true servant leaders must beware of associating with those who do not value community. He shares that "servant leaders relish time with those who encourage growth and development. They know the devastating effect of too much time spent with people who are negative or undermine community." The company that administrators keep is critical because not everyone in an academic institution values or is dedicated to addressing the issues happening in society.

CHAPTER 4

The Same Sheet of Music

A Villainous Assembly

A tribe is part of a community.
Rival types try to test its unity.
Evilish vibes move with impunity.
We groove to improve opportunities.

X stands for any means on many nights.
Band by hand on the scene, beacons shine bright.
This chess, we plan and hop hurdles like knights.
Take flight, our kites climb heights, for what is right.

Through uncertainty we'd be a unit.
Tirelessly every week, our truth speaks fluent.
In harmony, we formed this meek union.
Blackness, the power that makes us mutants.

Schools, Stores, Streets; feet, on many boulevards.
You studied, shopped, and chilled, we stood on guard.
We struggled to lift every voice till heard.
We forced you to see Mike despite how hard.

You called us villains and loony.
You called us stupid and unruly.
You called us reckless, goofy.
We saw our heroism and beauty.

August–September 2014

Throughout August and September, I experienced a lot of stressful situations. I often felt like my work was meaningless. All I could think about was what traumatic experiences I just survived. I remember watching a young Black woman being attacked by a tank on Ferguson and West Florissant Street. She kneeled in front of this tank as it propelled tear gas canisters and pepper spray toward her and into the night. A tank was attacking her, moving in her direction as she kneeled before it. She held her umber arms, yellow-brown, up in surrender, like Mike Brown Jr. I immediately left Mama Lola's van, where I was sitting nearby at the time, and went toward her. I ran at a quick pace, grabbed her by her shoulders, and hauled her away from the tank to a nearby grassy area in front of the McDonald's.

I later learned the young woman's name because *St. Louis Post-Dispatch* photojournalist Robert Cohen captured her experience. This woman, Cassandra, was wailing and drenched in pepper spray. I knew the feeling. Someone came out of the McDonald's with milk, which I quickly opened and poured onto her face. The tanks were still propelling canisters, and some bulleted into the McDonald's, breaking the windows. Ironically, this gave us demonstrators access to the inside, which we used for shelter and supplies. Cassandra was helped into the McDonald's for cover to protect her from further attacks. Like many putting themselves out there, she was a *bad motherfucka*—not simply for putting herself on the line in direct action like that but for believing the state would see her humanity in that moment. I ain't know her from a can of paint, but witnessing her bravery, you could tell when she gets pulled over, she gives the cops a warning. She cut her own umbilical cord at birth. At presidential inaugurations, the commander-in-chief swore her into office. When she was a student, she gave the teacher homework. *Bad motherfucka*. I'm just thankful she was out of harm's way.

During the time on West Florissant Ave in August and September, there were droves of protests. When folks tried to allegedly rob the Family Dollar on West Florissant Ave, Mama Lola acted, with a group of Black men. You didn't hear about this in the media: my people, who protected the entrance of a store they didn't own from those who felt they needed to vent their anger. Rather, there was this assumption that everyone was behaving like animals. My people knew that security cameras might come back to catch folks without masks, so to help prevent this, we blocked the store door.

There was a five-second rule in Ferguson where if you stood flat-footed for more than five seconds on West Florissant, you were subject to arrest. What kinda shit is that? The state was hypocritically trying to police the way my people expressed their right to assemble. During the nights, after a long shift at work, my people walked laps in defiance of the practice. This policy was meant to prevent people from demonstrating under the guise of crowd control. The law was later ruled unconstitutional because it prevented folks from expressing their rights.

On Tuesday, August 19, Dr. Bradley coordinated an interview between Chris Hayes of *MSNBC* and my homeboy Trevor, Alisha, and me. Trevor was ocher, brownish-yellow, clever, and stood at about five-six with an athletic frame. He had a knack for entertainment and aeronautics. That evening, though, he had a serious demeanor. Dr. Bradley came out in sweatpants, a T-shirt, and sneakers. In the interview, Trevor talked about what activated him to come out to Ferguson. He discussed the unnecessary presence of the National Guard. Alisha talked about the priorities of demonstrators, such as holding Officer Darren Wilson accountable. I talked about the need for students to be involved. I cited historian Derrick Bell's critical race theory to explain why Ferguson was connected to America's larger racial issues. What we were going through had a history. I felt privileged being invited to share a Black student-activist voice about issues in my hometown on a national platform of millions.

Around September, Tribe X, my protest group, formed. Many relationships were being created in Ferguson through demonstrators becoming more familiar with each other. Tribe X started as concerned individuals coming into regular contact with struggle. I remember meeting Rockit, EJ, and Darius with Alisha. Rockit was terra-cotta brown, wore glasses, and had a tall slim build with a friendly demeanor. Darius was sepia brown, had a midsize athletic frame, and was easygoing. Rockit and Darius were both passionate creatives with a strong bond that complemented their intense love for music production and Black people. EJ was reddish brown, about six feet, and was an adamant health aficionado. Talal was sepia brown, stood about five-ten, and was an outspoken intellectual. Our meeting was coordinated with Queen Mother Romona, Mama Mix, and Mama Lola. Mama Mix was sepia brown, about five-four, had a mesmerizing smile, and spoke with a frank voice about Black unity.

It was on one of the nights that the Lost Voices protest group was hosting its encampment action on West Florissant. Lost Voices, preceding Tribe X, was one of the earliest protest groups out responding to the uprising. Theirs was one of the earlier organized examples of direct action in Ferguson. I admired their initiative in committing to stay out overnight on the streets. As a student at SLU with many assignments, it would have been a challenge for me to have stayed out as they did.

After that check-in at the Lost Voice's encampment, we agreed to meet at the McDonald's on Ferguson and West Florissant, where we had a meeting of minds. Here, we discussed personal, core, and commonsense values as they relate to Black consciousness. This included drafting organizational philosophies and mission beliefs. We ensured we were on the same sheet of music: getting wins for the local Black community. I believe the name Tribe was supposed to mean *unity*, and the X was for Malik El-Shabazz, once known as Malcolm X. However, that's only my interpretation as I did not personally create the name.

In the meeting, I remembered reading Malcolm X's "The Ballot or the Bullet" during my first year of college. The speech was delivered at a meeting sponsored by the Congress of Racial Equality. It was delivered to bring attention to the failed promises of politicians, the persistence of Black disenfranchisement nationally, how voting disenfranchisement plays out in the North versus the South, and the fact that Blacks are still not afforded American citizenship's full rewards. Throughout the speech, Malcolm called for Blacks to employ whatever tactics they needed to advance their cause of freedom. This proved fitting given the mantra of Tribe X: to educate, empower, and organize. The group later expanded around new members such as Dhoruba and HJ. Dhoruba was umber, dark yellow-brown, and about five-seven with a witty and determined creativity that was embodied in his love for drumming. HJ was umber, about six-three, and in construction, which reflected his knowledge of real estate. The mission of Tribe X became *to counteract global injustices and systemic racism through issues organizing, education, empowerment, and building strong alliances.*

By the time of our #OccupySLU encampment that October, we rolled eleven deep. Tribe X members even developed a handshake that I use with my younger brother Christopher. It was such a dope formation with different walks of life, skill sets, and personalities being together. After the meeting, Tribe X would start having regular check-ins near Redbud and Carter in Saint Louis City. The location was at Bro. Zuhdi's market in the 21st ward, which is the same spot where M-SLICE would conduct briefings when I was younger. We tried to establish decorum, plan actions, develop organizational leadership, and advance our cause. Mama Mix, whom I first remembered meeting on the streets of West Florissant, was already sister-friends with Mama Lola. Along with Queen Mother Romona, these three brilliant Black women (affectionately dubbed "the Mamas") were our advisers. They ensured we had an intergenerational perspective, were focused, and kept abreast of issues and events. More importantly, they made *damn* sure we were aware of mistakes and pitfalls that happened throughout the trajectory of Black freedom movements. This helped us to stay sharp.

SLU tried to downplay the events surrounding Ferguson. Except for particular staff and students, there was no genuine university-wide response to supporting justice. Being on campus and in off-campus protests, I saw the disconnect. I was disappointed that the internationally known institution was moving past issues in its own backyard. I felt in my body about how SLU leadership seemed to treat the Ferguson uprising as peripheral. Only select groups such as distinct staff, student organizations, and Black student activists made noise. I wrote about this in an article for the *University News*. In the piece, I called out the need for the school's executives to be sincere. As Dr. Bradley would say, leaders lead from the front. My question was as follows: Why was SLU backstage? The title of my article is "*SLU: Moving Slowly and Taking Credit*":

> I feel compelled to speak—quite frankly, I'm disappointed.
>
> Within five days of Michael Brown's shooting, students and faculty (Christopher Walter, Joshua Jones, Briana Moody, and Trevor Woolfolk) issued a response in solidarity with justice for Michael Brown. As a member of the Black community, I initially felt proud to see a collaborative response calling for justice. Our engagement and criticism has to be internal as well as external; it cannot be selective.
>
> SLU makes it sound like it's doing a lot. SLU did not issue a formal response. In reality, a handful of student organizations and an equally small handful of staff and faculty members are carrying the campus. This is unacceptable when there is no fundamental change happening on an institutional level and the public is being placated with a distorted view of the university's commitment.

However, I then felt shortchanged. I wondered, "Where is my university as a whole? Why is it that only a few faculty members are willing to engage publicly with students on this?" I was upset that my university was unwilling to take initial action. To ignore the points being brought here is to perpetuate a bandwagon culture.

We are supposed to be a campus that speaks out. This is why I appreciate the joint letter issued by representatives from a coalition of staff and students: SLU's Black Student Alliance (BSA), African American Male Scholars Initiative (AAMS), National Society for Black Engineers (NSBE), and Society for African American Studies. The opening of their letter starts, "The life of one of our own was tragically taken by those who are required to protect and serve us—the Ferguson County Police Department. Michael Brown was an unarmed, Black 18-year-old boy who was shot multiple times by a Ferguson police officer and was left for hours to lie in his own blood upon his departure from this world."

Together, they deliver a collaborative response calling for two types of justice from the Ferguson authorities. The first request is the immediate redress in this situation (the firing of Darren Wilson). The second request is recommitting to the fundamental ideals of justice.

When SLU decided to respond, it held a vigil. The predominantly white campus ministry's summer candlelight vigils (Aug. 12 and Aug. 24) have a place, and that is not anywhere near the battle for justice. There are too many areas of administration, university committees, faculty pools, and student organizations that have settled for the meditative approach. Without what Campus Ministry director Sue Chawszczewski describes, paraphrased, as "peace with a sense of justice," prayer becomes an end in itself—a safe route of calling for an incomplete peace divorced from justice. The willingness of some members of our community to accept a responsibility beyond holding melting wax should be a source of honor to the whole university. SLU needs to reevaluate its approach and make stronger investments.

> SLU gave a lackluster response to Ferguson, taking credit for a few program actions with the support of ideal faculty, students, and staff. Their name is on the event—it's great publicity for the institution. This is not the goal and should not be the case. The university should be responsible for meeting its own standards. Standards that are set by the mission and supported by swift action aligned with Jesuit values. The truth is when the university, itself a member of the St. Louis community, does forget and gets the credit for program-initiated reform or progress, it distorts the reality. We do not want random pocket responses but for our highest levels to take the lead.

During the same time, I was applying for (and would later be awarded) the 2014 Jamala Rogers Young Visionary Award. This was an award aimed at promoting youth activism. I felt thrilled knowing that my actions merited such acknowledgment. It was sponsored by activist Mama Jamala of the Organization for Black Struggle and the Youth Council for Positive Development. Mama Jamala had sepia, reddish-brown cheeks; a warm smile; and a storied passion for Black organizing. I appreciated that there were programs such as hers and support for them that help young activists feel they have the capacity to further their passions. In the same way there are funds for sports, performative and visual arts, and other niches, so, too, is it necessary for advocacy work. In my application, I continued to stress the need for the crisis of SLU to be addressed. To this end, I wrote the following:

> [SLU is a] school where a scholarship in Martin Luther King's name rarely yields local Black recipientship, the Black undergraduate headcount is decreasing, Black faculty headcount is low, white billikens humiliate other Black billikens behind social media message boards, and the response to recent events in Ferguson shows how the structure never tends to a local anti-Black racist issue unless it catapults into national headlines. The only relationship between the institution and surrounding is one of expediency and distance. This is a tactic that aims to dismiss the frustration: we would not have this problem with

> SLU if it didn't say that it values truth—but it does and fails to materialize the fruits of its word. In effect, it also fails to serve its duty to St. Louis Black residents.

I first got in contact with Mama Jamala as an M-SLICE youth member and senior at my high school, Crossroads College Prep. Mama Jamala and her committee put out a call for student essayists to tackle the question of food security in their 2012 session. My younger brother Christopher Pulphus and I applied. We ended up being awarded first and second places. In my paper, I talked about how difficult it was to get access to healthy foods in food deserts. A lack of grocery stores or access to healthy food abounded in my environment in North Saint Louis. In addition, I connected the issues of racism and poverty. Contests and programs such as this hosted by the coalition helped give young people like me and my siblings platforms to express our advocacy.

Throughout my application, I was sure to emphasize that youth activism concerned with race issues was key to ensuring that SLU's community is held accountable to living its purpose. Benefiting from Black conscious discussions with Mr. E and the content explored in my African American studies classes, I learned the ways in which systems operated to Black detriment. Our lives are affected by the workings of systems. Just as rules can create a social, economic, and political forum for justice, they can also lead to bullshit like injustice. As a student, learning how these systems affect how I perceived myself and my ability to operate as an agent against institutional wrongdoings was integral to my education. Unfortunately, many are not correctly encouraged by their institutions to pursue this level of understanding in a way that tailors to the student's mind. Justice is placed in conversation with capitalism (the market) and colonialism (the land). As a result, money and monopoly are placed over my people.

Addressing the Apathy of Predominantly White Universities

The apathy permeating predominantly white universities today is traced back to the fact that Black people were never supposed to be graduates of white colleges in the United States. Since the inception of the United States, there were laws put in place to keep Black people from reading, writing, and talking, so the thought of us gaining a formal education was laughable. The purpose of antiliteracy legislation was to keep Blacks in a subservient status and prevent them from self-determining their own destiny. When the late, great Malcolm X stated that "education is the passport to the future," he affirmed the significance of learning even without having a high school diploma, let alone a college degree, himself.

Some of the oldest and most prestigious predominately white institutions in America were built by enslaved Black people. Blacks were good enough for forced unpaid labor in building these white colleges but were not deemed fit to be students of these same institutions that they helped construct. Currently, there are efforts from descendants of enslaved Black people to hold these institutions accountable for this damning history, such as Robin Proudie, founder of Descendants of SLU Enslaved. From Alexander Lucius Twilight to present-day Black graduates, having a mass of Black graduates from predominantly white institutions continues to be a near aberration.

The attack on affirmative action policies meant to level the playing field and provide disadvantaged communities access to higher education reveals the tone deafness of schools' administrations. The national attitudes toward specific support of disadvantaged groups in education reveal the disconnect many have associated with race and academia. Justin McCarthy, a journalist and analyst at Gallup, shares about the "we have arrived" post-racial mindset and opinions of Americans on affirmative action. Using a survey to illustrate how unpopular the policy is among people in the United States, he goes into detail about responses to recent efforts to dismantle it. McCarthy shares that "two in three Americans (68%) say the Supreme Court's June 2023 ruling to end the use of race and ethnicity in university admission decisions is 'mostly a good thing.'" This comes after *Students for Fair Admissions v. Harvard* ended race-based admissions at colleges. McCarthy shows that Black students are split on the topic yet more likely to view it as negative: "about half of Black adults say the ruling will negatively impact higher education in the U.S. (50%)."

The need for affirmative action policies emerged because of efforts to counter the residual impact of the enslavement of Black people in the United States. Assaults on affirmative action policies operate from a false understanding of the state of race relations in America, grounded in post-racial lies. Dr. Linda Darling-Hammond, a professor emeritus of education at Stanford University, published an article on the eve of the twentieth century naming this issue of the American aversion to affirmative action practices. Unraveling the source of the tension with the policy, Dr. Hammond writes that to "many Americans who believe that the vestiges of discrimination have disappeared, affirmative action now provides an unfair advantage to minorities." This mindset that a policy seeking to remedy centuries of harm to Black people or marginalized groups is unfair comes from a racially disingenuous posture at the least and racist gaslighting at the best.

After being derailed in education due to 250 years of enslavement (1619–1865), the flop of Reconstruction (into 1877), emergence of Jim Crow (into 1965), and ongoing ills, affirmative action policies are far from unfair. Hammond continues her analysis, stating, "Affirmative action is needed to protect opportunities likely to evaporate if an affirmative obligation to act fairly does not exist." Without efforts to specifically benefit Black and marginalized groups as they pursue educational opportunities, white schools make it clear that they've abandoned these populations.

Some of the white schools located in cities and urban environments with a critical mass of Black residents have the most racial audacity. They operate as gluttonous, gated, policed, and insular ivory towers with racist colonial and capitalistic aspirations. They take land and resources from the proximate neighborhoods and are sometimes the largest real estate owners of the local area. An overwhelming number of these white educational institutions are nonprofits, meaning they typically do not contribute to the tax base of the surrounding community. While gaining the rewards of tax cuts and accumulating land, they mainly recruit white students from in and out of state, overlooking the Black youth and adults in their own backyard. For example, SLU, which is situated in a city that's nearly half Black, mowed down an entire Black neighborhood named Mill Creek Valley to satisfy its colonial quest. To date, SLU does not recruit, retain, and graduate a mass of Black students. To be sure, these white schools will permit Black residents for hire to satisfy their service industry in cafeterias and maintenance. Of the handful of Black students they do admit, the most visible are Black athletes. Locating the sparse Black faculty of these white academic institutions is like playing "Where's Waldo?" The ways in which predominantly white institutions have enriched themselves to the detriment of Black residents is racially bold, egregious, and disrespectful.

The subjugation of Black and marginalized people to their detriment existed for the enrichment of white universities in America. There are different ways in which institutions of higher education have caused racial destruction with impunity in the name of academic advancement. Dr. Sharon Stein, an academic in educational studies at Idaho State University, published a journal about the ways in which racial colonization helped birth the present-day university. Dr. Stein mentions that universities have conducted "extractive research relationships . . . gentrification of areas surrounding institutions, and the erasure and invalidation of nonEuropean knowledge systems." This is generating knowledge without centering the experiences of Blacks and disadvantaged groups, displacing communities of color, and placing a premium on Eurocentric culture. Institutions of higher learning leaned on the manipulation and degradation of Black people and marginalized groups to thrive.

In her book, Dr. Stein continues to write about the colonial beginnings of universities in America. She describes the role of racial brutality in the conception and maintenance of institutions of higher education. Looking at the history of the present-day existence of universities, Dr. Stein states that "violence is foundational to US higher education's structure and organization . . . [it] is in the marrow of the bones of contemporary institutions." Without destructive forces at play, US universities would not have been made or continue to exist. Prior to the Civil War, US colleges were all beneficiaries of enslaved labor. This is not unique to schools in the southern states; "all schools built prior to the Civil War are implicated in slavery." The utilization of the system of enslavement of Black and marginalized groups in the United States was foundational to the birth and maintenance of American institutions of higher learning. The impact of resources gained from the enslavement of and violence against Black and minority communities continues to enrich colleges and universities. This toxic reality is evident in the "wealth that was expropriated from Black and Indigenous peoples . . . then donated or granted to various institutions of higher education . . . [and] continues to circulate and produce more wealth for these institutions." Dr. Stein also explains that the reason why universities such as Harvard have such a massive endowment is directly traced to the colonial conquests and subjugation of Black and marginalized groups.

Dr. Oriel Maria Siu, in an article based on a speech she gave at a Graduates of Color ceremony at the University of Puget Sound in 2015, speaks to the history and present implications of colonialism in higher education. She shares how, across the United States, academic institutions were enriched and rewarded by the dispossession and degradation of Black people. Speaking to this dynamic, she states, "Universities all throughout the nation supported the economy of slavery, benefited from it, and played a crucial role in retaining the racist and racial order of things." The wealth accumulated from racist unpaid labor and land grabs served as the basis for the ongoing financial prosperity of US academies.

Black students, marginalized groups, and allies have always kept white educational centers of learning honest. These youths tend to have a pulse on the racial climate of their institutions and find ways to navigate. They make the most of their white school experience, participating in extracurricular activities in and out of the boundaries of their academies. There's an endless list of hobbies that Black students and allies may partake in to keep themselves occupied, including volunteer groups, arts, sports, various clubs, leadership societies, school government, and affinity groups. These activities help round out their experience, helping to enrich their journey despite the sometimes bleak realities that come with being at predominately white institutions. It is important to name this because while issues of race at these white schools abound, Black students find ways to center joy and hope.

Before they enter these white academies, they're well aware of the dearth of Black students. As they attend their white schools, Black students are aware of the campus culture and the relationship race has to it. They are also sensitive to and aware of the contradictions in the stated mission statements of their white institutions versus the practice of these formal summaries. Therefore, when Black students finally organize and protest at their white schools, it's typically not due to trivial matters or an infantile desire to make noise. These Black youths have gotten fed up to the point that all it takes is a catalyzing event to lead to a collective quaking beneath their feet as they march, taking action to affirm their sense of dignity.

Black students find ways to make space for themselves despite the racial perils of white academies. The ambivalence and afterthought given to them by predominantly white institutions is not encompassing of all their experiences. When protests or campus uprisings occur, they are products of an overbearing racial climate that has motivated Black students to put down books and pick up bullhorns. Dr. Antar A. Tichavakunda, an academic at the University of California, Santa Barbara in the Department of Education, published a work articulating the nuances of Black experience on campuses. Emphasizing that issues of campus racism are only an aspect of their stories, Dr. Tichavakunda explains that "Black students are more than the manner in which they cope with hostile racial climates." While bias, microaggressions, and overt and systematic racism abounds, Black students still make the most of their university experience. He writes, "Black students are people leading normal lives—they go to the gym, party, have lunch, watch TV, etc." rather than simply getting by in the face of bigotry. Black students, like any other racial group, are focusing on their health, social lives, and entertainment interests.

Therefore, when Black students deploy activism to address issues on their campuses, it's not happening in a vacuum. Efforts to interrupt the business of their campus come from feeling invalidated and undervalued in the face of mounting racial incidents. For example, Black students, angered by police killings, turned to their campuses to fight for change. Dr. Tichavakunda explains that in 2015–2016 and 2020, "students across the nation protested inequitable campus experiences" in response to police shootings of Black people. In the face of issues on their campus, Black students made efforts "demanding more Black representation of students, staff, and faculty, the removal of racist campus monuments, and other changes that might foster a more inclusive campus racial climate." In these ways, Black students hold their academies accountable to making welcoming and conducive environments for their development. When these students go to teach-ins instead of the gym, attend organizing meetings instead of parties, skip lunch to draw signage, and write opinion editorials rather than watching TV, it is a reflection of their desire to get just treatment from their campus.

The truth is that white silence in the face of injustices that Black students experience is just as violent as the racial assault. It is a betrayal of the human project, which demands people stand in solidarity and affirm each other in the pursuit of justice, for whites in academic settings to abandon their Black peers. To do so often requires them to wrestle with their white privilege, which includes recognizing the power of racial hierarchy.

The refusal of white people in academic institutions to understand the function of their privilege and work to undo racism contributes to the apathy of schools. It's often difficult to have conversations with white students and professionals who cannot comprehend their complicity or role in the perpetuation of systems of racial dominance. Peggy McIntosh, an anti-racist and feminist researcher at the Wellesley Centers for Women, brought the term *white privilege* to its present-day consciousness to articulate this. In an article published at the end of the '80s, McIntosh writes, "I have come to see white privilege as an invisible package of unearned assets that I can count on cashing in each day, but about which I was 'meant' to remain oblivious."

White privilege is less about obvious rewards that racism has endowed than about the unseen benefits. It is not about intent or maliciously aimed individual actions that create the benefits that white people have, to the detriment of Black people and marginalized groups. White students have an "invisible package" of benefits of which they are not consciously aware as they matriculate. Dr. Sharon Stein unpacks the interplay of white privilege and higher education. Citing W. E. B. Du Bois, Stein writes how whites are "compensated in part by a sort of public and psychological wage," which in turn "promises superiority, entitlement, and exceptionalism." This wage that white people—including white students and staff of academic institutions—gain comes with levels of certainty and comfort at the expense of Black people (students and staff).

Dr. Nolan Cabrera, an academic at the University of Arizona in the Center for the Study of Higher Education, published a work wrestling with whiteness and its impact on universities. After the passage of civil rights legislation and policy shifts following the execution of Black liberation movements, Dr. Cabrera names how racism became publicly unpopular but still persists. He explains, "By the early 1970s, it fell out of favor to publicly state that White people were inherently superior . . . racism . . . did not magically disappear. Rather, it was driven underground." Just because something is not surface level and apparent does not mean it does not exist. Similarly, racism not being overtly displayed as acceptable does not mean it's not just as potent in society and on campuses.

Highlighting the dearth of Black students in higher-education white schools, Dr. Cabrera articulates that "the lack of access to higher education for People of Color exists only if there is concurrently an unwarranted advantage for access to higher education that White people experience." It is due to systemic forces and ambivalence toward white privilege that whites arrive in droves at universities, and Black students are few. Once they've arrived on campus, the tension that Black students experience around the racial climate of white schools is distinguishable from the feelings of white students. Dr. Kira Banks, an academic at SLU in the department of psychology, unpacks this in a journal article. She describes how "research has found that even when students of color and White students report similar levels of racial incidents, students of color rated the climate as more racist and less accepting compared with White students" (Rankin & Reason, 2005). White students, due to their privilege, tend not to have the same pulse on the problematic nature of racial incidents that occur on campus and may view racial indiscretions as harmless.

Scrutiny of white educational establishments' ties to problematic entities and individuals repeatedly reveals their infatuation with profit over people. Majority-white universities depend on the material resources and networks of companies, donors, alumni, board members, and organizations to build endowments, scholarships, research, and infrastructure. When these white schools are not concerned about the ethics and morality of who they receive a dollar or referral from, therein lies a debilitating issue. Some schools look away, pretend not to notice, or just do not care about the connections to militarism and systems of oppression that the sources from which they receive resources have. However, this is not unique to them as it's also a characteristic and reality of some historically Black colleges and universities.

CHAPTER 5

I Have My ID and a Lot of Guests

The Occupation Heard Round the World

For 6 days we toiled in the rain and cold.
Drained but never folded, our words heard bold.
Pains and scoldings, refused any less sold.
Til chains were broken, Ferguson was told.

Ashe, sista Assata.

West Florissant became West Pine real quick.
Clicked up, we challenged the school's politics.
Called lawless, pricks, rapists, like we punched bricks.
Clocktower, quick, air was thick as time ticked.
Our power made them sour; came with no tricks.

Pizza, tents, co-conspirators, covers.
Home, no rent; knew who did not see color.
Von's fam sent the thumbs up, we went longer.
Intent was well meant, they were our brothers.

The encampment shook the nation, that's fact.
Number #1 on twitter despite attacks.
A bitter campus' steel bubble was cracked.
No quitters, we showed the world how to act.

Sunday, October 12–Saturday, October 18, 2014

The week of the encampment was full of joy and pain. We were able to host teach-ins with the students around racism, Ferguson, and activism. Relationships were built; food and supplies (tents, water, trash bags, etc.) were sent in as support. When the university restricted the access of "guests" to buildings like the campus ministry, students resisted. Nonstudents, such as those in Tribe X, who wanted to use the bathroom met apartment-leasing students who let them use their facilities. The *New York Times* correspondents Monica Davey and Alan Blinder briefly touched on the action in an article titled "Ferguson Protests Take New Edge, Months After Killing."

Before Ferguson October, which was a national call for organizers and demonstrators to come stand in solidarity with the local community, Talal Ahmed and I were discussing to organize a major action at SLU. We did not know what it looked like and could not have imagined what it would materialize as. Alisha and I discussed the matter regularly because as SLU students we were intimately inundated with a desire for solidarity on West Florissant in Ferguson to translate to that of West Pine at SLU. One of the events that was part of the national call was a panel of clergy and civil rights leaders hosted by SLU at its Chaifetz Arena, which was disrupted by youth with their anger articulated by Kareem Jackson (Tef Poe) and Ashley Yates. Those that made the highest risks were not interested in hearing from national clergy and the "old guard" about solutions—particularly from those that had not been in the streets. Following the spiraling of events, Talal called me in a breathy cadence and explained "if we're going to do that thing with SLU, tonight is the night. Be ready."

When we stood at the gates prior to entering SLU, I paused. I was thinking about how far the demonstrators had traveled to make it to campus. Tribe X (including Talal Ahmed, Brandon Ali, Darius Ali, HJ Rodgers, Emmanuel Jones, and Dhoruba Shakur) in concert with other Ferguson organizers such as Kayla Reed, Freedom Fighters (Shermale Humphrey, JaNina Jenkins, Autumn Mae, and Damon Latchison), and Peacekeepers (such as Amir Brandy) helped coordinate the march to come to SLU. I learned the march began near the Shaw neighborhood, where VonDerrit Myers Jr. was murdered by Officer Jason Flannery. While I never knew VonDerrit, I got to meet his mother, Syretta, and father, VonDerrit Sr., that night. His mother was tawny brown and had a warm presence. She had a reserved yet sassy style with attention to detail when it came to her wardrobe. His father was sepia brown with broad shoulders and a businesslike expression. He dressed comfortably, held his chin high, and presented an attitude that was unshakably focused. Both of his parents' backs were erect and strong. Photos of VonDerrit Jr. show he had his mother's smile and father's eyes.

VonDerrit's father was an employee at SLU. Traditionally, the scholars at the institution would receive a campus-wide email or text alerts about a loss but not in this instance. Just as SLU was largely silent about Mike Brown Jr., the institution treated Myers's murder the same. SLU did not seem to reach out with care around therapy, legal resources, scholarships, and any other meaningful assistance. The university's treatment of the VonDerrit family following the tragedy was appalling.

I didn't anticipate campus police from the Department of Public Safety meeting us at the gate. They stopped our group of freedom fighters and stared us down. We were good troublemakers, in the words of John Lewis.

Dhoruba gave me the megaphone. I grabbed it and quickly yelled, "I'm an SLU student. I have my ID and a lot of guests to accompany me." Alisha and other student activists in the crowd lifted their IDs with me, and it was a standstill as we slowly motioned toward the guards. The campus security moved from the gates and let all the demonstrators in.

The encampment took place during midterm examinations. In my *Art of the African Diaspora* class with Dr. Gbadegesin, students were allowed to go to the clocktower to learn. The residential halls hosted sessions about Ferguson and protests.

There were several conflicts in the encampment. Dhoruba had an American flag hanging upside down to symbolize the distress of Black America, which drew the ire of many. The veteran student leaders and Reserve Officers' Training Corps members were insulted. They claimed the positioning of the flag was disrespectful and ignored the violence being done to Black people.

The encampment was rainy and cold that week. Participants in the occupation of the university slept in tents and relied on donations to keep the movement alive. I would later learn that a call center was set up to keep parents up-to-date on what was happening on campus. Parents and alums were calling in, asking, "How are you sure my daughter won't be raped by a Black man if they walk past the encampment?" In the midst of this, the university installed campus-wide security cameras for "safety."

Tribe X didn't get access to SLU president Dr. Pestello until later that week. He was new to campus, having come from the University of Dayton. When we did, we discussed our concerns in the Sinquefield Room in DuBourg, the administration building. Dr. Pestello was receptive to our calls for addressing the university's complicity in the ills. However, we didn't have an outline of what we wanted from the university. Many within Tribe X were reasonably distrustful of the university's promise to honor any commitment. We footnoted the meeting for a follow-up one later that week. Dr. Pestello urged that we settle whatever disputes we had as soon as possible, giving us a small window to work.

We held an internal think tank on possible demands to ask of the institution. Two Tribe X mentors, Mama Mix and Mama Lola, guided us through this process with Queen Mother Romona's feedback. We each got a piece of paper and wrote a list of points we felt would help advance the betterment of Black community concerns. Different ideas came up like a K–12 pipeline to assist with the recruitment of Black students from Saint Louis, a monument to honor the encampment, a center to host workshops for the community, and an anti-racist speaker series to educate the campus and public.

Once we returned to the encampment, there was a division within Tribe X over whether or not to submit the list. There was reasonable distrust in SLU's faithfulness to carry out the demands. Back in May 2014, before Michael Brown was murdered, Black students submitted demands to the university and got nowhere. *St. Louis American* reporter Rebecca Rivas covered this effort in a piece titled "Black Students Make Demands of SLU After Campus Hate Crimes." With OccupySLU, the fear of the university backtracking on its promises reemerged. Even within the BSA, which I was a leader of, there was disagreement over whether or not to present the demands. Some leaders felt we didn't have the capacity as an organization to support the demands and program. The BSA held programs around Black campus life with events to enrich the campus culture. Some examples included the Soul Food and Jazz (SFJ) and Cultural Extravaganza (CE), which was a visit to a nearby city to learn about Black history. Dedicating our focus to holding SLU accountable while also meeting the requirements to keep funding coming in for programming was challenging. To me, there was no either/or but *both*. Addressing these concerns, BSA had an emergency meeting, where our executive members voted and ended up with a lack of support for the demands. As a member of BSA, I tried to help the rest of Tribe X make sense of it, though I did not agree.

BSA's move was ahistorical in that it had always been a risk-taking and daring organization oriented toward social justice. During the first year it was founded in the 1960s, BSA (then named the Association of Black Collegians) led an occupation of Ritter Hall on SLU's campus. Then, its members presented demands for increasing Black faculty, Black students from inner-city schools, Black campus security officers, and an Afro-American studies institute. Despite this tradition, a majority of members of the BSA committee did not find it wise to join with Tribe X in making the demands. Despite this lapse in judgment from the committee, a trusted BSA adviser, Dr. Bradley, intervened. This and some change of hearts created an overhaul that led to BSA cosigning the demands that Tribe X had assembled.

Dr. Bradley was knowledgeable about Black student movements and had published about them, so he had a pulse on the past. When we finally met with Dr. Pestello a second time, Rockit, the Tribe X president, read the demands. The president of SLU agreed to the items and suggested adding a point that would help facilitate the process. The basis was to introduce a new position for a university leader who would be responsible for the accord's enactment. We moved forward with signing the OccupySLU demands, which would later become known as the Clock Tower Accords (CTA), and are as follows:

1. Increased budget for the African American studies program
2. Increased financial aid resources for retention of Black students at SLU
3. Evaluation of SLU's current scholarship programs to better serve Black populations
4. Additional college prep workshops for students in the area's most disadvantaged school districts
5. Establishment of a K–12 bridge program, including summer programs, in the Normandy and Shaw neighborhoods to help increase the numbers of college-bound students from neighborhoods in those areas.
6. Establishment of a community center
7. Mutually agreed on commissioned artwork
8. Development of an academic center for community and economic development to be integrated with the community center

9. Creation of a race, poverty, and inequality steering committee
10. SLU sponsorship of a national conference on racial equality
11. Appointment of a special assistant to the president of diversity and community engagement
12. Establishment of a Diversity Speakers Series
13. Biweekly meetings with an inclusive group, including the president, to continue to advance SLU's efforts to address inequality and poverty in the community

At the time, it felt like there was a level of inclusivity. I truly believed that a billion-dollar institution like SLU agreeing to carry out these assignments carried weight and possibility. More inner-city attending students like those at Vashon, Sumner, Roosevelt, or Northwest would be recruited to, retained by, and graduated from SLU. Signing the agreement seemed like a game changer for justice. VonDerrit's family played a huge role in making it all happen. Recall that the march that led to campus began at a vigil lifting his name. I am forever grateful to them and families such as theirs who fought for justice with us.

There was still friction over whether or not to end the encampment after the signing of the accords. Dhoruba explained that he did not have faith in the institution to live up to its values, and many within Tribe X agreed. Some of us were offered full-ride scholarships by university administrators like the vice president of retention and enrollment, Jay Goff. The decision to remove the encampment followed the president of SLU's agreeing to actualize the demands. The university agreed to U-Haul the encampment supplies. It was hard seeing our encampment come to an end.

The officer-involved shootings were going to stop and be addressed correctly or else. Whenever corruption and derelict of duty popped up their heads, there was no way around it: you'd see us. I felt proud to be a part of this fight for freedom with my people.

Making Community Demands as a Student

It is critical that students seeking to make change at their school center understand the purpose that calls for it: transforming communities. Young people issue commands seeking to ameliorate their campus conditions because the past is antiquated and the present is awful. Youths pressure their academic settings in order to self-determine a better future. The progress or gains made will sometimes be reserved for future classes of students. Since learning environments do not exist in silos, no matter how isolated they seem, what students fight for on the inside of the university impacts the community at large. While it's encouraging to have support, sometimes backlash is heard loudest.

Young people wrestle with complex problems that are sometimes decades to centuries old. Dr. Jerusha Conner, in the department of education at Villanova University, wrote a book that speaks to the centrality of student involvement in movements. Dr. Conner writes, "Youth have played vital roles in the abolition, suffrage, antiwar, Civil Rights, LGBTQ, environmental justice, immigrant rights, and labor movements, among others." One would be hard-pressed to find a cause or an issue that students have not participated in or been of consequence to. In higher education, Dr. Conners argues that youths being on their own creates a window of opportunity for them to deepen their involvement with causes. Describing the outcome that stems from this freedom that comes from being on campus, she states, "The college environment presents students with abundant opportunities to connect with others who share their values, motivation, and political persuasions." The transition to the university creates space for students to be activists due to their independence. For many young people, the exposure they have to issues in their community early in life necessitates taking stands at ages younger than the traditional undergraduate student.

Issuing demands is an authoritative act, not a request for favors. It is a command, not an ask. One has to recognize that the power is in the students and related people—the campus decision-makers. There's a saying that those most proximate to an issue are closest to the solution. Student demands are thoughtful responses grounded in everyday interaction. Youths are not seeking handouts or charity from leadership. Young people are not asking for acts of kindness and gestures of goodwill. Students are emphatically petitioning for what is owed: justice. Demands are the culmination of efforts to address debts a governing body has not paid. Schools have an obligation to provide students with a healthy and positive learning environment.

Young people pointing out and lifting up problems that need to be addressed is a gift to universities. Gari De Ramos, a journalist with

Worcester Magazine, penned an article illustrating the efforts of Black students at Clark University in Worcester, Massachusetts, making demands of their administration. The students were calling for action items such as campus divestment from local police, disarmament of campus police, and anti-racist training. Ahiela Watson, Black Student Union president and protester, is quoted making a salient point on the demands being issued: "I did come here to be a student . . . it feels like I'm doing other people's jobs for free." The typical duties of students are to study, pass tests, and graduate; however, having to tell career professionals how to do their work is unpaid labor.

Associated Press (AP) News journalist Noreen Nasir and two co-contributors published a news report around the Columbia University encampment, where student activists occupied their campus to call for antiwar and pro-Palestinian measures. The student protesters demanded that Columbia University cut financial ties with Israel and companies that support Israel as it wages war on Palestine. These student activists made it clear that they "intend to continue their encampment until their demands are met." They are putting their bodies on the line to call for what they believe to be a just outcome.

Taking the time to conduct an assessment of one's campus climate is essential when crafting calls for justice. Students should study the ways in which people and collectives in the academy interact and exist. There will be positive aspects that bring peace, joy, and hope that are salvageable. Students should learn to articulate their feelings as they relate to the conditions of where they learn, live, and laugh. Reading the news on and off campus is helpful because it exposes students to information connected to updates happening in and out of their learning environment. Through frank dialogue, students will learn different attitudes and sentiments on topics, which will inform organizing strategies. Should the processes and practices of the educational institution fall short of what's just when trouble surfaces, one must dream up ways to resolve them. This is the homework phase. If everything in the academy climate were copacetic, there'd be no need to issue demands.

Demands are like milk; they come with an expiration date. No matter what the command is, it is imperative that there's a deadline and timeline associated with an agreement to demands for justice. A tactic that decision-makers and administrators of schools may use is to filibuster a response to the demands. In other words, they'll kick the can down the road to nowhere. The strategy behind this deceitful and sluggish response is to bide time because those in positions of influence know that students have a short stint at school. An institution of education may even agree to demands, but that doesn't mean it will implement them. For example, students made a demand for change on topic A in 2024; it's now ten years later in 2034, and the demand is still not met. By then, the students have long graduated. When administrations do not meet deadlines for demands as promised, other mechanisms for pressuring the institution become viable options.

Another tactic to be wary of is when decision-makers offer to create and designate committees to address student concerns. If reciprocation of intent and action was actually happening, it should've taken place before students forced an administration to move. If a school wants to slow student activists' momentum, they'll make committees out of committees to do so. Rev. Dr. Martin Luther King talked about the urgency of now; demands call for a sense of urgency. To keep the campus's proverbial feet to the fire, there must be a window when students' commands should spoil.

Just like schools give students deadlines, young organizers should provide cut-off times for when demands should be met. Those with the power and wherewithal to meet the needs articulated by student organizers already know in their minds and hearts whether or not they will agree and actually follow through. There's no guarantee that the posture of the administration will necessarily shift, so it's wise for student organizers to get a commitment followed by a timeline for a meeting that is agreed to.

Dr. Joseph DeVitis, a retired educator, published a book with an additional editor capturing several perspectives on student activism. In their work, contributor Dr. Cassie Barnhardt, a professor at the University of Iowa who is based in the Public Policy Center, shares about the contours of demand making with youth organizers at their schools. Analyzing the precipitating factors that lead to activism, Dr. Barnhardt writes that "activism tends to emerge when conventional processes have fallen short of either conferring attention on an issue or of bringing about an adequate resolution to the matter being raised." Activism often emerges in response to the failure of formal efforts of pushing for change. When voting, meetings with governance, showing up to town halls, and polite requests for change fail, activism becomes a viable option. One trick that campuses may try is to create committees around the demands that student activists present. Dr. Barnhardt addresses this diplomatically, stating that "it is evident that the formation of a committee alone doesn't constitute a buy-in organizational response . . . however, the formation of a committee has the potential for buy-in." A university recognizing issues or forming subgroups around the problems raised by student activists does not necessarily translate into sincerity in meeting demands. Young organizers hedging their bets and pursuing a list that includes moderate to bold demands position themselves better.

Dr. Stefan Bradley, of the Black studies and history department at Amherst College, penned a book about Black Columbia University student activists in the 1960s who made demands of their administration. Articulating their "shoot for the stars, land on the moon" strategy to demands, he explains, "The strategy was to make exorbitant demands with the idea in mind that the university would most likely respond to only a few of their demands." Students made unreasonably high demands of their institution coupled with less cumbersome (for the university) commands as a cerebral mechanism of achieving their goals. In the course of issuing demands, students should consider strategy tied to their development of their need and a time limit on decision-makers accepting it.

Presenting demands is a carrot-and-stick relationship when pushing those in seats of power to cooperate. There has to be a consequence or reaction, the *or else*, should schools not follow through with the commands that students have put forth. Without any teeth behind the bite, students' concerns can be dismissed as just words. Just as students are having conversations about what they want from decision-makers, they must explore what organizing efforts they're willing to commit to if the university ignores them, fails to agree, or falls short on any commitments it makes. In an ideal world, campus administrators would acquiesce to what's just and fair. This is not the reality. Having plans to mount substantive pressure creates an incentive that holds decision-makers to their word. There are several organizing vehicles for doing so, but they come at academic, health, and legal costs that students have to be mindful of in their responses.

To be sure, students can employ an infinite number of tactics to express themselves. Exposing the school in the media by holding press conferences, organizing petitions, and hosting rallies to garner support are less escalated acts. Protesting by conducting walkouts, interrupting campus functions (board meetings, schoolwide events, libraries, donor visits, and more), holding hunger strikes, shutting down neighboring streets, and having sit-ins are effective at interrupting business as usual yet are riskier acts of civil disobedience. Student organizers should be mindful of how far they, allies, and accomplices are willing to go and have safety plans for when retaliation may happen.

CHAPTER 6

An Ounce of the Game

Respectable Thug Nigga (Flowers for Ahk)

Crowned with class but hood, and brown in one name.
Pure sound, called you cool when they called you lame.

August 9th just did something to his soul.
A patrol left a boy's body laid cold.
He strolled with one goal, justice was like Gold.
Stared down tanks and would never bend nor fold.

Organized with risks: you got bond money?
Dismiss, Dissed, Kicked, but never a dummy.
Saw Mike's Flicks and Pics, nothing was funny.
Chalk Sticks in the Loop seen round the country.

November 2014

Early in the month, Tribe X participated in an interview with the brilliant journalist Ms. Robin Boyce of STL TV on our experiences around Ferguson and our role in the OccupySLU action. During this time, we all had a chance to share what it was like fighting, despite the state violence we endured, and how we were persisting in different ways. Ms. Boyce gave us a platform to counter the clout-chasing negative media. Many on my team dubbed their last names as X for the interview, and I followed suit (Jonathan X).

My love for Malcolm X was different. Reading Alex Haley's autobiography on the brother eternalized my fondness for him. Saddled with a tragic childhood—his father died under mysterious circumstances and his mother was committed to a mental institution—Malcolm X spent most of his formative years in foster care and later partook in petty crimes. He spent time incarcerated growing in knowledge, crediting the Nation of Islam with his spiritual growth. This prepared him to be a formidable speaker and ushered in what would be a pattern of lifelong learning. Due to his example, I have also found that some of my greatest lessons have been grounded in practice combined with study. Malcolm attributed his knowledge to his unique life experiences and research as well.

One of my jobs at SLU was undergoing a recruitment push for resident advisers (RAs) for the next year. The number of Black students who held those positions was sparse. You could dump a pile of pebbles from the sky in a room filled with the campus RAs and miss every Black one. I talked with some of the Black RAs about doing what we could to increase representation in the field. This meant reaching out to Black students we knew whom we felt would be good for the role.

I ended up reconnecting with a thoughtful and generous SLU alum named Mr. Brian Shelton. When we connected, he explained that he graduated from the College of Arts and Science back in 1980. He was very encouraging of my passions around addressing racism on and off campus. Mr. Shelton was always willing to help. At the time, he was talking about starting up a social justice scholarship in the name of a Jesuit saint, called the Saint Peter Claver, S. J. Service Scholarship. When we met and talked on campus, it was always about how to advance the Black community at SLU. Mr. Shelton supported Black undergraduates by pushing the majority-white SLU student government association (SGA) to fund a fellowship retreat for BSA. He was aware that leadership development had its costs and pushed for SGA to help fund it.

My younger sister, T'Mya Pulphus, attended Saint Louis Immersion School (SLIS), where she studied every subject in French. The head of the school, Mr. Wildsmith, had a son named Eric, who was my classmate at my high school, Crossroads. Mr. Wildsmith reached out, seeking input on how his institution should address race in Saint Louis at the elementary level. He admitted that his typical approach to controversial issues was often limited. I told him to create space for the students to discuss their opinions and feelings. My other recommendation was to have youth organizers from the community come through and share their experiences.

Universities should be involved in helping promote activism in practical ways. I was happy to work on a proposal that created SLU's Community Skill Share. I ended up forwarding a proposal created by other activists to SLU's vice president, Kent Porterfield. Waiting for the jury's verdict in Officer Darren Wilson's case, members of the community wanted the public prepared. The proposal's points of contact were Tribe X's Talal and Sarah. Topics that were going to be touched on included knowing your rights, live streaming, talking to the media 101, protest-art making, nonviolent street tactics, and basic protest first aid. The speakers included Professor Roediger (from SLU Law), Rebel Z (live streamer), Janina (activist), Elizabeth (artivist), Kayla (activist), and Andrea (a medic, I believe). Dr. Porterfield ended up approving the SLU skill share.

The phone contact messaging field 90975 was a movement tool for spontaneous activity. These numbers represented a text cloud that guided the work of those invested in justice. Anyone who subscribed to the account could gain access to Ferguson uprising events. The first time I learned about the organizing instrument was through mass meetings hosted by movement organizations OBS and Missourians Organizing for Reform and Empowerment. Various groups were given access to this bullhorn for strategy, including Tribe X. The benefit to this tool was that it created alerts, beyond social media and directly to subscribers' cell phones, about ongoing events, ranging from healing to food, services, and direct action. The premise of this application was that *anyone* could subscribe to it. This included opponents of the Ferguson uprising.

There's a storied history of COINTELPRO, wherein malicious clout chasers, propagandists, and social architects utilized media, art, and printed words to discredit, dismantle, and destroy organizing efforts. This is depicted in Ava DuVernay's *Selma* in the scene presenting comrades Malcolm X and Martin Luther King Jr. in adversarial positions. Dr. King receives a letter that, at face value, conflates his insecurities and personal activities with the core values of movement in one scene. J. Edgar Hoover recruited members of the Federal Bureau of Investigations (FBI) and launched a crusade against those in opposition to American capitalism and colonialism. This included leaders who spoke truth to power around the United States' hypocrisy on many fronts. COINTELPRO's aim was clear: destroy those deemed to counter America's racist interests. As a result of the program launched by Hoover, many leaders were targeted, attacked, and murdered, leading to the destruction of their organized life. *This theme of surveillance later emerges on the full screen in Ryan Coogler's Judas and the Black Messiah, wherein Fred Hampton is depicted being trailed, harassed, and backdoored by an FBI agent.*

Given that the subscription to the 90975 was open, this gave those with access to the platform a license to access information around events, locations, dates, times, and resources. Alongside those invested in supporting those on the ground, there was a reasonable suspicion that a window was open to those who followed Hoover's legacy. Once a mass text was sent out, the information was free for all (even the police and counterprotesters). Mindful of this, those responsible for utilizing the tool accounted for possible disruptions and interruptions to the cause. Tribe X was of the groups charged with having access to the messaging system and the knowledge that came with ensuring its integrity.

To the benefit of Tribe X, there were minimal outrageous reactions to its usage given our strategic and mindful application of the 90975 platform. Whenever there were efforts sponsored by Tribe X, we moved with sensitivity to the history of surveillance using creative means. This meant accomplishing our promoted events and actions without diluting the foreseen goals. Tribe X conducted many of its actions outside of its social media and used word of mouth. While we could not account for every police or counterintelligence effort, we ensured that participants did not suffer the cruelties associated with Hoover-esque programs.

An example of this was the #DelmarLoopDieIn. On Sunday, November 16, furthering our pressure on Saint Louis to face the ugliness of its racism, Tribe X (by way of Talal) became the parent of one of the dopest protest actions: the Delmar Loop die-in. Die-ins have a historical root wherein participants lay on the ground to exaggerate an idea. Talal's idea was to conduct a die-in within the Delmar Loop to raise awareness of the need for the community to stay informed of the Ferguson uprising—in particular, to dramatize the need for public attention to the upcoming grand jury decision on Monday, November 24, 2014. This tactic had never been used in this way since the start of the Ferguson uprising. Tribe X was constantly thinking of creative and inventive means of expressing our platform. This moment was no different.

While working on the Delmar Loop action, I was taking classes with Dr. Hatsephi Kushma on African American film. In this course, we looked at Black films focusing on Black life in the United States. One particular film we looked at focused on youths addressing Jim Crow during the civil rights movement. Dr. Kushma had our class watch Robert Houston's *Mighty Times: The Children's March*, which undergirded my involvement as a youth in risking myself to lift a larger cause. For instance, journalist Robert Boyce invited Tribe X to tell our story; this gave us a platform to clarify our position while naming our pains, gains, and goals.

The day of the Delmar actions, two meetup points for demonstrators were set up to distract counterefforts using the 90975 service. One was at the Delmar Loop metro station, and the other was at the Washington University in Saint Louis (WUSTL) metro station off of Forest Park Parkway and Skinker Boulevard. I was at the WUSTL station as the crowd grew. Members of the Freedom Fighters were present, including but not limited to Shermale Humphrey, Autumn Mae, Nina Jenkins, and Damon (formerly known as Diamond) Latchison. They were a group of powerful women who were out in Ferguson early and stayed involved in protests and meetings.

Together, we marched down Skinker to Delmar, where we linked with the second meetup group. We must have had a group of at least forty as we marched in the middle of Delmar alongside the commercial centers, coffee shops, and tourist attractions. So many onlookers were puzzled by the presence. Talal had the action organized where, at a signal, one individual role-playing a cop would "shoot" the marchers to represent police brutality. Once shot, the marchers would fall in the middle of the street, and another individual would outline their body with chalk like a crime scene. After the demonstration, we left the chalk to leave a visual for onlookers to understand the message.

Throughout the action, many intersections were blocked. This upset a lot of drivers, who were angrier about being delayed than they were about our message about police killing Black youth. Some commuters honked in support, and many did so with malice. It did not make a difference to the Ferguson uprising, given that our purpose was strong. When you walk in your purpose, fear and hate bounce off you like raindrops.

The Children's March by Robert Hudson and Bobby Houston is a film about Black youth sacrificing for freedom in the 1960s. It is a documentary about the strategies that young activists employed and how their energy undermined Jim Crow in Birmingham in 1963. The documentary filmmakers follow the movement in Birmingham, the "fill the jail" tactics that defined its constituents. The movement's demographics range from Black to white, old to young, and include various professionals, activists, working-class people, store owners, teachers, students, and politicians. More than one hundred eyewitness interviews, including Dick Gregory, Harry Belafonte, and James Bevel, present storytelling that brings to life their personal experiences. Recordings of Rev. Dr. Martin Luther King Jr. inside the Sixteenth Street Baptist Church, where youths worked in strategic meetings, reminded me of the sessions at Greater Saint Mark's and Saint John's Church, two hubs for the Ferguson uprising. Imagery of children marching to Kelly Ingram Park—where officers, armed with batons and dogs, were standing at the ready—angered me. Film shootings of children behind bars after being piled fifty deep into paddy wagons helped bring the historic moment to the present in real life and left me incensed.

The message of the film creates a more honest look into the 1963 Birmingham Black youth movement because it brings to the forefront a sector that is often seen as the last to be involved in political action. Youths are often presented as apathetic, naive, and self-centered. Examples of how society undervalues youth politics are legal restrictions on voting and a lack of support for efforts involving their political education. This is done to portray the image that all youths care about are their self-interests and not those of the community. Yet the Black young people in this film are on the front lines of a moral battle. When the film is exploring steps that the Southern Christian Leadership Conference (SCLC) activists took to involve the Black community, the camera presents youths as the first and only to volunteer. Parents, teachers, and other professionals are presented as spectators. The film utilizes still shots of young people at home with their parents looking at them with concern.

The SLU AAMS initiative was an on-campus organization focused on the recruitment, retention, and graduation of young Black men at SLU. It was cofounded by SLU faculty and staff Dr. Bradley, Queen Mother Buck, and Andre Benson. I joined this group in my first year and continued to be involved in my sophomore year. By my sophomore year, Joshua Jones, a trusted Black graduate student, served as the point of contact and facilitator for AAMS services. AAMS would host informative panels, check on grades, hold enrichment events, give tours of local job sites, and match its Black male student members with mentors. In November, they were sharing a range of events to keep everybody focused and involved with SLU's upcoming finals week. We got invited to several opportunities to check in and advance our holistic development. AAMS shared how State Representative Michael Butler was seeking interns, Saint Louis icon Julius Hunter was having a book talk sponsored by African American studies, a panel on race and mass incarceration was happening through the Cross-Cultural Center, and an opportunity was presented to speak at a male youth summit.

Sitting in those AAMS meetings about grades with Dr. Bradley and Dr. Buck was everything to me. Having SLU Black professionals who were trustworthy, credible, and resourceful pouring into me as a Black student was key. I remember having a check-in with them about my grades during my first year. I didn't have any Ds or Fs at the time, but I had entirely too many Cs. I feel like they played both sides as a strategy to build me up. During grade check-ins, Queen Mother Buck would say to me, "This isn't bad for the first year; it'll all work out." She made me feel like I had room for growth. Dr. Bradley scoffed at her response and said, "You being soft on the boy. Look, you need to get these up." They both were very real about academic success and just had different styles of conveying it. AAMS provided such a framework around my studies that proved critical to accomplishing my goals while working on movement tasks. While it was easy to get caught up in the justice work of the Ferguson uprising, I was held accountable for my scholarly endeavors.

The work of the SLU's BSA didn't stop. As academic chair of the BSA, I was still doing my best to stay on top of attending meetings, programming events, and advocating for Black students. After OccupySLU, BSA president Christopher Walter reached out to SLU president Dr. Pestello to have him give updates and share his support for the work. Dr. Pestello spoke at the BSA's November 24 general assembly. It went well insofar as having students get an opportunity to ask him questions and receive feedback.

BSA had a lot of work to catch up and stay abreast of after the occupation. There were several announcements and updates to get out to the constituents of the organization. One effort was around the CE visit to Nashville, Tennessee. CE was more than a trip out of town. It was an immersion experience grounded in principles of *Sankofa* (Swahili for "go back and get it") and community-building. It was an annual traditional event, and we welcomed all from the SLU student body to join us in visiting a historical site significant to the history of Black people and the African diaspora. This trip allowed SLU students to explore and be further educated on aspects of Black history. I believed in its capacity to reaffirm history and challenge racism, which are two of BSA's building blocks. CE challenged our worldviews through education inside and outside the classroom, thus enriching the culture of ourselves (and, by extension, SLU). Previous locations included Little Rock, Arkansas (2012–2013); Memphis, Tennessee (2013–2014), and now Nashville, Tennessee (2014–2015). I regretted not being able to attend the visit to Nashville as my heart was faced with the upcoming realities of the Ferguson uprising.

Before the non indictment, there was a social media advocacy campaign that I participated in around Missouri governor Jay Nixon's decision to call for a state of emergency. The idea was to take a picture, adding the Twitter hashtag #WhatsTheEmergencyJay? Dr. Jonathan Smith, a SLU African American studies professor, helped push the social media campaign. It was aimed at questioning the reaction of the state to the upcoming decision. The government was paying a lot of money to have National Guard protection. Many found it odd that no announcement had been made by the prosecuting office, yet there were thousands for police. The idea was that the state was enacting a contingency plan in case Officer Darren Wilson would not be charged because the city officials feared the Ferguson uprising demonstrators would shut down the city. With all that money invested, Dr. Smith and those sharing begged the question: Why would there be an emergency allocation of resources unless the state anticipated there would be no indicting Officer Darren Wilson to begin with? Not that the presence of the guard mattered because the demonstrators were still going to get down to business.

The night of Monday, November 24, was tragic. While I did not have faith in prosecuting attorney Bob McCulloch's office to fulfill its duty, hearing the decision not to indict Officer Darren Wilson was unreal. For months, hundreds of thousands of people were petitioning to have McCulloch recuse himself due to his unwavering loyalty to Saint Louis police. His father, a police officer, was allegedly killed by a Black man in 1964. Perhaps this trauma contributed to his racist bias in how he approached officer-involved shootings. In 2001, two white undercover cops killed two unarmed Black men in Dellwood and claimed they were fearing for their lives. McCulloch didn't prosecute them.

The night of the decision, I was on campus and had a staff meeting with Residence Life. Throughout the semester, I was already getting hints that I needed to be more visible on my job's floor, which was challenging to me. This meant less time off campus engaged in the work of the Ferguson uprising. I received a bit of leniency from my supervisors because they understood my passion for advocacy. I did not want to keep taking the room my job gave me for granted. Yet it made me feel out of place not being in Ferguson on the night of the indictment. I was in Fusz, a cafeteria and residence hall on campus, with a small group of Billikens gathered around the television. I had to calm down as it took everything not to "Falcon punch" the screen after prosecutor McCulloch's announcement: no indictment.

I remember reading article after article about the response from the community. The way a lot of media covered the response to the horrible nonindictment was trash. My people were called "animals" and all kinds of names by clout chasers. Listening to the slandering of those rebelling as "rioters," I kept thinking, *Nigga, please.*

Studying Black history courses kept my mind sharp on how the past met the present before my eyes. It was like these architects of negativity didn't care that an infuriated response to injustice was inevitable. If you weren't angry along with my people, you weren't paying attention to history. The white Boston Tea Party protest of 1773 isn't called a *riot* but an *American rebellion*. These white demonstrators looted, threw away tons of products, and rioted to get their message across. White people were ready and willing to go to war over tea and taxation. How should the Black community feel about the murder of and lack of justice for their babies? The nonindictment and clout-chasing response to it reminded me that only certain groups of people in America are allowed to express outrage.

Overcoming Disappointment as a Student Organizing for Social Change

Student organizers should prepare themselves for a lifetime of servant leadership rather than relegating their organizing to an on-campus identity. The short time that students spend at their university is infinitesimal compared to the time they'll spend over their lifetime off campus. This is not to suggest that fighting for change in the academy is futile and an unworthy endeavor. There's a saying that you organize where you live. However, not limiting oneself to the four or so years that will be spent in one setting when the problems that communities face are decades old helps keep scholars focused on strategy. There's only so much that can be done to enact transformation in a college environment. Depending on what the cost of institutional difference being sought is, decision-makers will do everything in their power to resist acquiescing to demands. As Chicago activist Phil Agnew shared at Alex Haley Farm during a Knoxville Children's Defense Fund National Training in May 2024, "The university is not your friend . . . it's a business."

The stubbornness of the academy in the face of noble sacrifices and efforts may generate feelings of disillusionment, disappointment, and despair within youth organizers. Substantive change often happens over time rather than immediately. Therefore, it's astute for young people wrestling with the contradictions of their schools to play the long game rather than the short one. They must politically educate and experiment with the younger classes matriculating after them as a way of passing the baton so that the fight does not end with them. Form a commitment to a tradition of struggle that is longer and larger than themselves.

Exercising patience with passion is critical to student activists accomplishing goals. It is sometimes easier for student activists to identify a problem; however, the tedious work is in the execution of the solution. Issues abound, and the ways young people can articulate and describe that which is flawed have no limits. The process it takes to deal with a difficult situation and provide an answer to the question requires deliberation, discipline, and dedication. Microwaveable solutions to deeply rooted issues do not have substantive outcomes. It takes commitment, consistency, and care to deliver desired results. The issues within young people's schools are often not new but an old reflection of defects in the community. Erin Logan, a journalist with NPR, interviewed two activists from the 1960s, seeking advice from them on youths protesting gun violence in 2018. Mark Naison, a student organizer from Columbia University who was involved in the Congress of Racial Equality and Students for a Democratic Society, shared his thoughts on guidance for present-day youth activists. He explained that change-making work takes time, so students pushing for transformation should pace themselves: "this is a long distance run, not a sprint." Meaningful change does not typically happen overnight because the moving parts that maintain the status quo did not happen overnight. This can help student organizers feel relief because while the need they are advocating for is pressing, the mindset should be that the work is bigger than themselves.

Naison's advice is not unique to him, as other seasoned activists have echoed a similar concept using the track-and-field metaphor. In a profile conducted by Forward through Ferguson (FTF), an organization founded after Missouri governor Jay Nixon's call for actionable steps following the uprisings in response to the murder of Michael Brown Jr., there's an interview with two storied activists based in Saint Louis, Jamala Rogers and John Chasnoff. Rogers and Chasnoff serve as cochairs of the Coalition against Police Crimes and Repression, which addresses policing and state violence accountability. Asked by FTF why they continue to do movement work after decades of service, Rogers explains, "I was told many years ago by an elder, 'This is a long haul. It's not going to happen soon. You've got to be a marathon runner instead of a sprinter.' So you adjust your mindset as well as your body to facilitate that."

When student activists are fighting to create better communities, they have to think about the ways they're investing in developing healthy practices for themselves. This lens of looking at movement work as a *marathon runner* helps young people pace themselves as sorrows, regrets, and letdowns inevitably arise. Dr. Marie Cieri, a former professor at Ohio State University, cowrote a book about longevity within movement work. Dr. Cieri writes, "Effective activists need to be strong enough to read reality and to do what's required to maintain momentum . . . Each one sees activism as a lifelong enterprise . . . this takes place in the face of the slowness of real change." Activism is not a fad but a faith that carries sincere changemakers throughout life. Youth organizers should commit to a level of endurance because as long as injustice exists, while they're in school or not, the need for their efforts to address it does not end.

Embracing conflict is a part of the work. The democratic project implies a diversity of opinions that means sitting with and accepting the fact that all will not share the student organizer's vision. This truth applies from the peak of universities to its valleys. What is common sense and obvious to one person may be complex to the next. The urgency and priority of another may be inconsequential to their neighbor. It can be frustrating when a cause that one deeply cares about is not shared by others. After all the efforts of debating or demonstrating, conflict can cause one to feel deterred in their drive toward their dream. It can breed emotions of uneasiness and discomfort. Being at peace with the fact that others will disagree and challenge youth activist theories and tactics is monumental to the pursuit of communal transformation. This calls for students to be strategic and creative in whom they cultivate relationships with, how they build power, and where they lend their attention. Rather than talking to the proverbial wall, locate allies and form strategic partnerships with individuals and groups that identify with or are impacted by the issues you care about. This will remind students that they are not alone on an island and that there's support for the work. Instead of focusing on a tepid audience, it offers opportunities for untapped people to get involved and implement leadership development vehicles for growth.

At times, the expectations that young activists may have for their counterparts are not fulfilled and fall short. There can be debates that turn into disrespect, discussions that become discourteous, and decisions made that are disdainful. At times, addressing the issues that student organizers seek to solve becomes impeded by external and internal feuds that emerge. Being unable to wrestle with this reality can incapacitate and immobilize progress toward achieving goals. Dr. Aidan Ricketts, of law and arts at the Southern Cross University based in Australia, writes extensively about how critical it is to unpack and engage conflict in activism. Speaking to why it's important to not avoid strife and to accept discord, Dr. Ricketts explains, "Conflict is an opportunity. Although conflict usually conjures up a negative mental image, it is also what attracts a lot of attention in our society. Conflict can be an important precursor to beneficial change." Student activists' understanding and embracing the reality of conflict, as opposed to facing it with paralysis, is a healthy mechanism for ushering in possibilities of growth. This diplomatic attitude on disputes helps young organizers not fall for the temptation to meet disagreements with withdrawal and jaded energy. Instead of closing doors, conflict becomes a window of opportunity.

According to Dr. Randy Janzen, an academic in the peace and justice studies program at Selkirk College, Canada, rather than hiding from or avoiding tension that comes up, facing it head on creates space for the possibility of change. Dr. Janzen states, "Conflict transformation is a process where parties in a conflict strive for outcomes based on peace and justice. . . . [It] emphasizes the vision that conflict can be a catalyst for positive social change." By engaging in sincere efforts to bridge disagreements and arrive at an understanding, student activists can effectively resolve friction that comes naturally in doing movement work.

Student activists taking care of themselves is a radical act. Movement work is a contact sport. This means it's critical to have a healthy mindset, practice, and routine. Staying focused on their classes, investing in holistic care, and leaning into a support network help student organizers to sustain themselves. If youth organizers place a primacy on movement work to the point that they are neglecting their well-being, it is a disservice to both the cause and themselves. Anybody suggesting that students are less committed to social change because they prioritize their well-being is unrealistic and irresponsible. When students spend an ample amount of hours in movement work and an insufficient amount of time on their studies, they jeopardize their organizing and academics. The purpose of going to school is to gain knowledge and skills that one can apply after graduation. Skipping class, missing assignments, and taking shortcuts to get through studies hurt the larger cause. Making sure that they eat regularly, monitor their physical fitness, ground themselves spiritually, partake in fruitful social activities, and tend to their human needs stabilizes their capacity to show up in and beyond movement. Having a life outside of social justice activities gives students a stronger overall sense of self and affirms their ability to operate at their full potential. Building relationships with trusted adults, peers, family, and people who genuinely love students provides a community of accountability and care. This network will check students when they are overzealous or wrong but also affirm and protect them. Burnout and deep fatigue happen in movement when actors involved are overwhelmed, drained, and paralyzed by regular high levels of stress. The opposition counts on organizers to spiral into physical, emotional, and mental exhaustion. Centering health and joy makes it easier to navigate the pitfalls that come with activism.

Without question, it can be challenging for youth activists to protect their peace and prioritize themselves because, in so many ways, movement work is a dance of altruism. It's often a selfless effort that undergirds genuine participation in pushing for change. While a specific issue may impact young activists, the solution that requires organizing means that the cause is truly larger than them. As a result, it can be hard for young people engaged in social change work to take a step back and refill their own cups after pouring so many for others. Andee Tagle, a reporter with NPR, cowrote a piece that unpacks the importance of joy for activists. Featuring the work of Karen Walrond, who is an activist and author from Trinidad, they wrestle with questions of joy in organizing. Paraphrasing Walrond, Tagle shares, "The first thing to remember is that rest and joy are integral parts of the process. Just as the seasons ebb and flow, so too should your activism work."

Finding time away from the noise and bustle of community work by centering happiness and gratification is key. Walrond is quoted as stating, "Joy is how we gather the energy to go back in, to do the work. Joy is how we remind ourselves what we're fighting for." Student activists replenishing themselves with whatever makes them feel happy and recovered helps with their longevity. It also gives them the wherewithal to have a healthy outlook on problems that emerge so that they become architects of the solutions instead of being engulfed in the issues. The late, great Audre Lorde is a renowned feminist author, professor, and activist who wrote an essay on the importance of self-care and investing in one's well-being. Lorde writes, "Caring for myself is not self-indulgence, it is self-preservation, and that is an act of political warfare." Student activists taking the time to care for themselves in the midst of the cacophony is movement work. It is essential for youth organizers to listen to the song of their hearts that tells them to invest in their well-being.

Celebrate victories, whether small or large. Movement work is a marathon, not a sprint. Never let anyone downplay accomplishments that are won in fighting for a cause. The audacity of uninvolved observers and sideline commentators in giving unsolicited opinions on gains that organizers make can be endless. Decision-makers may agree, concede, or just resist demands that student activists make. Simply raising awareness and disrupting the business-as-usual culture of an institution can be a gain. Getting an audience with those who have power is not the same as actually getting what is sought, but it is commendable. Often, there can be a feeling that all the countless resources and time spent organizing adds up to nothing or is meaningless when one's ultimate goals are not met. This line of thinking is far from the truth. Impact from activism is not limited to just the calls for action. Building leadership and bases of support, educating others, and asserting dignity by calling out injustices are milestones that must be accounted for in doing the work. When organizers nurture and appreciate the seeds that they plant today, it gives room for the fruits of larger possibilities tomorrow.

The reality is that student leaders may not be able to enjoy the full rewards of their labor immediately. It may take weeks, months, or even years before the conditions for which they fight actualize into material change. The sense of urgency to make a difference should not capsize the small steps along the way. The motivation behind the struggle for justice is to leave the world better than how one found it. Whereas before, others were silent, ignorant, uninspired, and uninvolved, student activism forces their campuses to listen, become aware, feel compelled, and act. Acknowledging the efforts that are made in the movement for freedom gives youth activists grace and enthusiasm in their pursuit of transforming the community.

CHAPTER 7

If It's Bigger than You or Me, It Ain't Bigger than Us

Ode to Mama Mix: Jingle Bells, Life Is Hell

"I do it and do it well," she would say.
Cast a spell to cause hell, she comes to slay.
Yell and close citadels to start her day.
Risked jail, never fails, gets busy and plays.

What's Beethoven to Lauryn Hill silly?
"Fur Elise" versus her "Every City"
What's Shakespeare to a Lorraine Hansberry?
"Hamlet" versus "Raisin in the Sun" play?

Composer and playwright; Justice her Muse.
Holding back on the carols she refused.
Stacked by the Christmas tree, rest was a cruise.
Red book in hand, she gave shoppers the blues.

Friday, November 28, 2014

President Barack Obama promoted a color-blind, "rising tide lifts all boats" message in his campaigns. When I was a child and did not critically assess the outcomes of this kind of idea, I believed that it was all right. As a result, I naively went along with the go along. I mistakenly believed that if everyone saw each other as human and *not* Black, LGBTQ+, low-income, differently abled, woman, there'd be progress because we're all one. Instead of looking at the ways in which our injustices are tied to identity, we could look at all backgrounds as one. Furthermore, policy informed by such a lens would cease the need for racism and the additional *isms*. Trayvon Martin reminded me that I was wrong. There was no color blindness in George Zimmerman or other white supremacists. Zimmerman did not see a human being in Martin but an animal. The consequences were deadly and very much centered on color.

At SLU, I was able to form close relationships with white antiracist communities because they understood the importance of agitation internally and toward their peers. White privilege was unchecked and inseparable from the school, which was in a bubble. The school that began with several Jesuit slave owners paid little attention to Black neighborhoods north of Delmar. White mediocrity was deemed acceptable in terms of shallow efforts to increase Black enrollment, retention, and graduate rates at the school. White apathy was largely apparent in how funding for Black academic life was subject to the whims of white will. In the face of these challenges, I felt relief knowing there were white student activists who questioned this status quo. This set of white students was like family to me because they understood the power of using their privilege as empowerment in the face of injustice. Even if they felt uneasy navigating their proximity to white privilege, they unpacked it all and encouraged their white peers to do the same.

I enjoyed making *silent* white people uncomfortable because that was the only way change was going to come about within our predominantly white campus community. If no one agitated, the don't-give-a-fuck attitude many white students had would go on. I focused my energies on students who were fine with the everyday life on campus. These were often white people on campus who participated in acts of microaggressions. For example, there were incidents wherein Black cafeteria staff members were insulted by arrogant white staff members and students. Sometimes white students treated them like *animals,* as if their lives and livelihood were dispensable. The Black staff would be harassed, and because they did not pay tens of thousands of dollars to attend the school, their voices were treated like they were nobody. In response, I would speak with management and Black staff about their experiences. It angered me that many white people on campus saw the Black staff as inconsequential.

In addition, there were incidents when white students would host holiday parties and smudge makeup on their faces to impersonate a cultural group. One example of this was the *brown face* incident, where white partygoers were mocking the appearances of Latinx people. In response to this, I joined a protest on campus that called out the horrible event and demanded accountability. This disturbed white students because they felt the partygoers' disrespectful actions were just a harmless joke. White baseball players had group chats that were filled with slurs, including the word *nigger*. One player even called Barack Obama a "watermelon eating baboon." In response to this, I organized with anti-racist students to demand justice. Disagreeing with Obama's political stances did not merit racism. With other student activists, we marched with a bullhorn through the administration building and library on campus. If no one called out the bullshit going on, its odor would simply persist. Much of this campus context existed prior to the murders of Mike Brown Jr. and VonDerrit Myers. It didn't bother me when silent white folks felt bothered.

However, Tribe X was undergoing a tough transition period. Following a series of incidents, our group was reduced to only Alisha, the advisers, and me. One evening, members of the team called an *emergency* meeting, excluding our mentors, to talk about the future of Tribe X. I felt it was odd that this gathering about the affairs of Tribe X included all but our advisers. Since it was a meeting about the state of the team, I figured it made sense to have them present. Alisha and I walked into a room and sat down to join the spontaneous meeting. The air in the room was thick. Rockit, as Tribe X president, attempted to facilitate the meeting. The typical Robert's Rules of Order structure went out the window as formalities shifted to conversational. It became clear that the meeting was called because there were competing visions for the future of our organization. The following two points raised by some in Tribe X unsettled me:

1. Autonomy from the advisers: Claims were made that removing the position of our advisers would help in fulfilling the mission of Tribe X. The power to make decisions should be with those in the front line moving forward: finances, membership, actions, meetings, and marketing.
2. Micromanagement of advisers: Claims were made that the organic work of the team was halted by the intrusive voice of advisers.

The complaints above reflected concern that the advisers were stewards of the nonprofit and of social media, and they utilized veto power. I understood the desire for autonomy and self-determination; however, I felt saddened that the above points were seen as the solution.

On the topic of autonomy, I disagreed with the idea of removing Tribe X's mentors because they proved critical to our genesis, success, and stability. Tribe X would not have formed as it existed without our mentors. Helping procure the CTA agreement with SLU was a glaring example of their ability to help the organization achieve. I felt it was honorable that our advisers volunteered their professional and educational skills to advance Tribe X's work. I did not agree with the narrative of the advisers not being *frontline* and, by extension, without the need for a voice in decisions. They helped use social media to raise awareness and to launch Tribe X and had been protesting since August. Relieving them of responsibility for the budget was unwise to me. I felt that their role was a relief as the team could focus on programming, recruitment, and advocacy.

On the matter of micromanagement, I did not agree with the claim that halts in the work of everyday affairs were the advisers' fault. To help balance Tribe X's efforts with nonorganizational activities, there were interventions. This was meant to ensure the integrity of how time, labor, and donations were spent. This looked like checks and balances to ensure proper guidance around the allocation of resources.

Regardless of the above, some members felt like alignment and synergy were off, so moving forward without our advisers was the best move. I felt like the real issue was that members did not want to honor the accountability processes in place.

Dhoruba and I were the two who bumped heads the most. He felt strongly in support of the two-point argument. Both of us were tender-headed in our disagreement with the proposed measures. We felt annoyed and made sly comments to each other, and quickly the four walls in the meeting room were about to become the ropes of a boxing ring. This had nothing to do with Tribe X and everything to do with our egos. A shouting match ensued. I allowed myself to get out of my body about the situation, felt ready to fight, and no longer wanted anything to do with him. He felt similarly. We understood that our disrespect was evident, names were called, and all of this led to further distrust.

All of the above helped lead to the split of Tribe X. Former members of the team went on to form a separate group named Black Souljahz. A void was created, wherein Tribe X had to figure out how to stay involved and effective with less capacity. I knew we had a lot of supporters who were looking to us. This meant we had to continue seeking sincere partnerships and thinking of creative means to advance the cause. While the fallout was not easy, there's no testimony without a test.

Following the split, one of the biggest moments for Tribe X was our action at the Galleria mall. Bob McCulloch did not indict Darren Wilson for murdering a Black, unarmed, eighteen-year-old Michael Brown. So we helped the call for a boycott of shopping outside of the Black community for the holidays. After the government didn't give us justice for the death of Mike, we had to send a message that business would not continue as usual. Until a change was going to come, we fought to reduce money spent in US retail corporations.

On Thursday, November 27, Tribe X members did their research on the mall. It was simple: look at space for a significant amount of people to begin our interruptions. We ended up choosing a space not too far from where a big Christmas tree stood in the heart of the mall. Letting our imaginations run, we watched as the direct action played out in our heads, thinking of risks and faulty logistics. A security guard doing rounds asked if we needed help with anything before walking past us.

On Black Friday, Saint Louis, like many other cities around the nation, boasts many malls that are busy and filled with people. The Saint Louis Galleria, like the other malls, hosts comfortable spaces for shopping, dining, and entertainment options. For many shoppers in Saint Louis, Black Friday at the Galleria was an opportunity to get a discount on early Christmas presents or simply visit a luxury mall. For us, the Galleria was a setting for direct action.

That morning, we got up and met at an office in Clayton that was donated to a White accomplice. We ended up filling the suite we worked in with supporters. Christmas carols were written by Tribe X's Mama Mix, with radical eloquence. One song was from the Artivist Collective, a group of artists involved in the Ferguson uprising. The plan was to go to the mall and disrupt business by singing carols of justice. The goal was to call for federal intervention in the Mike Brown case given the nonindictment.

Sending two waves of supporters to the mall from a meetup location nearby, we were ready. Early that morning, supporters were recruited to review, get a copy of, and learn the carols. Beginning our session with an icebreaker to get a feel for who was present, strangers became acquaintances. Their final instructions were to walk in at different entrances of the mall to avoid suspicion. At a certain time, we would all assemble near one of the mall's Christmas trees. When they had a good grasp of the carols, we exchanged numbers and listened to placement directions.

When enough time had passed, Tribe X representatives met with the second wave, a larger group, at another meetup location at a park. Media, police, and people I had never seen were there waiting after receiving our mass meeting text sent through the 90975 number. Worried that the police would interrupt our plans, we whispered random group instructions. Eventually, we asked DeRay McKesson to share our plan on social media.

When Tribe X and participants got to the mall, we immediately got to work. By the time we finished, the mall was forced to shut down. Standing at the Christmas tree, punching our fists in the air to signal the beginning of our action, we led with the first of our five carols, "Life Is Hell," included below, sung to the tune of "Silver Bells."

Busy racists, busy racists.
Dressed in KKK style
In the air
There's a feeling of bias

Bigots laughing
Racists passing
Every mile after mile
And on every street corner you'll hear

Life is Hell, Life is Hell
It's a racist time in the city
Ring-a-ling, hear them sing
Slim hope for justice today

Taps of Keyboards
Even keyboards
With a slur and a meme
As the trolls troll
Protesters with hatred

Feel the gut punch
From the bad bunch
This is a racist's big scene
And above all of this bustle
You'll hear

Life is Hell, Life is Hell
It's a racist time in the city
Ring-a-ling, hear them sing
Slim hope for justice today

Our singing drowned out shoppers' conversations and the rings of cash registers near our vicinity. After singing, we held a die-in for four and a half minutes, the length in minutes for how many hours Mike was left lying in the summer street. Our group grew in number as the second wave finally joined us, and we began marching the three stories of the mall. Jewelry stores were one of the first locations I noticed locking their doors. In about thirty minutes, the National Guard was outside. By then, it was too late; the entire mall was closed.

People vilified the action. In online articles and social media blogs, there were comment sections that included racist and criminalizing reactions from the public. One called us the "Ferguson Mob." One said we went to "harass shoppers." Maybe if Prosecuting Attorney McCulloch had done his job, we wouldn't have gone to protest.

Several media outlets provided coverage of the demonstration, helping to amplify our message. It was a major boon to have reporters tell a story about what was happening so that our truth could be heard. The *New York Times* correspondent John Eligon wrote a piece called "Protesters United against Ferguson Decision, but Challenged in Unity" that described our carols and events surrounding the Galleria shutdown. He interviewed Alisha, who emphasized the significance of protest having an economic impact. *St. Louis American* reporter Rebecca Rivas also wrote about how the mall was closed for at least thirty minutes by "1,000 protesters." Having the media touch on our actions helped create a better picture of what happened and its impact.

Tribe X's Galleria shutdown and additional local demonstrations were in concert with an entire nation that was up in arms about

McCulloch's decision to not indict Officer Darren Wilson. Following the outcome, hundreds of people from around the United States took to the streets and protested. News reports spoke on this national uproar in service of accountability. *Reuters* correspondents Ellen Wulfhorst, Daniel Wallis, and Edward McAllister wrote about the national response in their article "More than 400 Arrested as Ferguson Protests Spread to Other U.S. Cities." In *USA Today*, reporters John Bacon and Gary Strauss wrote a piece titled "Ferguson Decision Triggers Nationwide Protests." All across America, people of character were expressing outrage and righteous indignation at the corruption and failure of the criminal justice system in Ferguson and America.

The police-involved shootings of Black people, children and adults, are not a Ferguson issue but a national problem. There were many instances in which cops simply murdered Black youths with impunity. This included the 2010 story of seven-year-old Aiyana Stanley-Jones of Detroit, Michigan. On Sunday, May 16th, Detroit police officer Joseph Weekley shot and murdered her during a raid while she was sleeping at home. As is typically the case, the cop claimed it was an accident. An accident is a baby peeing on themselves or McDonald's getting your food order wrong. Nothing about a trained servant getting away with murdering a baby is acceptable. The unchecked murdering of Black children by police seemed to be as American as apple pie.

Two days before the nationwide coverage of Bob McCulloch's racist decision to not indict Darren Wilson, another Black child was killed. Twelve-year-old Tamir Rice of Cleveland, Ohio, was murdered while playing in the park by Officer Timothy Loehmann. Since Rice had a replica airsoft gun, a damn toy, the officer's reaction was somehow deemed reasonable. Reading about the loss of this child further angered me. I didn't think too much about healing or healthy ways of managing these realities. I was focused on being TTG, trained to go with my people.

Responding to the decision and police-involved shootings with demonstrations such as the Galleria shutdown was cathartic to me. Did the state expect the movement to stay silent and back down in the face of atrocity? There's a risk associated with every protest, and you have to make peace with it. I got joy from interrupting and agitating because I knew that many of my people live in communities where there is a lack of services, and our access to resources is shut down. Such divestment is a result of systemic injustice. I found therapy in making white people uncomfortable as they faced the consequences of their racism. Michael Brown Jr., VonDerrit Myers Jr., and more would still be alive if racists didn't treat Black youths as animals. Every action I participated in affirmed my sense of self and certainty that while times may be bleak, the fight was far from over.

Addressing Internal Conflict in Social Movements as a Student

Conflict's basis is disagreement.[1] When engaged in movement work, just because there's a collective dedicated to the same cause does not mean there are no nuances in opinion. There are a lot of different ways that people look to transform a community, from tactics, ideology, and goals to governance, resources, and more. The methods of organizing that make sense to one person may seem insufficient or overboard to another. The stewardship of time, money, and people invested in pushing movement work forward may be negligent to a couple and diligent to many. Social justice work is a democratic experiment, and it demands that participants openly share their views, critiques, hesitation, and hopes. When serious conflict emerges, finding ways to deal with the disputes in a way that is reasonable, accountable, and transparent can strengthen the bonds participants have with one another. Not taking controversies seriously can implode and impede a movement's progress.

Egos can ruin a beautiful thing. Being self-centered and unable to see outside of one's own interests stunts growth and advancement. Some small-minded participants in the movement believe and behave as if they have all the answers, refuse to take feedback, and belittle others. As the saying goes, in their infatuation with self, they believe that their Kool-Aid is sweetest and ice is coldest. Nothing's wrong with being confident when there's a level of humility. When fighting for justice, it demands that one be self-assured and unwavering, but this certainty is predicated on the support of the community. No one is able to accomplish any substantive change in isolation, alone, or in silos. However,

1. *This chapter references a peer mediation model developed by staff of American Friends Service Committee (AFSC) and their "Help Increase the Peace" manual. The author, who previously served as a peace program associate with AFSC St. Louis, implemented the model in high schools, violence prevention sessions, and community organization settings.*

there are those who subscribe to the notion that they themselves are the solution to the problems. If a lock is unable to be opened, it is because they are the missing key. When activists bring more attention to themselves and their accomplishments than the issues they claim to want to address or when organizers are more critical of their own ranks or allies than they are of the opposition or those in power, this unhealthy sense of one's importance damages relationships and harms the larger cause. Leaders with this mentality in the fight for justice sabotage the struggle due to this character flaw overriding the selflessness required for the work. Participants working to transform communities on their campuses or in their communities must be mindful to keep their egos in check.

Mediation can be a helpful tool for remedying serious conflict when it emerges within the ranks. It requires all parties to be willing to put aside their pride and pick up positivity. This process reminds those at odds with each other that at the end of the day, everyone is fighting for the same cause and there are more unifying characteristics than that which is divisive. If both parties agree to partake in mediation, it's a show of good faith that they're willing to resolve issues and move forward.

Once they've agreed, there are four steps toward beginning the process. Step one is identifying facilitators. The facilitators of a conflict resolution space can be trusted mentors, reputable third-party representatives, and unbiased peers. Preferably, there should be two facilitators involved in the process. Whoever is leading this problem-solving space has to understand that their role in the process is not about right or wrong but about rebuilding community through transparency, accountability, and truth-telling. It is not their job to lend their judgment but to allow the opposing parties to come up with their own opinions and solutions.

Step two of the mediation process is preparing community agreements. After identifying those who will hold the space, preparation for the conflict resolution should be thoughtfully executed. They should have community agreements identified that will help guide the procedure. This is a social contract that participants will actually develop on their own to hold each other accountable. However, facilitators should be prepared to contribute ideas for what should be included in this contract. Some example agreements include participation, respect, openness, confidentiality, silencing of cell phones, having one mic, and sharing space. Step three is logistical: locating a space, date, and time to host the mediation. The space and schedule should be somewhere neutral, private, and in alignment with both parties' availability. Students have varying responsibilities juggling classes, student life, basic needs, and more. Finding a time for at least 1–2 hours that is uninterrupted at a space with minimal to no distractions ensures the process is done in good faith. Step four is convening. Facilitators will sit in between the parties and explain the purpose of the space. Conveners will start by articulating the following format that outlines the six stages that will drive the mediation: (1) overview, (2) roles and community agreements, (3) storytelling, (4) clarification of narratives, (5) locating a resolution, and (6) documentation of agreement.

During the mediation overview, facilitators summarize the purpose of the mediation space in terms of its flow and goals. Each of the six stages will be articulated and explained. In stage two, rules and community agreements, facilitators lead participants through a process of making and cosigning community agreements. Participants should be asked to think of what guidelines would help ensure that the dialogue remains healthy. If they are unable to come up with their own, facilitators can volunteer ideas for agreements such as those shared in step two above. During stage three, storytelling, each participant has an opportunity to share their perspectives on the root of the conflict, how it made them feel, and its impact on them. It's important they use "I" statements and speak for themselves. It's critical to emphasize the community agreements during this stage, as well as the entire process, so that each person is unfettered but accountable in their sharing. During this storytelling process, facilitators should take notes of important details and concepts that the participants explore. Stage four, clarification of narratives, is where facilitators summarize what the participants shared and identify any gaps or conflicting facts. This is the synthesizing of the knowledge shared to make sure that both participants are on one page regarding each disconnect and conflicting opinions on one another's points of view. It calls for the participants to make sure they understand each other's stories now that facts are established and narratives are clear. Participants will wrestle with the impact of each other's actions from an enlightened perspective. Stage five, locating a resolution, involves facilitators guiding participants through what they feel would be the best solution to address the problems or conflict that they have wrestled with in the space. Each participant should have an opportunity to share what they feel is the best way to move forward. If the two are unable to come up with reasonable resolutions, facilitators can recommend their own suggestions. Stage six, documentation of agreement, is where, once all involved have arrived at a solution, facilitators write down what the participants have agreed to, and both parties sign their signatures, committing to the next steps.

Mediation is a vehicle to give those willing to go through it an opportunity to resolve their issues when problems emerge. It's not a one-stop shop and can involve multiple sessions rather than just one. While it can be an anxiety-inducing process, the real work is what happens after the conflict resolution. Students or participants have to honor their word and make their best effort at actualizing the commitments they've made to one another. It helps for the facilitators to check in with students over time to get updates on how they are making strides to do what they've agreed to.

Some conflicts are deep, and it can be challenging to get parties to even desire to sit down together. Participants have to be able to get past their own personalities and grievances in order to make this conflict resolution process work. It cannot be just one person; both must see the process as a worthwhile endeavor. Mediation is a model that works for those who are inclined to work it.

CHAPTER 8

Ain't Fattening No Frogs for No Snakes

Trauma on Olive

We occupied the damn occupiers.
We allied, took strides, and jammed the liars.
We brought water to those that set fires.
We chide those that scam us like apartheid.

Held the state's door open, I was attacked.
Black police grabbed my sack, and that's a fact.
I was taken aback, had to backtrack.
Wanted him cracked, whacked, laying in a shack.

At headquarters, fed up with the bullshit.
Took the police's pulpit, we commit,
Brutality, hits, spits; made hard to sit.
Arrested, thrown in pits to make us quit.

Did not reach our goal, made a show of poise.
Boys in Blue cursed us, ignored it as noise.
Killer Kops, anger you couldn't avoid.
Can't continue playing with us like toys.

December 2014

Tribe X conducted an action against the production of *Annie* at the Fox Theatre on Sunday, December 7. This was a part of our string of work since the nonindictment of killer cop Darren Wilson. We felt some kind of way about the business-as-usual attitude that seemed to plague Saint Louis. Mike Brown's family could not attend a production like *Annie* during this time. They were wrestling with the murder and lack of justice around their son. The Ferguson uprising refused to allow residents of Saint Louis to focus on entertainment during this time.

I recall many participating in Tribe X's *Annie* action. One of the protesters was Dr. Jonathan Smith of SLU. During the action, Saint Louis American photographer Lawrence Bryant got a legendary close-up of Alisha Sonnier. It's notable because it's a headshot of her with red tape over her mouth reading "I can't breathe." Notwithstanding the misspelling, that phrase was one of the last spoken by Eric Garner, a Black father murdered by police in New York. It reemphasized that the work being done in Saint Louis/Ferguson was connected to a national crisis.

Also involved in the *Annie* action were my younger brothers Christopher and David Pulphus. They held down the action. Earlier in the month, they, and hundreds of students across the nation, participated in a school walkout through their high school, Cardinal Ritter College Prep, as a means of protesting the nonindictment decision. My brothers and their peers were reprimanded for this action and required to do community service. It is inspiring to see young people such as them stand up for a cause larger than themselves.

We didn't step to the *Annie* show to simply disrupt the production but to highlight that there would be no forgetting that the fight for justice is still on. Many wonder what a Fox Theatre production had to do with redressing the pain caused by racial injustice and state corruption. American apathy and privilege help create conditions where incidents like Ferguson happen. In "Protesters Gather at the Fox, Hoping to Send a message to Annie Patrons," Jacob Barker of the *St. Louis Post-Dispatch* covers the demonstration. Barker interviewed Alisha and a white ally named Melissa Krause. They both hit the message on the head in emphasizing that white families should have regular family talks about racism. White parents should have to explain to their children the relevance of injustices such as Michael Brown Jr.'s murder.

A few days later, I was participating in a discussion hosted by the Saint Louis Coalition for Human Rights headed by Mama Jamala Rogers. The event was a two-part effort: a student essay contest and a panel. The topic the young people addressed in their writing was the question "Are police department policies and procedures in violation of citizens' human rights?" Panelists wrestled with similar questions. I sat beside Brittany Ferrell, an activist with Millennial Activist United, and Rev. Mike Kinman, a preacher activist with Christ Church Cathedral.

Together, we spoke frankly about our ongoing efforts and challenges of movement. It was a well-run event and a timely conversation. I feel public events like this gave me the ability to process my emotions while raising awareness.

Tribe X dodged many invitations from clout-chasing media. Media outlets that Tribe X courted, such as Rebecca Rivas's reliable reporting with the *St. Louis American*, were critical. Journalists like Rivas helped us control narrative, promote events beyond social media, and keep our following informed of ways to support efforts. There were right-wing efforts to promote agendas way off or inconsistent with the goals of Tribe X. For example, there were conservative efforts to present protesters in the Ferguson uprising as aimless, animalistic, and anarchist. They saw the Ferguson uprising as composed of people who were jobless, uneducated, and hungry for liquor or destruction. Bill O'Reilly did a segment titled "What the Ferguson Protesters Accomplished" following the nonindictment. In this video log on national television, he attempts to villainize and criminalize my people. No one on the ground asked for pundits such as O'Reilly's opinion on the effort. His using a national platform to spew lies helped embolden white supremacist organizing. I felt diplomatic in listening to such narratives because it helped to identify oppositions to the work being done. Such clout-chasing presented our activities as ill-intentioned and faulty.

Instead of the public listening to demands for justice, a handful of conservative journalists took advantage of the public ear. They pigeonholed my people's humane pain and disparaged it as simply unruly trouble. While O'Reilly's role was to help cover events happening, journalists like him stigmatized and diluted the truth of those demonstrating. Without fair access to local or social media, clout-chasing journalists would dominate the public narrative. To prevent the intended harm and hindering of the Ferguson movement's efforts, Tribe X engaged race-conscious journalists. For example, when Ms. Robin Boyce covered the #OccupySLU segment, it helped clarify for its audience our humane and positive efforts. Rather than the only narrative being "those animals," other journalists helped counter with our truth. I feel thankful to have had their support.

It was nice to see that the efforts and sacrifices of those involved were reaching levels where the nation was forced to listen while wrestling with the issues. One of the ways this became apparent was through an issue of *Time* magazine on Wednesday, December 10. Contributor Alex Altman wrote a piece in the "People of the Year" issue titled "Ferguson Protesters, the Activists," highlighting the work. Describing more visible demonstrators, the article also named how the efforts of everyday people in Ferguson shook the nation. The reason why the movement formed was to promote fairness and equity. The local movement community being in an issue of a national magazine in the midst of the struggle gave me hope.

After a long semester of protesting, working, volunteering, and studying, I was now facing SLU's fall finals week. I felt nervous despite all the preparation I made toward my studying. The week started on Wednesday, December 10 and went on until Tuesday, December 16. I had a series of papers and tests that I had to write and review. Although I felt the semester seemed long, it also went by very quickly for me. Due to all that was happening, everything felt like a blur. Without the support of my family, friends, and fellow movement communities, I would not have made it as far as I did. Without my people, I would have stumbled.

I was wrapping up a class with history professor Dr. George Ndege on the history of Africa since 1884. During this course, we looked into the timeline of events that shaped modern Africa. I penned a paper on the relationship between the United States' Jim Crow and South Africa's Apartheid. In it, I explained the similarities around the two systems of oppression. I addressed a couple of questions around my topic. The one that I leaned on most asked what the history was of those who were challenging these systems. Studying and generating content around this reminded me that the Ferguson uprising was not simply local but a global struggle.

I was reminded of a lot of things in my research and learned new facts. Jim Crowism is a combination of racist local and state restrictions deeply rooted in the *Plessy v. Ferguson* ruling. Apartheid is a structure of de jure racial separation administered by the emergent 1948 National Party of South Africa. These were points of which I was aware through my rearing in Black consciousness. However, I was learning how South Africa's movement overlaps with the United States' struggle.

In the United States, Black power leaders promoted messages of Black pride and self-determination while advocating for self-defense and knowing one's rights. In South Africa, the Black consciousness movement empowered Blacks through self-dependence. Black power organizations were working to transform communities. There were groups like Stokely Carmichael's Lowndes County Freedom Organization. Also, Black consciousness groups like Steve Biko's South African Students Organization agitated for meaningful changes. The themes of self-determination and self-dependence between these two movements were jewels of knowledge that I valued. This demonstrated to me that no matter where systematic oppression existed, Black people took radical approaches to seek redress and justice.

In Saint Louis, demonstrators were protesting and utilizing space with lawyers in order to make headway in addressing the criminal injustices. One of the issues that were highlighted was the predatory municipal courts that targeted poor Black people to increase municipal revenue. *St. Louis Post-Dispatch* writer Jeremy Kohler discusses this in "Lawyers Sue 7 St. Louis County Municipalities over Court Fees." Lawyers from ArchCity Defenders, SLU, and more firms were seeking damages for the predatory methods of courts such as those in Ferguson. Just as protesting through street demonstrations is important, legal battles create change.

In late December, I recalled looking at social media and seeing another name, another hashtag: #AntonioMartin. This young brother was gunned down by police in Berkeley, Missouri, which is not far from Ferguson, on Tuesday, December 23. This was two days before Christmas, and activists responded immediately. I looked at the attacks on activists Bruce Franks, Calvin "Cap" Kennedy, and other members of the Peacekeepers organization by police. Bruce and Calvin had umber, dark yellow-brown skin and were donning hoodies with "Peace Keeper" in bold letters. A photo showed Bruce with a bruised face after being assaulted by the police for trying to deescalate the incident following Martin's murder. This reminded me how the Ferguson uprising participants promoting peace still meant nothing at the hands of the state. As the list of names and injustices continued to grow, so did my anger.

I remember helping plan the occupation of the Saint Louis Police Department. For weeks, Tribe X sat in a room with other like-minded people building direct-action capital. We discussed the risks, objectives, and rewards. We agreed that this had one of the highest risks of arrests, where participants would have to be trustworthy and willing to assume charges. There's no question that it takes bravery when engaging in high-stakes direct actions. Those who participated in the #OccupythePolice actions are a prime example. If the occupation was successful, this would force a negotiation between residents and the city. The goal would be to present some demands before the chief of police, Sam Dotson, and ourselves. This occupation ended up being the first time I'd been arrested. I recall loved ones warning me, "Don't do it! You do not want a charge!" They were worried about my safety first, regardless of whether the effort would even be successful. Me being me, fed up with the ongoing injustices, I was ready to risk jail anyway.

Before heading to the action, I knew I risked arrest. With the department being the target, this reality just made sense. The direct-action team came up with two strategic plots. This included an occupation from the inside of the department while another group agitated outside. The occupation team would take the highest risk of arrest because they were in the belly of the beast within the police department. The planning team for the action put some creative work into it. The Artivists, a Ferguson movement group that featured brilliant artists, created a huge banner that listed our demands.

Tribe X pushed for several demands to be made front and center to contextualize the demonstration. We didn't want the narrative to be that crazed, savage, and unruly protesters aimlessly "attacked" the police. There had to be a reason for what we were doing and willing to put on the line. Reporter Rebecca Rivas of the *St. Louis American* wrote about the action in her article "Protesters 'Reclaim' STL City Police Headquarters." Below are the demands we were fighting for:

1. Immediate meeting with Police Chief Dotson, Mayor Slay, and Board of Alderman President Lewis Reed
2. Firing of Officers Hayes and Flannery
3. Clear and transparent protocol when a person dies in police custody
4. Immediate medical attention for victims
5. Immediate release of the officer's name
6. Appointment of a special prosecutor for *all* deaths that occur in police custody
7. Whistleblower program that protects officers who act with integrity
8. Amnesty for protesters who have been charged with nonviolent offenses, including those who have been charged arbitrarily with third-degree assault with no actual violence

9. Creation of a diverse citizen review board with subpoena power (The board will be appointed by the community, not politicians, and will be a reflection of victims most subjected to police violence.)
10. Seven-day release of all information regarding police shootings, including transparent release of unedited videos and audios
11. A substantive plan with implementation dates for mandatory diversity training
12. Restoration of the residency requirement
13. Screening that prevents hiring of officers fired from other departments
14. Implementation of a youth summer program that creates opportunities for young people to serve in our community

To market the action, a video of the youngest member of Tribe X crying out and denouncing the shootings of people in the area was made to help illustrate the intergenerational need to stand against injustice. If kids can tell there's a problem, responsible adults should be able to recognize and fix it. Another marketing tactic included the creation of a social media handle through Twitter. This handle was named @OTHEPOLICE and would update the public on the direct action, similar to 90975. Attached to the handle were the hashtags #OccupythePolice and #ReclaimOurPolice.

There was a rationale behind each of the fourteen demands. Similar to the OccupySLU effort, we hoped that the OccupythePolice demonstration would bring dialogue. Through discussion following agitation, substantive change could happen. We demanded to meet with decision-makers. We demanded the officers responsible for murdering VonDerrit Myers Jr. and Kajieme Powell be terminated. We demanded a better process so situations like those involving Kimberlee Randale-King, who was arrested in Saint Louis for damn traffic tickets, never happen. She ended up mysteriously dying while detained in police custody. We demanded a protocol that protects officers acting with integrity who wish to hold their counterparts accountable. We demanded that bogus charges against demonstrators such as that faced by activist Rasheen Aldridge, who was tried for assault, be no more. We demanded that there be a community-based committee that could impartially review police-involved shootings. We demanded the delay and dragging of feet on releasing public information, such as what happened with cop Darren Wilson, be ceased. We demanded the required anti-racist training of all police officers. We demanded that police be required to live in the municipality that they work in. We demanded that if an officer is fired from one department, such as cop Darren Wilson, who originally worked in Jennings, they should not be allowed to work in the profession again. We demanded that quality jobs be made available for young people to give them more opportunities and access.

Tribe X did not operate under any circumstance or belief that cops could ever be trusted to train youth in any of its organizational promotions. Each member of Tribe X was well versed in the negative impacts that policing has on communities. The mission of Tribe X was tied to holding representatives of the state, such as police, accountable for derelictions of duty. Tribe X did not support industries aimed at surveilling, intimidating, and attacking youths and families as police have. Tribe X encouraged accountability and investment in social services.

The action was a tough one. We were able to occupy the department, but this did not last long, as the police reacted with brute violence. Many involved, such as leaders Jelani Brown, Kristina Vidovic, Jessie Sandavol, Daniel Aguilar, DeRay McKesson, and more, risked cases. On the outside, there was a huge march that became a rally of people demanding justice. Once the crowd started to thin, several activists blocked traffic until the police came to arrest them. I was one of those in the group.

DeRay McKesson's involvement with Tribe X was to help counter harmful narratives, such as those by pundits like Bill O'Reilly, that misrepresented the efforts of those on the ground. I supported McKesson's ability to control parts of the narrative alongside his desire to agitate for justice. He had a gift for communicating the grievances of people tied to the Ferguson uprising. There were times when McKesson did not explicitly credit Tribe X in the promotion of our activities. There were doubts about his sincerity as an outsider who was not from Ferguson (or Saint Louis). Concerns became deeper as his media capacity grew (as did that of others associated with the uprising). McKesson's voice helped balance the harmful assumptions that were spewed. Support for several actions such as the above (including the #DelmarDieIn) was done using McKesson's platform. I was glad he supported our activities.

Following the action, I was disappointed there were no negotiations, meetings with the powers that be of Saint Louis City, or time to celebrate. I was assaulted by police staff, my genitals grabbed while I was holding the Saint Louis Police Department door open during the protest. I was pepper-sprayed by officers. My heart raced as I allowed its pain to, once again, seep into my skin's pores. Emotions of humiliation tingled in my bones. Eventually, I was arrested by officers. I was afraid that I'd be kicked out of SLU or unable to pursue employment in certain fields. The steel around my wrists felt cold and mercilessly tight. As I lay with my chest on the ground, an officer's knee pressed into my back while he twisted my arms into a fold like I was an animal.

HuffPost writer Andy Campbell wrote an article about the action, "Protesters Storm St. Louis Police Headquarters with Eviction Notice." Nothing could be more accurate in articulating the purpose of the action in words than that title. We came like landlords, tax-paying concerned citizens ready to serve our tenants, the police, with demands. In the end, I was sent to jail for this. For this moment, I felt doubt around the question of whether protest works. All we asked for was a meeting, and we were met with brute force. Being with my people reminded me to keep my head high.

Students and the Substance Nourishing Protests

Protest should be looked at as a last resort. Organizers need to exhaust methods such as dialogues, discussions, and appeals to authority before proceeding with protests. Civil disobedience is not a lightly considered tactic to force decision-makers to act. Those with power to deliver the needs articulated by students should be engaged to gauge whether they are willing to make good on the request. It is a tedious process because it often requires a good faith exercise of students and/or community having many conversations about and several attempts at gaining understanding on change. There's a saying that "if it ain't broke, don't fix it." If the conditions or system of a campus is not believed to be harmful, those with wherewithal to repair it will not invest resources in doing so. In their minds, there are more important duties and responsibilities for them to work on rather than occupying their time with nonissues. It is the call of student organizers to identify grievances, recommendations for resolving the issues, those who must be engaged with the capacity to address these issues. In other words, youth activists must locate what's broken, how it can be fixed, and the individual or group that has the power to move resources in answering the call. Sometimes it's not logistically convenient for students to have an audience with those who can enact the change. After all efforts to gain an audience or reach a resolution with decision-makers have been attempted with no desirable outcome, then it's time to consider escalating tactics to more serious methods including civil disobedience. Protest should be strategically timed because when it's the season to conduct that area of business, all discussion and dialogue has failed. When bullhorns are being yelled through, intersections shut down, quads are filled, and signage is in the air, it's past time to talk.

The indifference of campus administrators and decision-makers demands that young people take an extra step toward being heard. After students have exhausted every conventional mechanism to let their voice be heard, only to be met with campus officials refusing to address problematic campus realities, youths take activist approaches toward accomplishing goals. At times, there's a lack of appreciation for the value added by young people protesting and raising awareness of issues, and their efforts are dismissed as if they're just making noise. Dr. Georgianna L. Martin, of Counseling and Human Development Services in the University of Georgia, authored a chapter within a book she edited with another researcher. In it, Dr. Martin articulates how some organizing on campus may repel the sincere interest of campus officials because they do not have the wherewithal and bandwidth to appreciate activism as an articulation of substantive civic engagement. She posits, "Depending on the magnitude of the action, some activism may simply be viewed by campus educators as a distraction or nuisance to be managed rather than an educational opportunity or a step toward engaged citizenship for college students." When student activists' methods of being civically engaged are perceived as a problem instead of campus officials acknowledging the actual problem that young people are articulating, there's a missed opportunity for growth.

Dr. Judith Bessant, of the Royal Melbourne Institute of Technology University in Melbourne, Australia, coedited a work about youth studies and social movements. They write about the rigid definitions of and perceptions held about politics and youths in relation to civic engagement. Bessant explains, "What happens when we rely on conceptually constrained or narrow accounts of politics and political participation (for example, as engagement with formal practices such as voting, joining parties, or campaigning for electoral candidates). The result being that students and young people's political interests and actions are misjudged. It allows, for example, students, and young people more generally to be portrayed as 'politically apathetic' and disinterested in politics and the life around them." The harm in how politics is traditionally viewed is that it pigeonholes students as disinterested when, in fact, young people utilize activism as a vehicle for creating political change and self-determination for better communities and for themselves.

Prior to conducting civil disobedience, student activists should have internal conversations weighing whether or not the seriousness of this escalation matches the gravity of their recommendations. While there are varying levels in terms of methods for deploying protest associated with nuances in risk, the activities across the board come at costs regardless of what action is taken. Therefore, whatever participants are expressing public disapproval of must be worthwhile. What's pressing to some may not be grave to others. Students may identify shallow characteristics of their institution that are undesirable or outside of their preferences. Youth leaders should not major in the minors. A student's school losing against another school in a basketball tournament may feel unpleasant but is not corruption. A student's university dismissing their beloved football coach may feel unsavory but is not inequity. Those taking the risks associated with protest are at liberty to publicly express their disapproval with any and all manner of issues. It does not matter if the average person or opposition finds substance in what is being fought against. Relevance stems from the youth activists who are involved being in accord with and collectively identifying the importance of activities communicating dissent. However, the purpose behind the protest should not be tied to trivial matters. It is a waste of time, labor, people, and additional resources to rally behind a meritless cause.

Determining whether or not it is worthwhile to execute varying tactics of protest is grounded in an understanding student activists must have that there are associated costs with demonstrations. This is a strategic cerebral endeavor that calls for young people to calculate the weight of their grievances with the existing state of affairs and what they are willing to do about it. When it's decided that protest and direct action are a worthwhile investment, students should have already exhausted conventional means of asserting their self-worth and dignity. Dr. Micah White, an activist known for being the co-organizer of the original push for the Occupy Wall Street uprising against corporate greed in the fall of 2011, shared the arduous lengths to which organizers have gone to create change. Dr. White writes about a need to reinvent activism, given the series of tactics that have repeatedly been attempted yet have yielded little to no transformation. He explains, "Activists have not been passive. For decades, we have tried every tactic to shift the course of our governments. We have voted, written editorials and manifestos, donated money, held signs, protested in marches, blocked streets, shared links, signed petitions, held workshops knitted scarves, learn to farm, turned off the television, programmed apps, engaged in direct action, committed vandalism, launched legal challenges against pipelines . . . and occupied the financial districts. All of this has been for naught." While Dr. White's position is understandable in terms of the exhaustion of organizers in light of the ongoing persistence of societal issues, despite the best active efforts of activists, adjacent to the point he raises is the reality that student organizers must meditate prior to employing any tactic at all. There's no silver bullet to achieving substantive change, as there are many factors at play that can both enrich and diminish efforts.

Dr. Evgeny Morozov, a writer and former fellow of the Open Society Institute who focuses on the societal impact of technology, published a piece on the impact of digital activism as opposed to traditional avenues of organizing. Dr. Morozov argues that online activism is a slothful approach to pushing for social change because it does not require the labor and effort that conventional forms of organizing demands. He argues, "'Slacktivism' is the ideal type of activism for a lazy generation: why bother with sit-ins and the risk of arrest, police brutality, or torture if one can be as loud campaigning in the virtual space?" Dr. Morozov sharply weighs the effectiveness of digital activism; however, nothing replaces the impact of on-the-ground campaigns. It is essential, though, that student activists measure the gravity of the problems they want to address and total the value of inserting themselves in the equation of executing a solution.

Locating the nonnegotiable demand is the conduit for ensuring that protests are focused on the goal that matters most. There may be myriad recommendations that student activists are lifting up in civil disobedience. All of these demands may feel equally important, but the reality is that some will hold different impacts than others. Being able to arrange in order all the various issues one hopes to address to determine which one holds the most weight helps with prioritization. This is not to say that the other calls are afterthoughts. When meeting with decision-makers, they may or may not challenge all the demands. Speaking to what matters most to organizers helps tease out the critical concessions that youths wish to have granted. The other items can be further discussed or explored, as there's a level of flexibility associated with them. These are desired outcomes, but activists can live with them not being tackled as urgently and efficiently. It may even be the case that the less pressing demands are awarded. Student leaders have to determine whether it's worth moving forward with what's been granted even if what they ultimately want is rejected. If they find the other issues that they raised are positively received, then the prioritized demand was never nonnegotiable. It is the nonnegotiable demand that cannot be debated, conversed, or overlooked. If this inflexible command is not agreed to in the meeting with those in power, dialogue ceases. Protest returns as a viable option.

When the opportunity presents itself for student activists to create a crisis wherein decision-makers have to listen, youths must prepare to make arrangements for agreements. The purpose of protest and direct action is to create a necessity for discussions with those with power, getting them to the table to listen. At the point that young people have the attention of those in positions of authority, they must aim to broker a deal that's grounded in their values. Dr. Amy Finnegan, a professor of justice and society studies at the University of Saint Thomas, and coauthor Susan Hackley, former director of the program on negotiation at Harvard Law School, argue in an article about the interplay between negotiation and nonviolent demonstration. Dr. Finnegan and Hackley claim that negotiation and nonviolent action can work together to get parties in opposition to arrive at a sincere understanding. They state, "Negotiation, which is about 'getting to yes,' and nonviolent action, which is about 'asserting no,' can interact in ways that help us to get to the 'yes' we really seek, rather than an agreement just for agreement's sake."

Dr. Finnegan and Hackley's illustration of the power of negotiation and nonviolent action further emphasizes that student organizers, when positioned to discuss goals with those in authority, should keep in mind the power of peaceful resistance as a leverage. However, young activists should also keep in mind nonnegotiables on which they will not budge.

Katie Shonk, editor of a newsletter published by the Harvard Law School Program on Negotiation, discusses the contours of activism and negotiation using Nelson Mandela's experience with Apartheid in South Africa as a frame. Describing Mandela's decision to use skills of persuasion and pragmatism as a vehicle for bargaining for justice, Shonk articulates the importance of knowing when versus when not to come to agreements with decision-makers. She writes, "Not negotiating with an enemy on moral grounds can be a legitimate decision. But when we take a hardline stance without thoroughly analyzing the likely costs and benefits of negotiating, we risk letting our principles to get in the way of the greater good." As a result of Mandela's willingness to prioritize the collective by forming concessions rather than caving to his personal hatred of his adversaries, transformation was made possible. Shonk's analysis of Mandela's position on negotiation affirms the reality that young activists should strategically consider their posture toward engaging in agreements with decision-makers. In identifying nonnegotiables, these unshakable measures should be rooted in the good of the collective rather than individualistic reservations.

The fight for justice should center around tangible change versus fleeting compromises. When designing demands, an assessment should be completed that determines whether the commands are for the long or short term. The motivation for expressing grievances can be personal, but the impact should be communal. It's not about one single individual but about systems. The targets are those that can change policy and legislation. The effects are to be felt for years. Even if direct actions are not strategically planned and are more organic in terms of execution, they should still have an end goal tied to hearty resolution. The uprising or civil disobedience aim is to result in a soulful modification of the status quo. Dr. Victoria Canning, an academic within the criminology department at Lancaster University, coedited a book that explores lessons from seasoned to more nascent social justice movements. In this work, Dr. Stephanie Fohring, a professor of criminology at Northumbria University in the United Kingdom, coauthored a contribution that looks at the tangible benefits of hashtag activism using #BlackLivesMatter and #MeToo as backdrops. Dr. Fohring and her coauthor interrogate what criteria are used to measure achievement and transformation in campaigns for justice. They examine the ways hashtag activism has outcomes with merit, stating, "Most commonly, the impact is conceptualized as influencing the mainstream media, governmental reactions, legislative reforms, or reforms to the justice system or policy . . . but the ability to shape public opinion and articulate new solutions, create online communities, or raise awareness may also be considered significant achievements."

More broadly than hashtag activism, tangible change for youth organizers can mean simply moving the needle forward rather than changing policy alone. While these wins are instrumental, influencing societal attitudes, sharing innovative answers to problems, building power, and increasing public consciousness are all worthwhile endeavors. If a rebellion rocks the proverbial societal boat, but the business-as-usual conditions that previously existed are still maintained, it is futile.

CHAPTER 9

Don't Hop Fences—the Gates Are Wide Open

Delmar Divide

Honey, go to the theater called the Fox.
Funny, show starts soon, just look at the clock.
Flock 70 to Grand then a few blocks.
Pass up a jungle of stranded homes, shops.

Make this right on Grand and then go head south.
White water tower at night standing proud.
Plight and Blight, gunshot fights sound very loud.
A beggar in sight, change I can't allow.

We almost at the Fox? A while longer.
Blocks of fast food, grime when you face hunger.
Dime Real Estate stocks will make you bonkers.
Yet Crime so bad, nothing here but monsters.

Why don't they just take care of these nice homes?
Look at his hair he needs a line up, comb.
Remember Beaumont school, now it's a tomb.
Don't you dare stop there for gas

The shows will be very nice nevertheless.
On the fair side of town far from this mess.
Once we cross Delmar, the less we will stress.
God please wake them up, they need to be blessed.

Wednesday, December 31, 2014–Thursday, January 1, 2015

I began asking myself, Who in their right mind gets arrested on purpose? Why would you let the boys catch you? In hindsight, part of what helped me understand and process it all was the 1960 Greensboro, North Carolina, Woolworth restaurant sit-ins. In an article written by Mike Lillis of *The Hill* titled "MLK Receives the Congressional Gold Medal," he writes about civil rights activist John Lewis. Crediting his demonstrators as being a benevolent problem, Lewis is quoted as saying, "[We] inspired an entire generation to get in trouble—good trouble, necessary trouble." While many named the Ferguson uprising as ill-intentioned, I felt strongly about being in the company of those involved in "good trouble." My people and I strived to be the best troublemakers.

The first time I was released, I felt overjoyed about being let go from custody. During the time I spent in the cell, I met a lot of people who supported the Ferguson movement. One brother was inside with me on alleged terroristic threat charges against the Saint Louis police. I felt outraged when I got the backstory. Some other brothers were there on alleged gun charges. I got locked up with a down white brother named James Meinert. Everybody wanted to know what everybody was in there for. When we told them what we were there for, they laughed, saying, "Y'all wild! Y'all missed y'all holidays to protest?" Through the laughter, they showed love for us and our cause. I had to laugh at myself, missing the holiday for a holding cell. While I had a cool time in the holding tank, I could not stand the conditions. The holding tanks did not have a lot of room. There was one toilet and one sink. The food they served was far from satisfactory. One person drank from the toilet because he wasn't given water. It was a horrible experience.

When I got out, I was not deterred but ready to continue doing the work. I didn't even tie my shoe strings, which the jail staff remove once you are being processed. I jetted to the next action that I knew happened that day. This protest was an opportunity to lift Mike's name and connect the struggle to systemic issues around the Delmar Divide. Many Saint Louisans passed up North Saint Louis to celebrate the New Year in Grandel Square. The plan was to interrupt the evening proceedings. My restlessness helped lead to my going to jail again.

I got arrested twice in twenty-four hours. It felt as silly as it sounds, but I meant the best. The day was December 31, New Year's Eve. After the Occupy the Police action, I was released later that day only to be booked again later that night. I swore that the first time I experienced being processed and put in a holding cell would be my last. But my eagerness to force change too quickly put me on the track for other plans.

After leaving the Justice Center downtown, I walked to Grand and Delmar. I knew there'd be another action in that area. This one was about addressing Saint Louis's racist and classist Delmar Divide. Once I got there, I linked with Tribe X and supporters. My adrenaline level was as tall as a giraffe.

Dr. Ilene Berman helped start a Delmar Divide protest push. Dr. Berman founded NodHouse based on art and advocacy, and Queen Mother Romona worked with her with M-SLICE. They came together with the idea of highlighting the tacky nonsense behind the inequities in Saint Louis that was symbolized by Delmar's divide. At Crossroads, Mama Lola, my siblings, and I participated in the protest that was held on the first night: January 1, 2013. First Night was an art and activities festival hosted in the Grand Arts District. This area started at Delmar heading south on Grand. Nothing was wrong with the art; however, it was problematic for the same reason why SLU staff would tell students, "Do not go past Delmar." Cutting festivities off at Delmar implied that North Saint Louis residents were undeserving. To agitate, we held electric-powered signage that formed the letters I-N-V-I-S-I-B-L-E on the north side of Delmar. The letters symbolized how the lack of resources invested in North Saint Louis rendered its divested-from communities invisible. One year after graduating, we were agitating for the extravaganza to extend north of Delmar or not be held at all.

Participating in the demonstrations against the Delmar Divide made me apply what I studied about it in a real way. I read a lot of material about the issue in high school, and it gave me the language and analysis around the problem. British Broadcasting Corporation's Franz Strasser interviewed several residents on the reason for segregation in Saint Louis. This is captured in his work "Crossing a St. Louis Street That Divides Communities." Dr. Berman's organization NodHouse was also focused on tackling this issue. A piece by Nancy Fowler of *St. Louis Public Radio* covers the work done by Dr. Berman. Ferguson connected to this work because police brutality bears a relationship with policies of exclusion that deny majority-Black communities just access. This includes accessible opportunities for enrichment or art.

After I linked with everybody on the corner of Grand and Delmar, we marched toward the festivities in Grandel Square. I overheard that the plan was to remove the barricades to the event, so I proceeded. That was my mistake. What I didn't know was that doing so was a prior commitment made by select white accomplices ready and willing to be arrested. I ran to remove one barricade and already knew I was in trouble. One officer asked me to halt, and I, having just been released, wasn't ready to go back to jail. They'd have to catch me first.

I sprinted away from the boys down Grand toward SLU to make a right on Grandel Square Street. There was a police car waiting meters away. I changed direction and ran back toward the protest group, and another police car pulled up. I tried to maneuver over the hood of the squad car only to be blindsided by an officer. My heart was racing given the outcome: I was going back to a holding cell. I was pissed. A white ally legal observer harmlessly came to collect my information for jail support. They ended up locking her up too!

I was reminded of the valuable lessons of patience and humility. As a student, the only positive thing about the second arrest was that I didn't have any classes or finals. Forget confinement—what was up with my studies? Too funny. We were on winter break. I couldn't imagine that email to my professor: "Hey Dr. [such and such], I got arrested fighting for freedom. I need to reschedule my exam." I feared that process would've gone nowhere and left me hurting with an F, wasting a semester of hard work.

Family and friends checked in with me to make sure I was well after being released the second time. Mama Mix let Tribe X know that a counterprotest hosted by pro-police groups was happening. It was held at the Saint Louis Police Department headquarters, and this reminded me of the tone deafness in Saint Louis. All we asked for was a meeting, and some in the public were saying, "To hell with that." The blind gratitude for murderous and incompetent activities done by Saint Louis police puzzled me. *St. Louis Post-Dispatch* reporter Tim O'Neil wrote an article called "Friendly Crowd Gathers in St. Louis to Support Police, Who Return the Favor," shedding light on the trash. I guess the #OccupyThePolice protest we hosted struck a nerve. Yet I couldn't help but feel pity for these people who took the time out of their day to counter us. What were these pro-police demonstrators protesting for? Freedom? Justice? Fairness? Was it for life to stay the same? Back the blue, no matter the cost? The idea of freedom did not resonate with the stories and public data on Black residential experiences with police in our region, nor with me. I felt like being detained for being willing to put my body on the line for what I believed in was an honor.

Earlier in December, a grand jury decided not to indict Officer Daniel Pantaleo for murdering Eric Garner. Garner was senselessly murdered after allegedly committing a nonviolent violation. The truth is that, nationwide, there continued to be unjust outcomes that simply enraged my people. We referred to the national issue of police brutality as "Ferguson is everywhere." We understood that in the face of the impossible, we would stand together and make the difficult plain. If you fuck with our people, we would stand up and battle for ours. If that means we'd be labeled troublemakers and animals, arrested, or attacked, many of us were still willing to step.

Listening to music continued to help me process and reflect on the work. Since being at Crossroads, I have been a J. Cole fan. I loved that he was a reflective, honest, and lyrical genius. He ended up coming to Ferguson without the cameras to stand in solidarity with the community back in August. Four months later, he had recently dropped his anticipated album, *2014 Forest Hills Drive.* In this work, he had bangers like "No Role Modelz" and melodic tracks like "Love Yourz." His track titled "January 28th" seemed to reflect on his personal, professional, and political journeys. In it, he asks a critical question around race: "What's the price for a black man's life?" He, like many, understood that America uses its tools to render Black life as having no value. Yet, throughout the track, he inserts encouraging messages about faith, self-determination, and goal-setting that are critical ingredients in the dish of persistence. It was important for me to listen to artists like this, who lifted their voices for Ferguson.

I had to learn at an early age that not everyone is going to agree with you in your fight for freedom, and you will get pressure to stop. I learned this back in high school. At Crossroads College Prep, I played on the basketball team during my senior year. I averaged a triple-double: thirty minutes on the bench, thirty minutes getting water, and thirty minutes of rooting for my teammates. I remember standing in line for the Pledge of Allegiance. I researched Black power and found out about the protest of John Carlos and Tommie Smith at the 1968 Olympics. They simply raised their fists during the US national anthem. In the same spirit, I raised my fist while we stood in line at the beginning of basketball games until the national anthem ended.

After doing it awhile, it became a tradition that some of my fellow ballplayers would replicate. This started a trend where other ballplayers followed suit. My beloved coach Mr. Stephen Abdul-Hamid pulled me into his office one day during practice. He advised me to stop but told me he respected my cause. Coach Abdul-Hamid valued the intent of what I was doing, especially with his being Black conscious and its implications following Martin's murder. It was my understanding that he was getting feedback from parents and staff to have me stop. Out of respect, I chose to comply with his wishes. I may have faced repercussions, an extra lap in practice or so. More important was choosing my battles, which I had to decide for myself.

Despite being arrested twice in twenty-four hours, I felt discouraged but kept my head high. Some still dismissed our protesting efforts as just making noise. Who cared? The work we assigned ourselves to do was grounded in substance and high moral causes. We shook the city. We shook the nation. We shook the world. Not just one individual or organization—it took the work of countless brave souls willing to risk it all for something greater than themselves. It would continue to take that effort and energy. I knew I had it in my people, so no matter what we faced leading into the new year, I would continue to work.

Weighing Risks as a Student Organizer

Protecting oneself from the threats and dangers of pushing for social change is paramount to longevity. One of the exhausting and tiring encounters that student organizers can face is the retaliation and backlash associated with movement. There are academic, legal, and health risks tied to the battle that, when anticipated, can help young people make informed decisions when engaged in activism. Schools may suspend, expel, designate academic probation for, or withhold diplomas or degrees from scholars. On- or off-campus police may arrest students, charging them with trespassing, traffic impediment, building defacement, assault, and a multitude of other accusations of law violations. The physical and psychological cost of advocacy work can stem from hate speech/mail or assaults, including but not limited to spitting, sexual attacks, body slams, punching/kicking, pepper spray, etc. The toll endured by organizers can lead to delays in their educational pursuits, encounters with the judicial system, and medical expenses.

Civil disobedience can be a dirty game. In the face of these odds, students must be just as serious about defensive strategies as they are about their offensive ones. When discussing protest or direct actions, students should identify all of the retaliatory possibilities that come with their involvement. After compiling these, an assessment should be completed on risk reduction, designing strategies for eliminating or minimizing the possible threats. Examples include calling off the formal action once the threat of arrest comes, having jail support in place to aid those who are arrested, and having therapists available to help demonstrators. Finally, youth organizers have to make a decision on whether or not their methods of disruption are worth the risk. The above is not exhaustive, and additional discussion should be held before committing any civil disobedience.

Any responsible student leader will pursue reasonable wins, not a Pyrrhic victory. To be sure, in real time, a demonstration can lead to unpredictable reactions, results, and retaliation, and often, the aggressors are not the activists. Certain actions are less risky than others. Having these strategic conversations before committing to anything helps shield students from being blindsided and exposed to harm. The NPR journalist Leila Fadel hosted a segment about the risks of student activism, discussing the topic with Dr. Robert Kelchen, an academic in education at the University of Tennessee, Knoxville. When asked about what occurs following students employing specific protest tactics that may have led to suspensions and expulsions, Dr. Kelchen answered: "There can be a range of different consequences running from simply not getting as good of a grade in a class because you spent less time studying all the way up to expulsion." There are risks ranging from a student activist getting a less-than-satisfactory grade to being expelled from the campus. However, there's more at stake than academic perils, and that includes legal and health consequences.

The journey to complete a diploma or degree should not be taken lightly or disregarded, even though students are more than their studies. Especially for certain communities that are disproportionately underrepresented in the echelons of the academy, it's even more paramount that these scholars make it to that cap and gown.

When organizing, it can feel easy to be so sucked into the business of the movement work that students lay their academic commitments to the side. Students end up dropping out or getting put out of school. Every young leader has to ultimately make their own decisions and accept its consequences. The community needs skilled and educated advocates who will lead organizations and occupy powerful positions. A college degree does not automatically translate to morally sound and civically engaged graduates. However, those with a heart for social justice who gain talent and a knowledge base nurtured in this learning environment can have compounding impacts on society. One does not need a degree to be a legislator, policymaker, elected official, or leader of organizations (for- and not-for-profit). Nonetheless, going through the rigor and exposure that come from university studies helps with the professional transition and provides a theoretical basis that can be applied to ethical and efficient actions. A courageous use of student activism also means judicious and strategic exercising of one's capacity. Due to their school commitments, students may have to miss protests, organizing meetings, rallies, panels, media sessions, and more. Instead of holding a bullhorn, students are picking up a book. Rather than sitting in a planning session, students may have to go to a study hall. When a speak-out in the school quad is happening, students may have to be meeting with a professor during their office hours. None of this makes youths less serious about the issues they seek to address. It just demonstrates effective management of time and projects.

There must be ways to balance student activist involvement in organizing and the risk of veering away from the demands of schooling. Dirk Smith, managing editor of *Compete Sports Diversity*, wrote an article that advises organizers how to balance feelings of emotional, physical, and mental strain. Smith shares about the importance of exercise, mindfulness, letting go, positivity, and walks when engaged in doing work to transform the community. He explains, "Activism is how we change the world, so to be the best activists we can be it is important that we practice techniques to help us maintain our health and enthusiasm. The world seems to be growing quite harsh, but maintaining a positive attitude and building our own self-confidence cannot only help us become better activists but allow our activism to have an even bigger impact." Not taking care of one's physical health or exercising mental releases, holding on to toxic feelings, basking in negativity, and ignoring stress are counterproductive to the longevity of activists. Student activists in particular, as they juggle the demands of movement work, have to be just as serious about their studies, self-care, and health.

Journalist Lauren Lumpkin, a contributor to the *Nation*, and coauthor Devan Cole published a work that peers into the price that comes with activism, using race as a framing. Lumpkin and Cole share about the experiences that young people, particularly Black youths, navigate when advocating for change on their campuses and the costs associated with the process: "As the number of racial incidents increase at colleges and universities, more black students find themselves on the front lines of campus protests, defending their right to be there. But activism has a cost. Acts of racial bias draft black students into racial battles without warning, where they sustain evidence of battle fatigue, reporting skipping class, missing work, and sleeping less—all in service of making change at their schools."

When faced with racist incidents, Black students many feel called to respond through mechanisms of organizing that come with tolls on their academic, mental, and physical health. This is not unique to Black student activists; student activists in general, when faced with injustice, pay a cost in working to execute a solution. Less time doing class assignments, engaging in levels of truancy, and neglecting one's rest schedule are all examples of the downside to young people engaging in movement work. Heeding the expertise of Dirk Smith can be a remedy to help student activists thrive in the face of the whirlwind of academic neglect that Cole and Lumpkin describe young people finding themselves in.

All students, particularly working-class and low-income students, are vulnerable to the judicial ramifications that come with certain protest activities. Without question, whenever students perform escalated acts of civil disobedience, there is a likelihood they could be arrested, charged, and even found guilty of criminal acts. The charges that students may face vary depending on what the act or direct action includes. The mindset of being willing to go to jail for what one believes in is admirable. The practice of placing your freedom on the line for a cause is commendable. However, students should assess the threat level of legal retaliation when partaking in their expressions of resistance. There's a long lineage of activists being incarcerated and having to fight legal battles in their pursuit to transform the community. Fighting for advancement sometimes has necessitated a level of agitation in those with power and are responsible for "law and order." Interrupting the business-as-usual happenings and culture of academic institutions brings discomfort and anxiety to those who would rather enjoy the rewards and benefits they reap from protecting the status quo. So it's critical that students exercise their critical thinking when the threat or possibility of an arrest takes place.

When young people get booked for their activism, whether found guilty or not, their detainment will in some cases follow them for the rest of their lives. Their being in custody may show up on background checks when applying for housing, employment, and other necessities or opportunities. This is not to discourage students from fighting for what they believe in by any means necessary. The goal is to make sure that students, should they choose to take a risk and be arrested, are prepared to minimize the impact that being in custody has on their well-being and future. Students should be in contact with lawyers and be prepared to establish a jail support network. It's not required, but it's a wise way of handling the backlash that can come from universities and police. Attorneys equipped to handle group cases and First Amendment expressions and who understand the sensibilities of student activists should be readily available. They can give legal advice and representation should it be needed. A jail support fund is a financial account dedicated to paying bonds, citations, and legal fees associated with movement activities.

Taking the time to invest in a network of legal support in concert with the riskier activities of organizing helps youths have a sense of security and support. Journalist Rebecca Nathanson, a contributor for *Teen Vogue*, breaks down the dimensions and applications of jail support in social movements, historically to the present day. Nathanson cites Deborah Archer, president of the American Civil Liberties Union and professor at New York University School of Law, who shares the moving parts of jail support that serve the interests of arrested demonstrators, using police brutality as a frame. Describing the ways in which jail support functions and how it has looked in practice, Archer states, "Today, jail support includes legal observers, bail funds, and representation for protesters, and provides coordinated support for those who stand on the front line demanding justice. We saw all of these components of jail support in Ferguson and Occupy Wall Street. We are seeing all of them again today, supporting protesters who are demanding an end to police violence."

Jail support leans on volunteers who observe the activities of police behavior at protests, entities that collect money for posting bail, and lawyers who provide legal assistance. When student activists are demonstrating, it's essential they work to establish or coordinate with local jail support to ensure arrested participants receive expedient assistance. Lawyer and author Derecka Purnell published a memoir unraveling the contours of abolition, policing, and freedom movements grounded in her experiences in community, movement, and education, with Ferguson as a backdrop. Purnell shares the ways in which she and her peers were trained on jail support, along with the distance one of her colleagues was willing to go to ensure activists received assistance: "Several organizations trained us for copwatch, legal observation, bail, and jail support . . . I was shocked by the power and command of Black law students who organized the support networks behind the scenes, especially Marques Banks. Marques became part of the Black Movement Law Project . . . When we worked together later in Ferguson, activists would run away from the police when they escalated violence. Marques was one of the few people who would run toward the chaos to help others." Being trained on how to watch for police, document the violations of activists' rights to demonstrate, navigate the process of releasing arrested protesters, and implementing overall jail support were integral to Purnell and her colleague's experience providing services to demonstrators at protests. In an ideal world, student activists would have a jail support team that includes individuals like Derecka Purnell and Marques Banks, who will help young people navigate the legal landscape that comes with direct actions.

The pain and agony from the health inflictions endured while organizing and employing direct actions call for attention to safety measures to help shield students. There are physical and mental vulnerabilities that students expose themselves to when putting themselves on the line for justice. Some of it are situational and dependent on the activities that youth activists are partaking in. The more escalated the demonstration, the higher the risk linked to the harm that can be suffered. If students conduct a civil disobedience measure that includes shutting down public streets near their campus, they are at the mercy of public drivers. If it's an action that interrupts the business of a university (such as an occupation of or sit-in in a quad or library), campus police may use dangerous coercive methods to disperse participants. If it's a demonstration that raises the ire of peers in opposition, agitators may confront and assault student activists. While none of the above is guaranteed to happen, there's a precedent for all of these unfortunate and tortuous incidents. Their likelihood of happening matters less than the fact that if they do transpire, they can lead to bruises, broken bones, and blood.

In addition, by being vocal and raising awareness about issues with or without protesting, students leave themselves exposed to psychological trauma. Often done anonymously, keyboard warriors will exhaust every button on their QWERTY keypads to spew mean-spirited, disrespectful, and vicious messages. This includes hate emails, social blogs, direct messages, and letters. While it's not direct physical violence, being on the receiving end of these notes when they're unceasing and exaggerated can damage one's sense of security. A campus is actually supposed to be one of the safest spaces a student can be in at any moment. However, an onslaught of the threat of violence can impact a student activist's psychological well-being.

There is sometimes an ever-present threat of violence that youth organizers face. Dr. Charles H. F. Davis III, a professor in the Center for the Study of Higher and Postsecondary Education at the University of Michigan, coedited a book capturing practitioner and theorist voices on contemporary social movements in higher education. Contributors Sy Stokes and Donte Miller wrote a chapter speaking to the backlash student activists faced when organizing against the underrepresentation of Black students on campus. Stokes and Miller describe the fallout that came as a result of student activism, which Stokes was involved in and attacked for, following the digital promotion of their cause through posting the *Black Bruins* video on YouTube:

> Despite the success of our digital media campaign, it did not come without aggressive, and sometimes violent, resistance . . . Within the first two weeks, Sy Stokes, the creator of the video, received countless death threats from anonymous sources. Some of the threats promoted suicidal rhetoric such as "Go hang yourself, bitch," while some where more direct threats such as "I'm a student at UCLA. Watch what happens when I find you on campus," and "Kill all niggers." Regardless of the inaccuracy and blatant disregard for factual evidence to back their racist claims, these statements admittedly took a psychological toll on each member of our cohort.

In response to the student activism on campus, youth organizers alongside Stokes encountered racist death threats. This came from anonymous sources making statements with the intention to inflict pain as a means to discourage, dissuade, and derail the youths' efforts at the transformation of their campus.

The physical and psychological intimidation of student activists is not unique to any specific movement but is a theme that all organizers may face in doing work to make advancements in their schools. Author Dr. John Wilson, editor of *Illinois Academe* and co-organizer of the Chicago Book Expo, illustrates the plethora of attacks on academic freedom and expression of youth organizers pushing for change on their campuses. Dr. Wilson clarifies this in the way the 9/11 attacks on the United States had a chilling effect on the capacity of student and faculty activists to push their antiwar social and political views. Providing a myriad examples reflecting the repression of antiwar student activists, Dr. Wilson writes:

> During the 2005–2006 school year, suppression of peaceful campus protests reached its highest levels at American colleges since the Vietnam War. In just two days in September 2005, college officials at three different campuses illegally banned protests and violently attacked students who tried to protest military recruiters . . . on September 29, 2005, George Mason University student Tariq Khan, an air force veteran, stood near a recruiting table for the U.S. Marines while wearing signs that said "Recruiters tell lies. Don't be fooled" and "U.S. out of Iraq, Israel out of Palestine, U.S. out of North America." Khan was surrounded by three conservative students who yelled at him and ripped off one of his signs. Instead of defending Khan's rights, a campus police officer attacked Khan without reason, throwing him on the ground and putting him in a chokehold.

At several campuses, peaceful youth organizers faced violations of their First Amendment rights and experienced physical attacks for denouncing war and their universities giving agency to representatives of militarism. Tariq Khan's story of facing backlash for peace advocacy as a student activist is not an isolated event but a reflection of the possibilities that come with students pushing against the arms of the empire.

Student activists should develop defensive measures to support one another in the face of the above unfavorable possibilities. They should be prepared to utilize therapeutic support provided on or off campus. This will offer a cognitive and self-affirming resource to help them navigate trauma. Youth activists should also have regular check-ins with each other to make sure they are all copacetic. It's not enough to stand side by side against danger on a campus intersection; when the bullhorn's battery dies, they must recharge their batteries. There should be mentors, family, and support networks established for student demonstrators to vent to and lean on for help. In addition, those involved should be prepared to advocate for themselves and stand up for their livelihoods.

Finally, the media may publish about a demonstration that student activists organized. Students should not spend too much time focusing on the comments section, especially depending on the politics of the media. Anyone telling youths that they should just take backlash and not be prepared to respond accordingly is misleading them.

CHAPTER 10

You Know King; I Know Lil Mike

David Facing Goliaths

America did not love Dr. King.
Blood on Leaves, Hate dreams less it brings cha-ching.
It hates dreams unless they shine with bling-bling.
Hate for this winner, not one more winter,
Figures, America gunned him down in spring.

When we speak of him, speak of pariahs.
Seek out the meek, Talk of a defier.
One who saw fires, didn't shame riots.
Talk of David facing the Goliaths.

Settlers, You give him a holiday.
A predator, you took his life, like prey.
Meddlers, he prayed off demons you praised.
Regulars, crazed, his greatness left you dazed.

America did not love Dr. King.
His image they gloved then bleached with white cream.
White doves. A troublemaker made them scream.
A radical, they labeled him extreme.

But we remember.
Waterhosed us down, but left embers.
Miseducated us, yet we remain tempered.
We are immortal despite a bullet from a chamber.

January 2015

The #ReClaimMLK demonstration I participated in was a part of a nationwide effort to straighten out myths surrounding Rev. Dr. Martin Luther King's legacy. The MLK I studied, understood, and followed was leading sanitation workers, not simply parading for parade's sake. I was involved in a plan to disrupt the Saint Louis's MLK Committee in its forty-seventh year. Many in the Ferguson uprising felt the best way to honor MLK would be to go out in the streets calling out systems, not simply hosting a commemoration.

Dr. King was able to see through the injustices of a society plagued with devious ills caused by racist segregationist attitudes. Laws that led to sneaky housing, health care, employment, education, transportation, and voting practice outcomes slid by with impunity. Dr. King did not run from the problems of society and steadily challenged systems in the streets.

The Ferguson movement understood that any space honoring MLK given the climate after Mike Brown's death should be in alignment with the level of seriousness he brought to the work. I felt it cheap for city-wide efforts to settle for a tributary, ceremonial, and cosmetic expression of King's legacy. This comes off as an exploitative, dishonest, and backward use of his name. Dr. King once said, "A riot is the language of the unheard." While Saint Louis organized #ReClaimMLK, so, too, did activists in California for their Silicon shutdown and in Atlanta, etc.

Alisha and I woke up expecting to give speeches at an action in front of Larry Rice's shelter for the unhoused on MLK Day. Larry Rice was the meeting point given that funding for its facilities was in jeopardy. The Larry Rice action lasted for about thirty minutes and communicated that Saint Louis's unhoused community must be addressed. Residents who benefited from Rice's shelter were given a platform by Kayla Reed to tell their testimonies. Reed is a Ferguson movement organizer who played a role in various actions, including Occupy SLU.

After the action, Kayla directed folks to move the march forward to Harris-Stowe State University (HSSU). HSSU happens to be the only Historically Black College and University in the city limits. Fittingly, it was where the Saint Louis City MLK Committee's event would be held. I helped lead the marchers to pass police cars and officers on the way to HSSU's quad. Demonstrators were already on the inside disrupting the event and were exiting the School of Business. As the group I was with walked across the grass, you could hear retaliation from HSSU's event supporters. Some students screamed, "Fuck y'all!" at our protest. I believe many were confused about why we were interrupting the event.

When we arrived outside HSSU's Busch Hall, I was welcomed by the warmth of Elizabeth Vega's smile. Vega is a local organizer who worked with the Artivist group that put together many actions with creativity, substance, and flair. To help clear up myths that we were anti-HSSU or anti-MLK, Vega asked me to explain why we were there. I did so with pleasure and emphasized the need for MLK's legacy to be kept alive through radical action. For the past five months, fellow demonstrators and I had been lifting the names of those murdered by police. It was dangerous work, and we were not promised that we'd make it home. I explained that MLK risked everything, so we felt any public attempt to honor his name should be tied to the fight for justice.

We were joined by a group of mainly white police officers. Reacting to them, Ferguson protesters were chanting, "Who do you protect, who do you serve?" Up to this point, the police were never there to dialogue but to intimidate under the guise of keeping the peace. We participated in a standoff with the police for at least half an hour, when an unexpected scuffle happened. Some of the Ferguson protesters were getting into it with some HSSU students about the protest. This was all bad.

The HSSU students were shouting their school spirit refrains for fear that we were there to confront them, shut their school down, or damage their school's public image. I could hear the "I love my H, I love my S, I love my S, I love my U!" chants. Our goal was not to tarnish HSSU but to express our grievances with the MLK Committee. HSSU just happened to be the venue where this affair went down. Insults were being exchanged on both sides. Alisha and I quickly responded with other members of our protester community.

Some of the HSSU students couldn't be reached with reason because they blindly took the interruption as disrespect of their institution. To express their anger, they called some of the demonstrators "unemployed" and "uneducated." This just so happened to be the same kind of refrains that clout-chasing conservative pundits like Bill O'Reilly would use. This name-calling was regularly used to discredit the integrity and sincerity of protesters. In response, some demonstrators called them "house niggas." This came from a place of frustration with the HSSU students being blind to our grievances with the MLK

Committee. It was a terrible affair given that many of the police stood by smiling and enjoying the scene. We were not there to fight HSSU students, burn down HSSU, or defame their school. Rather, we were hoping to support them, uplift HSSU, and disrupt with the hope of properly contextualizing MLK.

In the *St. Louis American*, journalists Kenya Vaughn and Rebecca Rivas's "Protests Create Moments of Chaos during STL City Dr. King Celebration" details the action. We felt that by hosting that MLK event, their school was complicit in the ongoing Saint Louis tradition of commercializing and softening his legacy. The Ferguson uprising was letting Saint Louis City know that the use of King's image for "feel-good" reasons was unacceptable. Police looked on as Black people argued with Black people over a Black figure, and I felt embarrassed for my people. The insults on either side and the time and place were not acceptable; it was a shouting match that thankfully did not escalate to fisticuffs.

Toward the end of the month, I got an invitation from Diontrey Thompson, associate director of the Black Community Services Center at Stanford, to be a panelist in a discussion about Ferguson. The title of the event was "Ordinary People Who Do Extraordinary Things." This opportunity was a direct result of my relation to another activist, my older sibling, Ti Pulphus. Ti attended Stanford University (after blowing to the top of her class in college admissions and scholarships at Crossroads). Alisha and I were extended the offer and would later be flown to Palo Alto, California, to share about our activism and represent Tribe X. I felt thrilled to be going to the West Coast for the first time.

I'm from a family of hard-nosed fighters who were reared to respond to the issues of the day head on. My siblings and I all, in some way or form, refused to be silent or ignorant around Mike Brown's murder. Ti had been raising awareness in her campus community following the murder of Mike Brown. It inspired me to see Ti putting it all on the line, and it affirmed the work I was doing in the streets as her younger sibling. Alex Zivkovic, of the student-run newspaper the *Stanford Daily*, wrote about Ti and peers protesting for Ferguson back in October 2014. They reduced traffic at a busy campus roundabout known as the Circle of Death to agitate for public awareness of the Michael Brown Jr. case.

In addition to the campus effort, Ti and peers of the Silicon Shut Down group disrupted the entire San Mateo-Hayward Bridge that January. In the *Stanford Daily*, contributor Caleb Smith interviewed participants in the protest. The goal was to voice their demands about education, criminal justice, and policing. As a consequence of their direct action, there were sixty-eight arrests and eleven people detained. The bravery of concerned citizens and student activists such as Ti and their peers forced the locals and the United States to face the ugliness. Ti and the team risked jail to advance a cause surrounding somebody they never knew. All of my siblings put in work for my people.

At that moment, word was getting around that Bob McCulloch, the prosecuting attorney assigned to Darren Wilson's case, was being given a platform at SLU Law. This outraged Tribe X and many others in the Ferguson movement because of his mishandling of the Mike Brown case. I felt like SLU giving McCulloch a platform was slapping the faces of citizens impacted by systemic racism in the region. Tribe X adviser Mama Mix ended up drafting a powerful response to SLU Law dean Michael Wolff on behalf of our organization. Regardless, SLU Law moved forward with the event.

Rarely were there opportunities when I took time to work on healing within the movement. The trauma and burnout were real for me. Due to the pace and load of duties, it is challenging to sit back and focus on mental health and deepening connections with people. Few spaces are designated for camaraderie. One of these was organized by activist Charles Wade of the Operation Help or Hush organization. Wade coordinated a dinner for demonstrators with Chef Angela, known as the Kitchenista, for Saturday, January 17. Chef Angela put her foot in that food—seasoned it until the ancestors told her to stop. I just know it. The Kitchenista made a Southern-style dinner with mouthwatering fried chicken and some fire macaroni. Almost thirty of us in the Ferguson movement were invited to be in one space to break bread and network. Months had flown by, and many people knew of one another by name but never rubbed elbows. I attended this with Alisha, reconnected with several people, and networked. Efforts like this are critical to movement-building on a social level but also to the healing process. Sitting with people who can relate to challenges you've been through over a hot meal was therapeutic.

The Organization for Black Struggle put together a fifteen-week paid training program in partnership with the Deaconess Foundation titled the Next Revolution Fellowship Program. It focused on supporting activists to create their organizations or advocacy projects, giving participants the necessary tools for organizing. At the end of the training, participants were awarded one thousand dollars for completion.

Alisha and I applied together to be a part of the workshops. We ended up being mentored by activists like the longtime organizer Percy Green, Montague Simmons, Kofi Ansza, and more. Workshops such as this help sustain movements by creating the infrastructure that encourages agency, education, and action. This skill-development space was worthwhile given investments I made in myself and Tribe X.

Jason Ebinger, a white fellow SLU student and activist, invited me to write for Karen House. Ebinger was one of the few white counterparts I attended SLU with who gave me hope for the multiracial struggle. He, and many others, refused to be silent on Mike Brown. Through his affiliation with Karen House, a Catholic worker house and shelter, Jason invited me to partake in a panel for their *RoundTable* newspaper. Karen House's Jenny Truax asked that I participate in a panel on the same question in January. That white people were inviting frontline voices was helpful in controlling clout-chasing narratives.

CHAPTER 11

Due to #OccupySLU

My journey to and from helping garner the CTA agreement with SLU was my affirmation of the power of protest. Five months prior to OccupySLU, the BSA protested for similar demands that were simply footnoted. Dr. Pestello's decision to move forward with the named demands spoke volumes. Louder than SLU's pen was the organizing and strategy that made the possibility happen.

Without protest from the community, there'd have been no signed document. The involvement of the VonDerrit family, the faculty, staff, community, residents, and students opened the doors to the halls of decision-makers. Just as direct action resulted in the CTA, continued efforts would be needed to move the agreements forward.

OccupySLU worked differently from a BSA demonstration that happened in the spring of 2014 during my freshman year. The action happened because of an on-campus incident at SLU. Someone typed "Nazis Rule . . . Fuck Niggers & Fags" in a bold-lettered message on a smart board in the Busch Student Center, which set off a hell storm. I felt infuriated while talking with Mr. E about this on the phone. Outraged as an alum, he replied, "Would this happen at Harris-Stowe State University or Howard University?" I couldn't imagine such vitriol being spewed within the halls of a historical black college and university. The fact that it happened at SLU, as a predominantly white institution, reflected the writer's cowardice.

BSA agitated in Griesedieck Hall, inviting Rainbow Alliance and HALO (Hispanic and Latinx Leadership Organization). BSA organized a media-invited panel across identities on Tuesday, May 6, to articulate demands. BSA representatives demanded a meeting, later agreed to, with then-SLU president Bill Kaufman. As a panelist who stood in place for BSA president Christopher Walter, I felt nervous yet thrilled to be speaking out against bias alongside Brittany Kendricks and Kimberly Turner. Demands were tied to addressing Black student enrollment and the MLK Scholarship. *St. Louis American* journalist Rebecca Rivas covered the action in "Black Students Make Demands of

SLU after Campus Hate Crimes," capturing the moment. At the later meeting, President Kaufmann did not sign the demands, explaining that his role was only "interim." I felt saddened, believing that this protest was a failure.

The main difference between the spring 2014 action and Occupy SLU is that one was ground-setting, while the other rocketed off. Both the OccupySLU and the spring 2014 actions were effective in grabbing the attention of the administration and involving direct-action tactics. Both had disruptive activities as a means to bring attention to an issue, raising awareness through speeches and sharing recommendations grounded in research. Both had ways that overlapped in terms of tactic and demands. However, the spring 2014 events had a low level of community participation. OccupySLU included massive community participation.

OccupySLU was fully driven by the community. The murders of Mike Brown and VonDerrit Myers Jr. created a climate that put the country at the edge of its seat. The involvement of students and community forced the university to place its mission at its mouth. With the entire nation's eyes (see Twitter) on #OccupySLU, the procuring of an agreement was inevitable. Without mass involvement in collaboration with university students and staff, there would have been no CTA.

The CTA remind me of the power of will and protest. Every protest has power behind it that thrusts issues from the ocean floor to the surface. Without activities of agitation being expressed, neither the spring action nor OccupySLU would have happened. Protest worked to birth both of these actions, regardless of their different outcomes. I began to understand that protest works even during times when I second-guessed the impact, such as the spring 2014 action. I needed not believe that all outcomes were simply performative. It takes drive to make the logs of indifference spark into a flame of possibility. It took protest to make the CTA happen.

Orchestrating Your Protest

Student activists supporting one another fortifies their capacity to pursue goals in movement work. At times, movements can become more than just colleagues who just so happen to want to see change happen together. Through shared experiences, trials, tribulations, and joyous moments, they develop bonds of familiarity that in some cases become similar to kinship. Those who stand side by side with on that campus quad become not just classmates but cousins, brothers, sisters, and siblings. It comes to the point that y'all eat, study, play, cry, and celebrate together. Not that it is the case that everyone participating in social justice work has the same dynamic or closeness. Movements can come with cliques and intergroup dynamics that happen with any other collectives. Regardless of how tight or loose student activists are with each other, they ought to have each other's back. If an injustice is haunting some, all should be wrestling with how to defend their peers. If a blessing is bestowed to a group, all ought to be celebrating the achievement of their comrades. Building that connection and relationship with each other makes it easier to navigate the ups and downs that come with tackling social justice issues. Youth leaders who strengthen their communication, trust, and respect for one another are more willing to offer grace, understanding, and forgiveness when issues arise.

Even though it may be challenging to build synergy among one another based on a shared goal, it is an integral part of student activists pursuing outcomes. Dr. Ming-sho Ho, a faculty member of the department of sociology at the National Taiwan University in Taipei, published a journal article about the ways in which trustworthiness among movement participants is critical to the advancement of goals. The foundation of movement activities is on a strong confidence that those involved will be loyal to the shared cause. Dr. Ho affirms this:

> The expectation that others will fulfill their anticipated role is vital to all successful movements. Movement leaders have to demonstrate their genuine commitment to attract followers. Donors and volunteers need the assurance that their contributions will serve no other purpose than the movement's goals. In short, the mundane activities of social movement organizations tacitly rest upon trust among participants, including activists who join rallies and demonstrations, and supporters who contribute resources (Rossi, 2023). Given that trust undergirds movement activism in many ways, it is to be expected that the authorities would attempt to destroy trust networks in order to undermine the challenge. (Sika, 2023)

It is vital to have a movement infrastructure from those directly involved to those indirectly involved who share a mindset dedicated to the same goals. Opponents of activists may make every effort to thwart progress by breeding seeds of doubt and uncertainty to disrupt the synergy of activists involved. Student organizers should go through a process of vetting and interrogating one another's true interests to ensure they are all on the same page.

Dr. Michelle Benson, of the political science department at the University of Buffalo, and Dr. Thomas Rochon, former vice president of academic affairs at Saint Thomas University, penned a journal entry outlining the direct relationship between trust and movement participation. Unraveling the reason that social movement participants take on costs in pursuit of the benefits of activism, Dr. Benson and Dr. Rochon explain that interpersonal trust causes a push for change and is a leading factor in mobilization efforts and protest. They write, "Interpersonal trust increases both an individual's odds of protesting and the odds of becoming involved in more militant forms of protest. Trust in others increases one's likelihood of becoming an intensely involved protester and of moving across some thresholds of protest participation. The effects of interpersonal trust on the likelihood of protest and on the militancy of protest are found both in democratic countries and in those that are not free. This relationship is maintained despite an exhaustive array of statistical controls." The more that activists trust other organizers, the higher the likelihood that risks in demonstrating are taken together. If youth advocates lack a belief in each other's reliability and honesty, this diminishes the possibility that they will take risks among one another associated with direct actions.

When an agreement is made around a protest, it's important that student activists honor their word. Not every direct action is made strategically behind the walls of a room filled with markers, chart paper, and power mapping. At times, civil disobedience can be an organic, knee-jerk, and experimental tactical response. However, there should ultimately be an organized and thoughtful effort guiding ongoing disruptions to add sustainable direction to movement. It is in this space that student activists ought to determine the terms of how they'll conduct business when engaged in resistance. If a direct action is being developed, everyone who's agreeing to participate should stick to the boundaries set for the event. Roles that are assumed by participants should be followed through on. Some will be responsible for leading chants, others will be charged with creating and holding signage, a few will be looked to for communicating with media, and a couple will be interacting with decision-makers. No matter what responsibility is granted, activists ought to stick to what consensus was made. When there are those who deviate from the plan, it can cause confusion and disorganization, diminishing the power of the collective strategy. This is different from when audibles are called and shifts have to happen in the moment. However, there should be contingency plans for the serendipitous and unseen.

Student organizers should all be on the same page, which is connected to participants each being confident, aware, and comfortable in their responsibilities. William "Bill" Moyer, an activist and trained social worker heavily involved in the civil rights movement, wrote a book that describes the stages of social movements to explain the ebbs and flows that come with activists seeking transformation. Citing that there are several functions played by participants in social movements, Moyer articulates that it is essential that activists understand and fulfill the expectations that call for moving the needle forward in collective organized efforts. Moyer states, "We all play different roles in life. We are children to our parents and parents to our children. Sometimes we are conscious of the shift in roles and sometimes not. Activists need to become aware of the roles they and their organizations are playing in the larger social movement." Just as the cycle of life happens, where people can play a role as both guardians to their kids and still exist as kids compared to their own guardians, individuals engaged in the project of transformation must understand the ways in which their purpose calls for different responsibilities in relation to their positions.

George Lakey, a Quaker and former professor in the Peace and Conflict Studies Program at Swarthmore, wrote about the intricacies of organizing nonviolent social action. Addressing the topic of roles as a means of clearing the clutter that happens when activists feel conflicted about differing responsibilities in organizing, Lakey leans on the teachings of Bill Moyer as a means of explaining the importance of togetherness in the execution up to, during, and after demonstrations. Using Moyer's model, Lakey explains, "Bill's advice was to recognize that in successful social movements all these change roles do show up and it's best to make peace with that reality. Focus on your work with those of like disposition, he said, instead of wasting energy and time criticizing the efforts of those playing a different role . . . In today's political reality, we can't afford not to work together." Rather than spending time being infatuated with the activities and pursuits of other organizers' work, finding ways to be in alignment with others based on one's own skills and wherewithal helps move the work forward. Lakey emphasizes that it takes activists understanding how to mesh different talents together as a means of reaching a common end goal.

Learning is a lifelong endeavor, and it's to the benefit of activists to ensure that all involved are versed in the same knowledge base. It's one thing to feel fed up with injustice and want to be a part of change. It's another to engage in the business of studying and committing to practice informed by one's experience or education about the issue and solution. Those involved in the movement should have internal teach-ins and spaces to engage with literature, articles, informative videos, and other means of deepening their own awareness about the issues they want to tackle. Taking the time and effort to make sure that all are abreast of the essential history and current facts strengthens the collective expertise necessary to advocate for change. When only one or a few students have the core understanding tied to the work, it creates an unhealthy knowledge gap. The burden of developing shared language, vision, and comprehension should be shared across an organizing group. It is more challenging for student activists to challenge opposition or educate uninformed individuals when they themselves are only privy to the basics of their cause and not its intricacies.

There can be no robust transformation without learning and the application of those lessons. The late Aziz Choudry, an activist and former faculty member within the Department of Integrated Studies in Education at McGill University, wrote a text that closely examines the intellectual life of organizers, emphasizing the importance of learning tied to knowledge generation. Drawing attention to the necessity of study and devotion of time toward intellectual pursuit in conversation with movement- building, Choudry states, "People struggle, learn, educate, and theorize wherever they find themselves. The form this takes may change, but the importance of spaces and places for collective action, learning, reflection, and intergenerational sharing is crucial to building, sustaining, and broadening resistance. . . . This lens is necessary for those who want to link critical knowledge to action and for action to be informed by deeper historical understandings of how and why we are in the state we are in." There can be no expansion, maintenance, or growth of pursuits of change without critical thinking linked to reflection and learning.

The acquisition of knowledge and skill sets in service of movement dictates that participants spend time examining trends, history, and qualitative and quantitative factors related to their cause. The late, great Fred Hampton, the Illinois chairman of the Black Panther Party, gave a prolific 1969 speech at Olivet Baptist Church in Chicago, where he discussed the importance of practicing lessons learned in service of community advancement. While acknowledging the value of ideas intended to explain the dysfunctionality of societal issues, Hampton stressed that this is futile without taking strides to implement solutions. He explained, "I don't care how much theory you got, if it don't have any practice applied to it, then that theory happens to be irrelevant. Right? Any theory you get, practice it. And when you practice it you make some mistakes. When you make a mistake, you correct that theory, and then it will be corrected theory that will be able to be applied and used in any situation. That's what we've got to be able to do." One can have all the hypotheses in the world, but without experimentation toward achieving desirable outcomes, it is useless and pointless. Just as it is important to learn and study, there must also be a level of application of the ideas that organizers explore.

Presenting a united front even when participants are at odds is a mature and strategic asset in transforming a community. There will be moments when conflict happens, and it may occur often. Being able to put grievances, especially petty ones, aside when in public, on social media, during interviews, at meetings with stakeholders or decision-makers, and in other exposed spaces fortifies the integrity of movement work. All business is not show business. There is a time and a place to air out issues that peers may have with one another tied to protest. The time and place to do it should be procedural and internal. Giving others a window into the pains and tension that organizers feel offers an opportunity for deep irritation, infiltration, and instigation. The opposition would love to leverage publicly shared disagreements to their benefit and to the detriment of student activist's larger cause. This is not to dismiss conflict or not address the root of it. Movement participants must be able to put their pride to the side and stand elbow to elbow with one another despite their differences.

CHAPTER 12

Keep Campaigning, You Gon' Get Elected

Bob McCulloch Diss

Even your name leaves a bad taste, sounds nasty.
Clad designer, race foreigns, still tacky.
Too much of mama's DNA, Nancy.
Caused too much drama, you spiteful Granny.

Left a killer free due to your bias.
Caused fires, you liar, yet act pious.
Fumbled when times were dire, in crisis.
Cursed the choir, yet your voice was direr.

Karma is real and your time will arrive.
No love, no hopes that you thrive, no high fives.
The drive to hell is hot, forbid you die.
Who gone keep the fire going as you fry?

February 2015

In early February, there was an article written by *St. Louis Post-Dispatch* correspondent Koran Addo titled "Planned Protest Statue at SLU Prompts Online Backlash." This came about as work was being done to fulfill the promises of the CTA at SLU. One of the agreements included artwork. Clout chasers following the movement were doing what they could to smear SLU's name in the news due to its decision to exhibit the art. They called the possibility of a statue that would memorialize the occupation "anti-police." This was an attempt to appeal to blind "blue lives matter" folk to discredit and discourage the fulfillment of the accord.

In the grand scheme of things, the idea of a statue is wonderful, but it was only one of the thirteen agreements. Tribe X was happy there would be a monument that commemorates the dialogue and discussions. These were fostered by the occupation, so we felt that as a part of history, the art would be a time stamp and learning opportunity. *St. Louis Business Journal* reporter Jacob Kirn quoted Dr. Pestello, who stated that the sculpture would be something that "captures the spirit and importance of the demonstration and encampment."

I felt like SLU's willingness to confront the issues that face the Saint Louis region was applaudable. SLU would use the art to help tell the truth in terms of recognizing that there are racial inequities in this region. In addition, the university would step out in a leadership position on those issues. SLU would work with the community to help make Saint Louis a better, more just and anti-racist city.

The critics of the statue and the CTA should've taken the time to go and reread the demands alongside SLU's mission statement. At the time, so much negative publicity was focused on the art that the twelve other agreements did not receive as much press. A refusal to acknowledge and address systemic racism hinders Saint Louis from reaching its true potential. SLU's decision to do something about it was recognized as a step in the right direction for the region. Tribe X was hoping that more institutions and businesses would follow SLU's lead. SLU truly embodied its Jesuit principles and acted on them by signing the CTA. The mission statement of SLU refers to its desire to serve humanity. Tribe X felt that the October encampment and the resulting agreement closely aligned with SLU's principles.

The first time I saw good old Robert McCulloch in person was at SLU Law on Friday, February 20, 2015. The title of the event was "The Thin Blue Line: Policing Post-Ferguson." This was to be his first public appearance since his decision to not indict Darren Wilson. Before the SLU Law event, some talented organizers from a college network reached out to Tribe X. The name of the organization was Saint Louis Students in Solidarity (SLSS) and included students from different campuses. Some of the members included Reuben Riggs and Danielle Blocker. Christina Vogel, a SLU Law student with the Black Law Student Association (BLSA), was outraged by the event and contacted us. Vogel got the BLSA to come out with an entire press release against the event. They all wanted to demand accountability from

McCulloch given his coming to SLU Law and had an entire plan laid out. SLSS decided on a skit charging McCulloch with disbarment for his neglect of duty. The larger goal was to protest his being a prosecutor and denounce how he handled the grand jury in Mike Brown's case. All stakeholders met one night on SLU's campus in Xavier Hall. There, we went over the plan, hoping to make a scene. I smiled at how brilliant SLSS was to include a script for the action.

On the day of the action, I remember how we cleverly walked past the SLU Law desk into a security check. We made sure to disguise our signage in legal brief folders and dressed business casual. We got ready, not wanting to bring attention to ourselves and ruining our chances of making our point. I felt nervous as the security check officer patted down my pants and coat. In my hands was signage disguised in a legal brief folder with pens and pencils. With a security wand, a guard swept all my belongings.

Mid-sweep, the officer asked me if I had any weapons. I joked and told him, "Just these hands." The officer nodded and moved me along. Little did he know that we had all snuck our protest props in. Inside the folders, we had printed out tombstones engraved with the names of victims of police brutality. Some of the names were VonDerrit Myers, Kajieme Powell, Kimberlee King, and Mike Brown. As the team passed through the security checkpoint, we approached the sign-in table.

We had to register in advance to attend this event. Looking back, we could've used false emails, but we relied on our regular student accounts. While the event sponsors claimed that registration was in order to follow fire marshal codes, I begged to differ. A repeat of the mass response to McCulloch's nonindictment decision from November was their likelier concern. This plus the security presence led me to believe that it was all about discouraging a larger assembling of the public. The event organizers created an echo chamber for bigotry at the expense of the democratic project. The security guards divided us into cohorts to pass us through the middle room into a hallway that led us to the elevators. At the ring of the elevator, another guard was stationed nearby, awaiting our cohort.

Entering the Scott Hall mock courtroom felt like entering a colosseum. Our group of student activists divided ourselves across the room. I walked past the witness stand, plaintiff/defendant table, and the judge's bench to take a seat midrow in an emptier area. Along the way, we passed by many white men and women. One white woman, near the front, casually donned an "I love Darren Wilson" bracelet. I made gentle eye contact with her and grinned. I thought to myself, *Such trash.* When everything was settled, several people instrumental to the event, including dean Michael Wolff, spoke, and recognitions were made. Once it was McCulloch's turn, SLSS, BLSA, and Tribe X got busy. We didn't allow Bob McCulloch to speak for more than three minutes before we began our action.

One of the SLSS members screamed a phrase that shook the courtroom. Standing up in the audience, the student activist playing our bailiff yelled, "All rise!" Some in on the action obliged. Donning a judge's robe that she'd hidden underneath her business professional disguise, there stood Judge Danielle Blocker. Moving further toward the middle of her aisle, with her back facing McCulloch, Judge Blocker paused before starting her next lines.

Blocker read her script forcefully and with grace: "Good morning, ladies and gentlemen. Calling the case of the *People vs. Robert McCulloch.* Are both sides ready?" I saw many in the largely white audience grow confused after this Black woman interrupted their keynote. Behind Blocker, one could hear the *actual* event's master of ceremony banging the gavel to revert attention to the agenda. Blocker peered into the crowd with a serious and admirable presence. One could tell she put time into rehearsing this skit. Blocker's demeanor was chill. She yelled, "All rise . . . this court is now in session. The Honorable Judge Blocker presiding." Our student activist playing the "prosecution" responded aloud, "Your Honor and ladies and gentlemen of the jury, the defendant [Bob McCulloch] has been charged with the crime of intentionally showing bias by talking favorably of Darren Wilson and negatively of Michael Brown in the case against Darren Wilson."

To my surprise, SLSS was able to get through the entire script without officer intervention. Afterward, waves of the protesters stood up, holding signage with the names of those murdered by police. I held up Antonio Martin until I was escorted out by the SLU Law School public safety officers. Once everyone made it outside, we sang protest songs and chanted. We told passersby outside about why we launched our campaign against McCulloch.

Ebony magazine contributor Katina Parker's "'What Side Are You On': McCulloch Defends Himself, St. Louis Police" and *New York*

Times contributor Eli Yokley's "Officials Defend Handling of Ferguson Case" are pieces that describe the demonstration and McCulloch's reaction. Yokley describes the skit putting McCulloch on trial. The photo for the article by photographer Huy Mach captures several of us holding up the tombstones. The shape of an arch complete with black filling served as the background for the tomb on our signage. The names of those murdered by the state were centered on the tomb inscribed in bold, angelic white letters.

Just the semester prior, I was on campus studying under Dr. Olubukola Gbadegesin in her Art of the African Diaspora course. Students looked into the visual and performing arts of prehistoric to contemporary African artists. I reviewed many works such as Afro-Cuban artist Maria Magdalena's constellation piece on gender and race. Our class also studied African social pushes and the role art plays in activism. I ended up learning about and writing a paper on the role of artists in the Harlem Renaissance and the Black Arts Movement (BAM). This held many implications for the present-day struggle in Ferguson.

In this assignment, I posited that the Harlem Renaissance and BAM not only revealed the skill of their artists but also showed the role of art in bettering America. The two periods are of great significance to Blacks and America as artistic monuments, but the contexts of these moments are different, which must be highlighted. The Harlem Renaissance followed rampant lynchings and a wartime United States, while BAM came after urban neglect and the assassination of Black leaders. Despite the different levels of state terrorism, the visual artists captured what would make a more positive America given the United States at the time.

I looked into the works of artists from the two periods and concluded that in each moment, the arts were a place for agitation. Harlem Renaissance's Lois Mailou Jones and her canvas *Jennie* from 1943 fleshed out Blackness as normal and human. The canvas is an impressionist piece showing a Black girl cleaning fish. It is a painting with yellow spongy colors decorating the young girl's dress, near fruit on the table. Jones presented a Black subject minding her own business. Nevertheless, during a time of racist policies and dehumanizing of Black Americans, it was unapologetically an actual act of resistance.

BAM's Faith Ringgold and her canvas *Black Light Series #10: Flag for the Moon: Die Nigger* from 1969 emphasizes America's connection to white supremacy. Using the US flag, the artist inscribed the word "Die" behind the stars and "Nigger" within the stripes. This particular racial slur within the message is intentionally controversial for a flag that is supposed to unify all Americans. This piece was an indictment of America following a time when Black political leaders like Malcolm X and Martin Luther King Jr. were assassinated.

Looking at the work from past Black artists in both periods helped me better appreciate the present-day art in Ferguson. Just as artists in the Harlem Renaissance and BAM used art to reflect the times and push against marginalization, so did those in Ferguson. Artist Damon Davis's *All Hands on Deck* features photography capturing Mike Brown's signal of surrender. His work depicts the arms and hands of people imitating the moment as a call for social change. Hip-hop artists Tef Poe, T-Dubb-O, Darren Seals, Tank the Machine, and Ron G. used their medium to speak truth to issues. Early on, some collaborated under the umbrella DOA (Dead on Arrival) through the song "*Born Targets,*" which featured special guest Young Noble (from Tupac's T*he Outlawz* group). I felt inspired by their use of raw bars to articulate their dismay with Ferguson. They were able to humanize the uprisings through their creativity as a means of agitation. Dr. Gbadegesin's class afforded me the opportunity to wrestle with current art and its relationship to other work.

I felt happy to make the connections given the efforts on campus to explore Black history. SLU's BSA was moving and shaking during one of the busiest months of programming in its year: Black History Month. During this month, there were a variety of events including SFJ and the annual coveted keynote speaker address. Most of the events were free and open to the public. SFJ, just as the name implies, was a night of Southern cuisine and classical jazz music. I felt amused that we'd get white students who didn't attend a single Black student effort popping up to get a taste of the food and listen to music.

I was excited for BSA's keynote speaker event, which was an address given by an influential orator. BSA brought Michael Eric Dyson, the esteemed Georgetown University academic, in my freshmen year. For this year's February 25, 2015, keynote, BSA ended up bringing in Temple University professor Marc Lamont Hill. When Hill came to campus, he touched on relevant issues ranging from police brutality to the duty we have to our community. I remember seeing Ferguson activists Tef Poe and Tara Thompson, who came to support Hill. Back in January, they traveled with Hill to Palestine to show the connection between the issues plaguing the United States and the country abroad. In SLU's Pius Library archives, I spent time studying BSA's history of keynotes and learned we brought many notable speakers. There was BET's Ed Gordon, poet Sister Souljah, activist Angela Davis, coach Ken Carter, director Spike Lee, activist Pearl Cleage, academic Cornel West, comedian Dick Gregory, and journalist Touré Neblett. I felt proud to be a part of BSA for using its funding to create spaces open to the public to address systemic racism.

Tribe X got to share stories, lessons, and resources at a Black history event late in the month with the Washington Tabernacle Missionary Baptist Church on Friday, February 27. The pastor hosting the event was a brother named Rev. Rodney T. Francis. The event, titled "An Evening with Community Activists: Then and Now," was intergenerational. Storied activists Percy Green and Mama Jamala shared space with Diamond Latchison from Freedom Fighters, Alisha, and me. The facilitators were Dr. Bradley and Dr. Martin of Washington University. Here, the more experienced panelists shared their wisdom, grounded in overcoming their challenges in the past. One key lesson that stood out from what Mama Jamala and Percy Green shared around the movement is that it was long *distance and not a sprint*. They elaborated that freedom fighters burn themselves out early from rushing to accomplish goals. I felt fortunate to have had their advice and regretted times when I did not heed it.

Being aware of my limits to do the work of any movement activity so that I did not burn out became crucial to my academic health. There were days throughout the organizing when my will was zealous. This reflected in me taking on tasks with minimal to no delegation. I'd represent during CTA committee meetings and miss class time instead of asking for a substitute representative to be present. At times, this negatively impacted my ability to study and be present in (expensive) courses. While in good spirits, this did not always feel like a sincere way to express my commitment. At an extreme level, my flunking out would have interrupted my ability to finish the reason I started at SLU. Just as there were times when my will was unshakably high, there were times when my drive was low. This is exemplified by my resorting to unhealthy habits to make it through. I'd have a major exam for a class and spend more time focused on "the work" than my other work like studying. I'd pour a little Mike's Hard into a lemonade and keep it moving. This action often denied my capacity to feel emotionally available and operate with a level of focus. The best results happened when my will power was focused at sustainable levels. Uninterrupted stress, no matter how brave one is, carries a toll on the bearer. Fortunately, my people in the form of family, mentors, and peers kept me grounded.

There continued to be clout chasing in Saint Louis after Dr. Fred Pestello and his decision to sign the Occupy SLU CTA the previous fall. I felt at ease knowing many supported Dr. Pestello's decision; however, there were those who did not agree with it. As a result, this called for supporters of Dr. Pestello to make their encouragement known. An example of this was the SLU Staff Advisory Committee Board, which ended up sending out a letter to affirm the decision and leadership of Dr. Pestello regarding the CTA. In it, the committee celebrated Dr. Pestello's decision to stand against bigotry and ignorance. While Fred Pestello was no Fred Hampton, he was no Freddy Krueger and it was vital to support his move.

Engaging in Cross-Campus Collaboration as a Student

The issues that students wrestle with on one campus may overlap with the problems that young people are tackling at the next school. Challenges faced in one place are not limited to the walls and gates of that location. Whether it's an institution that's proximate to another or in a distant state, organizers should find ways to identify with others facing similar difficulties. While students at one school may be vexed by a specific complication, scholars at another university may have solutions for addressing it. In her book on the key function of student activists in justice movements, Dr. Jerusha Conner, of the department of education at Villanova University, shares strategies that some activists have deployed around coalition-building beyond their campuses. Dr. Conner writes, "Networking and coalition building emerged as common strategies deployed by activists as well . . . Cross-campus collaborations and connections proved powerful in sharing ideas and information as well as building a sense of solidarity and common cause." Developing relationships beyond the gates of their campuses created an avenue for youth organizers to unite with other students around shared interests.

When working to undo injustices that one also endures, it can be easy to be lost in stale ideas. When one is engulfed in the same people, issues, ideas, practices, and environment, it can be hard to think outside the box. This creates a monotonous and mundane outlook that stifles the growth of fresh perspectives and methods. In response to this, there should be a call for uncharted thought and untapped voices. By looking toward the strategies employed by others in response to their plights in different settings, one can open up windows toward rethinking how to address issues at home. It reminds youth activists that they are not alone or on an island with regard to the ails that plague them on their campus. Collaboration creates the space for students to build meaningful relationships that can be leveraged to accomplish larger goals.

Having cross-campus conversations naturally leads to exposure to tactics for successful organizing and humble revelations of ineffective efforts. These discussions reveal ways that students in one environment were able to get near or accomplish substantive change. If a win was gotten, students should explore and inquire about what precipitated that achievement. In the words of hip-hop and New Orleanian artist Percy Robert Miller Sr. (Master P) circa 1997, cross-campus questions should be asked, such as "How ya do that there?" Figuring out the thought processes and application of ideas that led to desired outcomes is essential. No query should be interpreted as stupid or ill-placed because it's a learning experience. Just as much as students sharing with one another, it should also be an exchange of ideas.

In the course of talking about what's worked well, discussions should also include real, modest conversation about challenges. Julia Conley, a journalist with *Common Dreams* news website, based in Portland, Maine, wrote an article about the solidarity efforts of student activists following the retaliation suffered by antiwar Columbia University students. Conley states,

> Undeterred by Columbia University's sanctioning of a crackdown by the New York Police Department in which at least 108 people were arrested on Thursday for protesting Israel's war on Gaza, dozens of students continued to camp out on the campus' West Lawn Friday as solidarity protests cropped up

> at other schools across the country. Students at the University of North Carolina, Chapel Hill (UNC) set up tents at a rally, while the Harvard College Palestine Solidarity Committee announced a walkout to express solidarity with "steadfast Columbia students" and emergency protests were announced at Boston University; Miami University in Oxford, Ohio; and Ohio State University.

The actions of students at Columbia University and continued war atrocities incentivized other antiwar student activists across the country to organize on their own campuses. In the course of organizing for change, being able to talk across campuses by observing lessons and successes is essential. Students should freely ask, "What went wrong?" or "What barriers were faced?" Identifying the errors that surfaced in the midst of the struggle for justice is just as important as locating the strategies that led to wins. While having these dialogues, students may learn ways to overcome elements that paralyze or halt their activism. Cross-campus collaboration leads to opportunities to learn from best practices, nuances, and mistakes.

Skill sharing is a vehicle for students to develop one another. Youths on one campus may have more fruitful methods for aspects of organizing than those on a different one. Students may have more creative chants and signage expressions that can help with articulating messages. Some youths may have more clever tactics for protest that reduce risk but maintain impact in terms of getting the attention of decision-makers. Activists may have more strategies for dealing with conflict in a way that's transparent and accountable to shared values in order to present a united front in organizing. Organizers may have strategies for engaging media in a way that keeps messaging succinct yet deep.

Dr. Sandra Jeppesen, on the faculty of communications at Lakehead University Orillia, and Dr. Paola Sartoretto, an academic in the media and communications department at Jonkoping University in Sweden, contributed a chapter to a book they edited peering into the interplay between communications and social justice movements. Drs. Jeppesen and Sartoretto write about the balance of scholar activists in unpacking the demands that research and organizing require. Speaking to the responsibilities of those pushing for social change, they share that "activism demands participation in events and dissemination structured as activism such as activist participatory workshops, community forums, general assemblies, popular education conferences, skill-sharing workshops, social movement convergences, and the like." Taking the time to learn new skills, attending meetings about topics tied to the work, and being in spaces where people ask questions about issues are avenues that activists take to keep themselves sharp. Exchanging talents and gifts is paramount in developing competencies that can aid in building successful movements. It provides an impartial lens and expertise that can advance outcomes. In some cases, students across campuses can unite and provide mutually beneficial support in a way that's hands on to amplify common goals. Especially in situations where students identify prevalent problems that are not just unique to their school, youths can organize together, increasing their resources, knowledge base, numbers, and stride toward their pursuits.

Investing in relationships with off-campus students is essential to deepening trust and community in service of the larger organizing project. Just as it's important to wrestle with dense and complex problems happening on campus, it's critical that students develop social spaces to unpack and lean on one another. The fight for social change and justice isn't just about the battle itself but how one struggles together with others. If the only reason why youths are coming together is because of work and there's no time dedicated to relaxation, camaraderie, and leisure, therein lies the issue. How do you regularly put your confidence into someone, and you've never shared a laugh together? How do you consistently take risks and put your body on the line when you've never had a meal together? How do you organize, and you don't know who you are organizing with? This is not to say that every relationship demands this attention. However, when engaged in the work on a steady basis, it's prudent to forge bonds. Have fun together and create social spaces to connect.

CHAPTER 13

This a Marathon, Not a Sprint

Ferguson to Selma
Walking on the Edmund Pettus Bridge felt surreal.
Joined by thousands to remember, gave hearts so many feels.
Couldn't get too caught up in the moment and swallow the pill.
Years later we still being chased down like animals in a field.

March 2015

As a part of my experience with Ferguson, I had several opportunities to travel, speak about the work, and visit sites of significance to Black history. An example of that was going to Selma, Alabama. Alisha and I got to attend the fiftieth anniversary of the Edmund Pettus Bridge march from Selma to Montgomery, which was a symbol for civil rights efforts for voting rights. It felt surreal being in the space where former freedom fighters walked. Funds were assembled for a caravan of Ferguson activists to take a trip to Alabama to participate in the commemoration. This was made possible in part through the leadership of Mama Julia Davis, a mentor to youths in the Ferguson movement. Local longtime activist Zaki Baruti helped coordinate the effort. I spent time reflecting about Malcolm X and his visit to Selma.

I felt like a kid in a candy store, as there were all kinds of vendors for food, clothing, books, and merchandise. Being able to spend time away from Saint Louis but still in proximity to the fight felt fulfilling on many levels. Before we got to the bridge, there was an entire row of places to shop. There were tons of vendors selling Black political art, clothing, music, and more. The smell of the food was delicious. It ranged from Jamaican jerk chicken to charcoal burgers, and it all looked amazing. You could hear civil rights anthems, such as Sam Cooke's "A Change Gon' Come." You could see families with youths smiling and having a great time. There were so many people from different walks of life taking in the occasion. President Barack Obama was in town for the observance to deliver a speech. This was the first time in my life actually considering an opportunity to physically see him. I did not take the chance; however, I looked up his speech, wherein Obama acknowledged civil rights and the need for democracy. I appreciated having the chance to see the nation's first Black president. This rang true, although I still felt he could do more locally with the Ferguson movement.

I felt awestruck, listening to various speeches and witnessing the connections among Selma, Ferguson, and other present-day Black freedom movements. The talks that locals made about Selma helped contextualize and connect the dots on a lot of issues. I was reminded that the purpose behind the Selma protest was more than about raising the issue of voter registration. It was about treating Black people as human beings. In Selma, the state not only responded with violence but also attacked women and the elderly. While the two cities of Selma and Ferguson were hundreds of miles apart, our struggle against state-sanctioned hatred brought us together.

While in Selma, I thought a lot about Malcolm X and his story. He visited Selma in 1965 to talk with Coretta Scott King. As stated throughout this text, few people outside my family and gang have been more influential in my life than Malcolm X. His ability to organize the masses and educate people about systemic racism was inspiring. The way he spoke out against oppression made him a heroic and impactful figure to me.

In Dr. Katrina Thompson's Contemporary Black America course in the fall, I recalled studying the Harlem uprising of 1964. In response to clout-chasing critics of the rebellion, Malcolm stated, "the riots, actually they weren't riots in the first place; they were reactions against police brutality." The language he used created imagery and evoked emotion that channeled itself into action. While businesses burned in Ferguson, my people did not become mired in that imagery. Similarly, Tribe X collectively took the opportunity to galvanize the people to rise against oppressive policies locally and internationally.

Our group also got the opportunity to hear Rev. Al Sharpton speak during the commemoration. He spoke about the connection among sexual health, Selma, and the larger Black freedom struggle. He spoke well. He's an interesting figure. I don't know too much about him, but he left a bad taste in a lot of people's mouths in Ferguson. Based on discussions, I felt that many understood him to be a liberal clout chaser.

Rev. Al Sharpton may have been well-meaning about the issues. I don't know what he did behind the scenes in Ferguson. His commentary about how people were smearing the name of Mike Brown by rioting and looting fell on deaf ears for me. This commentary sounded like a more polite Bill O'Reilly segment. You don't have to agree with the acts to understand where folks were coming from when they engaged in them. Following a boy being murdered, the Ferguson uprising did not equate the issue of murder with property.

I was not shocked when the Department of Justice released a report on the Ferguson Police Department naming what everybody already knew: Ferguson police practices were racist. It's funny because every demonstrator and most Black activists already understood this reality. That there needed to be a formal report naming this truth speaks to how little the state valued grassroot voices. *New York Times* correspondents Wilson Andrews, Alicia Desantis, and Josh Keller wrote a piece titled "Justice Department's Report on the Ferguson Police Department" about the findings in March. According to the release, Black people were horrendously hunted in Ferguson.

While Black people constituted 67 percent of the population, they represented 88 percent of those receiving use of force, 85 percent of vehicle stops, 93 percent of arrests, and 92 percent of cases with warrants. The police were clearly focused on generating revenue rather than safety. Ferguson was setting a financial goal every year and putting pressure on police to reach that number by any means necessary. It is in this climate that Ferguson officer Darren Wilson murdered Michael Brown Jr. While many already knew how bad Ferguson was, the facts and documented stories helped paint a grislier picture.

As a part of the CTA agreement, a committee was formed to sponsor the tenth accord around a national convention addressing race and racism. Dr. Bradley was charged with coordinating this effort and sent an email out in March seeking assistance. He was focused on generating support around a panel, possible keynote, and timeline to execute the event. I was thrilled to be a part of helping with the conference because I'd never planned one before. With Dr. Bradley heading the push, I knew it'd be powerful and honest. The need to continue the work of Ferguson and holding SLU accountable would ring loud.

Before I came to SLU in 2013, Black and social-justice-oriented students were fighting for the institution to open access to its Martin

Luther King Jr. Scholarship to current students. By mid-March, SLU's Cross-Cultural Center and the Retention and Enrollment Management office announced that it'd be open. I was excited because I knew I'd qualify and likely receive the award, which could be used to offset my academic expenses. Many current MLK scholars whom I knew complained about the apathy and passivity of current awardees. They complained that many of their counterparts looked at the scholarship as just another award. The privilege was not used as a means of advancing the cause for freedom in any meaningful way. As a case in point, few MLK scholars were physically involved during #OccupySLU. I would hear about applicants being awarded for loving MLK on paper but who didn't care about his values in action. Therefore, I was happy that student activists forced the university to make the scholarship more available.

The African American Scholars Initiative was continuing its programming in full force that month too. After months of hosting events and engaging the community around Ferguson and other issues, its signature event—"African American Males Scholar Symposium: Can I Live?"—was announced for April. It boasted a dope selection of orators such as Dr. Bradley, Dr. Walter Kimbrough (author and Dillard University president), Dr. Duane Warmack (Harris-Stowe State University president), Dr. Shaun Harper (University of Pennsylvania scholar), and BSA president Christopher Walter. All of the panelists were leaders in different ways who cared about issues surrounding Ferguson, with increased sensitivity to mentoring Black youth. The panel consisted of authors, university presidents, and student leaders. The only thing missing was a community voice or someone from the grassroots movement. Nevertheless, I looked forward to attending and supporting the event. As always, AAMS furthered tough conversations in real ways. I attended this and felt it was a good effort to highlight the importance of Black male mentorship.

One evening, I received an email from one of my residents about my job as a resident adviser. The student, Nicholas Jennerjohn, was a white first-year student who wasn't afraid to, in his way, speak out against racism and white supremacy. We had many conversations about Ferguson and the United States, agreeing that we had fucked-up systems. In my mind, he did his best to embody the floor's theme of leadership and social change. The title of his email was "Something I made that you may like." When I opened it, there was a video he created using the Black Eyed Peas' song "Where Is the Love." I understood the song to be about societal issues, but the overall message is around unity. I was proud of him. During this film, there were over ten clips of recorded incidents of police brutality. Even the recording of Michael Brown Jr.'s body laid out for 4.5 hours is presented. All of these scenes of unchecked police violence were disgusting. At the end of the video, though, he showed a clip of a band of demonstrators united in chasing down a platoon of police in riot gear. This made me smirk. There were many gratifying moments of my experience working for residence life. This video had to be near the top.

Reflecting on the Successes and Failures of Past Social Movements as a Student

There are many student movements, both throughout history and in contemporary times, that reveal the journey youths have taken to attain just outcomes. While in name and subject, the efforts may be associated with different focuses, that's irrelevant. The ways that youth activists were able to raise the temperature in their respective communities and campuses regardless of the matter are worth observing. It can be wins that were accomplished close to home or afar. Studying global movements in addition to those that happen in one's own backyard helps show the nuances and themes of effective organizing.

Emmaline Soken-Huberty, a contributor for Human Rights Careers, a platform for social justice professional development, published an article illustrating the efforts of youth movements throughout history. Emphasizing the need for a review and appreciation of past youth movements, Soken-Huberty explains, "In many societies, young people are looked down on. They're viewed as powerless, entitled, or even lazy. They're expected to obey authority without question. However, students have led many of history's greatest protests. They recognize oppression and injustice and organize in mass, often putting their lives and futures at risk." Youths have never been complacent and apathetic about their conditions. Students have always made efforts throughout history to assert their self-worth and dignity through activism.

Focusing attention on the power of past youth activism, Soken-Huberty cites the following eleven movements spearheaded by young people: (1) the Fisk University protest of 1925 in Nashville, Tennessee, against a pro-Jim Crow university president; (2) the White Rose activists of 1942–1943 against the Nazi regime in Germany; (3) the Greensboro sit-in in North Carolina against segregated businesses; (4) The Kent State University uprising of 1970 in Ohio against the Vietnam War, at which there was a police shooting; (5) the Tlatelolco massacre of 1968 in Mexico, a movement intended to be against police brutality; (6) the Soweto uprising of 1976 in South Africa against apartheid; (7) the Velvet Revolution of 1989 in Czechoslovakia against antidemocratic leadership; (8) the Tiananmen Square events of 1989 in China against political and economic corruption; (9) the March for Our Lives demonstrations of 2018 that started in Parkland, Florida, against gun violence; (10) the global climate strikes of 2019 that began in Sweden against forces precipitating climate change; and (11) youth protests in Thailand against dictatorship of 2020.

Looking at the ways in which young people have pushed for social change opens a window into the strategies they've deployed toward accomplishing goals. While the landscapes may be culturally, socially, and politically different, when students take time away from their studies for the streets, there is typically a valuable lesson to be received. Those involved face different levels of repression and barriers that impede their pursuit toward just ends. Observing the ways activists overcome these hurdles can inform present-day organizing efforts.

Movement work often comes at a cost paid by demonstrators, so understanding how past students have endured these and stayed the course helps reassure and recenter youths. The losses and setbacks that have happened to past activists, which have the potential to halt or debilitate their efforts, reveal the grit and resolve they had in accomplishing their goals. Kiara Alfonseca, a reporter and producer for ABC News Digital based in New York, published an article linking the lessons from past youth movements to near-present antiwar uprisings on campuses about Palestine. Exploring the civil rights movement, Vietnam War protests, and South African anti-Apartheid efforts, Alfonseca teases out the themes from these movements and juxtaposes them to that of the antiwar movements around Israel and Palestine. Alfonseca writes, "Students have adopted the building takeovers from the Civil Rights Movement and Vietnam War protests, the calls for university divestment from South African apartheid in the 1980s, the encampments of the Occupy Wall Street movement, and more . . . The movements of the past were polarizing, as are those of today, taking college campuses by storm and mirrored by today's mass arrests, police action against protesters and altercations between counterdemonstrators and protesters." Just as in past youth movements, there were tactics of resistance such as direct action associated with building takeovers, there were costs endured by student activists such as police retaliation and conflicts with opponents of their cause. Just as it is in the present day, past organizers had to figure out how to weigh physical, emotional, mental, and spiritual costs when engaged in the work. While problems that have happened back in the day may persist, looking at the ways resistors moved the needle forward in their respective communities despite setbacks can be rewarding.

Studying documentaries, books, films, interviews, art, and articles that present the losses endured by past activists exposes present-day students to a plethora of data that can inform today's work. It is paramount to watch and read material about the struggle, just as Malcolm X shared in his *Message to the Grassroots*: "Of all our studies, history is best qualified to reward our research." A solid footing in and understanding of the frustrations, disappointments, blessings, and curses endured in former times can influence youth's course of action this very day. Naturally, looking into material related to a student's topic of interest is a starting point. In doing this, youths get a lens to look into familiar issues and problems that were met, overcome, or are ongoing. Peering into the trials and tribulations endured in adjacent movements outside of the scope of students' focus is also rewarding. Wherever in history there was repression and losses around resistance dedicated toward the pursuit of just outcomes, there's opportunity for enlightenment.

The execution of one's learning helps create room for experimentation, knowledge development, and correction that's necessary for moving forward with youth organizing. As important as it is to study the historical activities of activists, present-day youth must equally exercise the best practices from what they've learned. Executing the steps that led to past successes and avoiding historical failures help develop a formula that can lead to meeting campaign goals. Scholars are going to learn what does and does not work, which is valuable intelligence. Refinement of action steps based on the insights gained from practice helps sharpen vision and the coordination of efforts.

CHAPTER 14

Early Bird Gets the Worm

Up Early Monday Mourning

Justice woke me up, not breakfast.
Purpose got me going, classes felt second.
The artivists did that and made it precious.
We'd move careful never reckless.

April–May 2015

The #MondayMourning actions were the offspring of the Artivist Ferguson protesters like Elizabeth Vega. Tribe X partnered with them to pressure officials and public servants to advance just outcomes. Mama Mix designed a crafty and substantive flyer that outlined the grievances of the #MondayMourning group. We would pull up to the homes of these officials before sunset and voice our concerns with coffee, signage, and a megaphone. In the morning, we waited for a 90975 mass text about a meetup point. This was a similar tactic and theme throughout most of our actions such as the Delmar Loop and Galleria shutdowns. We were confident that the police subscribed to the call line. To decrease counterefforts, once we met up, we'd give directions by word of mouth. This included instructions of which designated area to protest. The list of targets included, but were not limited to, the following:

1. Saint Louis City Mayor Francis Slay
2. Saint Louis City Alderwoman Christine Ingrassia
3. Ferguson Mayor James Knowles
4. Saint Louis County Executive Steve Stenger
5. Saint Louis Chief of Police Sam Dotson

I participated in the Ingrassia, Stenger, and Dotson actions. Being a student, and not being a morning person, made these actions a wakeup call. I remember the late nights of studying and early days of protesting. At the Ingrassia action, we were demanding that she support the Civilian Review Board referendum, a public accountability mechanism to oversee the incidents of police misconduct. Thankfully, the referendum later passed. When we arrived, we had cardboard signage cut out in the shape of fists with the names of Black victims of police murder. The names inscribed in thick letters included Michael Brown, VonDerrit Myers, Ladarius Williams, and Kajieme Powell. It turns out Ingrassia was not at home when we pulled up. However, that didn't stop us from making our voices heard. Ingrassia's neighbors heard our concerns, at the least.

With the Steve Stenger action, *St. Louis Post-Dispatch* contributor Steve Giegerich wrote about it in "Protesters Pay Early Morning Visit to Stenger's Home." In this article, our demands were made public and clear.

At the Dotson action, the police were on top of everything. Even though we had a fake meetup point to distract them, the cops had already pulled up right in front of his home. Officers were stationed to prevent us from even knocking on his door. We stood outside and spent time talking with Officer Rochelle Jones, a Black woman ranked officer (likely one of the few in the department). She heard our concerns. There were plenty of other officers on the scene as well. The demands for Dotson involved the following points:

1. Termination and arrest of Flannery and Hayes
2. 100 percent transparency in all police shootings
3. Support of civilian oversight board with subpoena power
4. Immediate psychological testing of existing force, comprehensive cultural sensitivity training, and training in deescalation of those in mental health crises
5. Whistleblower program that protects cops who report bad cops

Indeed, many of these demands were follow-ups from those we called for throughout the #OccupyThePolice (@OThePolice) effort back in December. We wanted Dotson to act on holding Officer Randy Hayes responsible for murdering Kajieme Powell. We wanted the same accountability for Officer Jason Flanery after murdering VonDerrit

Myers. With that, we wanted an honest and clear process on all officer-involved shootings. We demanded support for a community-driven oversight board. We demanded evaluations of the entire police department as well as training around implicit bias and de-escalation. Finally, we demanded a better program to protect cops acting with integrity.

It made me feel affirmed seeing my mentors participate in our protests. Mama Lola and Mama Mix participated in the Monday Mournings on the street. Mama Lola went to Mayor Francis Slay's house, and Mama Mix went to Dotson's home. Their participation is an example of how this fight for justice is intergenerational. It wouldn't be won behind a keyboard or phone alone, either. There was skin in the game and risks taken.

This action tested my fortitude as a student activist. It was not at all easy risking getting arrested (again) on any level, knowing that it'd disrupt my life. As a student, I'd possibly be kicked out of class. I had to be strategic about how I used my body. Refusing to be silent, I had to come up with creative ways to be involved and be heard.

I was still pushing SLU to live up to its mission even when I wasn't engaged in the fight to hold public figures accountable by pulling up to their residences. I took further steps to address the Martin Luther King Jr. Scholarship. The majority of the recipients of this award were white. One cannot put into words how angry this made me and students who looked like me. After speaking with select recipients like Jason Ebinger and Alisha, I felt annoyed that many MLK scholars did not participate in the OccupySLU efforts. How are you going to have an advocacy award named after a Black leader known for anti-racist work and produce a disparity in favor of white applicants? It was very typical of SLU. I was shocked that I, along with several of my Black scholar-activist peers, applied and did not receive it. SLU often uses the Jesuit term *magis* to talk about improvement. I wrote an article aiming to call the school to do justice to King's memory titled "MLK Scholarship Needs 'Magis'":

> St. Ignatius of Loyola emphasized the purpose of human existence as to "praise, revere and serve God," or "Ad majorem Dei gloriam." Related to this Latin phrase is the word "magis," which means "do better." Magis matters in university settings to students as they better themselves on their journey to

graduate, but it also matters to committee members who create rules for and oversee social justice scholarships.

Many saw the opening up of the Martin Luther King Jr. Scholarship beyond incoming freshmen as an indication signaling an end of its problematic tradition and as an opportunity. That current SLU students would not be rewarded for radical social justice work under a scholarship that incentivizes such work may indicate a symptomatic issue inherent to the MLK Scholarship.

The MLK does not prioritize radical social justice work but its optics. Radical social justice is advocacy in service of institutional change—not advocacy in service of perceived change.

The criteria for an MLK scholar needs a recalibration toward its supposed social justice tenets. The current requirements basically read as such: Are you a freshman, sophomore, or junior SLU student? Can you fill out this MLK Scholarship application? How well can you write a scholarship essay? Where is your resume? Let us see two letters of recommendation. Also, do you have the minimum 3.0 GPA?

Clearly how a candidate looks is preferred over who, where, and what the candidate has been or is about. For a scholarship that is supposed to prioritize social justice, one would expect more than a scholarship essay.

Once scholars join MLK, they are not held to any level of accountability for continuing social justice, and many current scholars take advantage of that. When there was an unprecedented occupation of SLU's campus, there was never any sign of organized leadership from our MLK scholars.

Finding out who is responsible for the tremendous apathy that week may lead to some sort of accountability. There are no measures in place to ensure that MLK scholars are at the forefront in carrying out Dr. King's ideals; Ferguson was just another predictable opportunity missed.

The real work of MLK scholars is praised, but often not backed by incentive. Incentives must integrate the real work with student life by providing assistance that will overcome simple limitations: retention, community, and transportation. Without any aid, a complex naturally emerges where students feel that they have to choose between fighting for the right cause and studying for the right grades—not to mention financing cost of attendance the right way. End-of-the-year-reception accolades do not come with increased funding to support ongoing efforts.

The MLK Scholarship remains a program without funding and focus required to encourage radical social justice work. The only difference between MLK and more highly incentivized programs is its social justice purpose.

For example, the Presidential Scholarship—which awards full tuition ($38,700) and a community program that provides up to $1,200 for scholar's projects—asks for exemplary academic and disciplinary standing, but nothing in terms of social justice standing. Meanwhile, MLK recipients receive an average amount of $24,000 a year.

The disparities between MLK and Presidential Scholarships suggest that if you get good grades, you will be honored, but if you are fighting for change, you are more disposable. The social justice component of MLK is rooted in our university mission's "service of humanity" just as much as the intellectual "pursuit of truth." Can you imagine if we valued social justice as we did academics?

MLK continues to struggle with issues of diversity. Part of this rests in the fact that SLU does not appeal to Black students for reasons stated below. This year, MLK received only two Black scholars for its incoming freshmen class. In the *St. Louis American*, I write extensively about how the purpose of a scholarship in the name and honor of an activist who rallied for Black uplift cannot be fulfilled without its recipients being majority Black. That is because Black students who are affected by racial oppression are best equipped to move the meter forward in terms of racial social justice. Therefore, we need to look for and support them.

Some of their struggles include having significant communal space replaced by a majority white SGA and being

> relegated to a closet in the Center for Global Citizenship; being tokenized or asked to "speak for" our race by often-well-intentioned white professors, on a predominately white campus, located in a nearly half-Black St. Louis (49.2% 2010 census); and forgiving racist insults by unassuming white Billikens. Meanwhile, Black student percentages at SLU remain at six percent. This is an issue for MLK because it has failed to live in the tradition left by its parent, the Calloway scholarship, which was established to recruit Black students.
>
> MLK Committee and Saint Louis University: We need "magis."

At SLU, I was taking Dr. Nathan Grant's course on Black literature. We read about all the Black literary giants from Zora Neale Hurston to Richard Wright. In one assignment, I read and wrote about Wright's 1942 text called *The Man Who Lived Underground*. This work helped me understand the skewed relationship between criminal justice and race. Just as with other Black studies courses, my involvement in Ferguson outside of class further cemented my analysis.

Wright's writing historicizes societal racism and expresses the alienation Black people feel from America. The life of Wright's lead character is arguably a reflection of larger Black life, belief, and struggle. The main character is Fred Daniels, a Black man forced to live underground in sewers after being wrongly accused of murdering a white woman. Societal racism is largely represented throughout the text by Black interactions with corrupt law enforcement.

Even if Daniels wanted to, he would be unable to find confidence in law enforcement because those with the badges are bigots who hunt him. Loopholes permit racist officers to work with impunity on the streets, harming Black people. Wright characterizes the protagonist's dilemma as helpless and uniquely Black. The idea is clear that no welcome space for Black people exists. Entrapped, Daniels is unable to exist literally above ground without suffocation.

There are parallels to Wright's writing on societal racism and Ferguson. Fred Daniels, who was not convicted of anything, distrusts law enforcement he knows to be corrupt. So, too, do many Black people living under the Saint Louis arch. So, too, did Mike Brown Jr. Daniel would rather live in a sewer than be subject to the danger and gaze of hypocritical public servants. Many Black people locally are forced to live in divested neighborhoods, such as North Saint Louis, in duress. In the same way that bigots hunt Daniels, racist officers terrorize communities in our cities, just as Darren Wilson did with Mike Brown Jr. Facing a platoon in August–September, I remembered being challenged by telling so-called good officers from bad ones.

New York Times contributor Jay Caspian Kang published a piece in May highlighting the work of Ferguson activists over the year as a precursor to the summer. The title was named "Our Demand Is Simple: Stop Killing Us." In this work, he speaks on activists such as Johnetta Elzie, DeRay McKesson, and Clifton Kinnie. Regarding Clifton Kinnie, Kang writes about how this student activist inspired many young people to fight for change. It is this kind of energy from young people that reassured me that the movement is in good hands. The fight is long and hard, yet every generation is doing its best to move the needle forward.

By the conclusion of my sophomore year, I decided that I'd focus the rest of my undergraduate experience on wrestling with Black movements. I wasn't sure how I would do it, but I wanted to explore Black freedom movements using Ferguson as a backdrop. It was the end of my tenure with BSA as an academic chair. Nothing felt wrong with committing to student-organized life. Being a part of the BSA in my second year at SLU provided me with another family and opportunity to serve. At the same time, BSA required a lot because the demands of Black student-organized life on predominantly white campuses can be high. It became difficult to show up and give my all since I was so intensely involved in the community. I had decided not to run for a seat on the board again because I didn't want my activism relegated to an on-campus organization. I was still employed as a circulation clerk / student worker at the Pius XII Memorial Library. I needed to keep some level of income coming in.

Reading *Assata* by Assata Shakur while at SLU was transformative. Alongside *The Autobiography of Malcolm X*, her story was captivating. The reading was originally assigned as a requirement in Dr. Katrina Thompson's class. In the text, the reader is given a lens into the experiences and journeys of a Black woman revolutionary. Shakur's bravery, selflessness, voice, and integrity were beyond admirable despite the sexism and retaliation she faced. Her autobiography provides a window into her life while making a more complete image of the leaderful roles of Black women. Through her example, Shakur coordinates a school breakfast program and even provides insights into one of the shortcomings of the Black Panther Party's political education. I reread my favorite parts from this text again and again during my free time.

The events of Ferguson intensified what I was already passionate about academically and socially on an everyday basis. When I came to SLU, I was an undecided major. Hearing Dr. Stefan Bradley speaking at a Students of Color reception in my freshmen year made me consider African American studies. At the same time, I wanted to understand anti-sexism as a man, so I picked up women and gender studies as well. While I demonstrated a lot in the community, I was in classes reading works from Black freedom fighters, which humbled and inspired me.

By the end of my sophomore year, many were locally talking about Ferguson, but there was a lingering conversation about who would write about it. This is just another piece to the whole puzzle so that those coming after us could have some guidance. Ferguson deserves to be understood within the larger narrative of Black resistance. I was committed to being a part of that process, which, for me, became a book. I understand that my voice is one of thousands. I understand my voice to not be unique. I understand my voice as being with my people.

Balancing Life and Study as a Student Organizer

Courage does not equate to popularity, though some mistakenly believe it to be so. Who wouldn't want to be known as brave? Tied to this, some may think that rocking the boat too hard or making a mistake is the be-all and end-all. Life is about learning from missteps. Everybody didn't agree, break bread, or want to be around the radical Dr. Rev. Martin Luther King Jr. According to a 1966 Gallup Poll, most Americans did not approve of King. Despite the naysayers and devil's advocates, King's stance did not falter. He didn't mince words when it came to his people, and he refused to back down when the rubber hit the road. It was what it was, and it was going to be what it was going to be. At the same time, King's bravery required a level of responsibility and temperature check with reality. He had to dot his Is and cross his Ts: be on top of the clock and keep track of what was in his backpack.

It is critical to be unashamed of rocking the boat, pushing yourself, and making mistakes during one's journey as an activist. It is equally important to know your limits. This cannot be stressed enough. When one realizes that one can easily commit to a million things, one does not always have a means of managing time to keep priorities together. Students have to balance class, work, community, meetings, check-ins, family, friends, and outings. This does not include taking time for praying, eating, bathing, studying, preparing for work, and commuting. It's a lot to do this work and practice self-care.

Having a planner or an e-scheduler can be a youth's friend. Entering one's obligations into an itinerary can help keep everything sharp. It's important to stay organized and push one's limits. It's okay to have multiple responsibilities to keep track of when students are able to commit to doing the work. Some of the heroes and sheroes in history held down multiple roles while doing the work and accomplished great feats. Harriet Tubman lived as a wife and a freedom fighter. Tubman went on to lead the underground railroad, which, along with her additional obligations, required significant prioritization. Malcolm X journeyed as a father, husband, religious follower, and freedom fighter. Malcolm managed these expectations while helping lead one of the largest rallies for freedom. It's critical to do the work and have a life outside of work. One only has twenty-four hours in a day and cannot stretch oneself too thin. When it comes to classes, prioritize assignments. If students have to miss class, offer to make up the work. Take extra credit opportunities. Get your syllabus and work on projects in advance.

When students are doing this work for freedom, they should expect to manage their everyday time and affairs more than their coworkers and peers. Scholars cannot always expect support from certain spaces and places, even if these entities say they are there to help. In so many words, students should cover themselves. Saying no is also critical to this work; as my Pops would say, no stands for "next opportunity." Some struggle with declining and refusing to commit to movement or community projects. Outside of having a full class schedule, jobs, and movement work, students are involved in a lot of on- and off-campus affiliations. As a result, they can feel stretched thin and cannot always give their best. Activists may feel bad about not taking up somebody's request for support; however, they're cheating that person and themselves if they commit, knowing they cannot fulfill their promise. Organizers owe it to themselves to give their all, and people seeking their help deserve to have them at their highest potential. Students have head work, heart work, and hand work and cannot afford to unbalance any of it. If youths say yes to everything, they'll be saying yes to failure. It's sort of like that saying about a jack-of-all-trades, master of none.

Getting rest may sound like a no-brainer, but it is not that simple. I've found that the more involved one is in terms of responsibilities, the less time one has to get things done in a day. As a result, sleep can sit on the back burner. This is not fair on activists or their bodies. Students may find themselves nodding off in class after a late night of protesting in the streets. Nothing about movement work is worth students diminishing their health and capacity to focus. Having a disciplined schedule and knowing how to manage it is worthless if you don't find time to rest your eyes.

Being prompt and on time for commitments is also essential. Being the one who's often late to a meeting or class is a bad look. Some professors and teachers may lock their classroom doors at the start of class to make students who were late to realize the importance of showing up on time. There's a saying that goes "If you're early, you're on time. If you're on time, you're late. If you're late, you're just late." This has a lot of truth to it because one should want to make sure that one does not miss anything. There's a reason why youths signed up for what they have to attend. The hardest part of a job, class, or commitment is often just showing up on time. Activists could be anywhere and doing anything else. Make the most of it.

Just do it. That's Nike's slogan, but it's also a practice that can be helpful against procrastination. Nothing is wrong with putting something off when you have time to get it done later. The issue is when one continues to put it off and ends up forcing oneself to get it done at the last minute. When student organizers have scholarships, grants, classwork, and event deadlines, they are at a disadvantage if they start working on these serious tasks at the final countdown. There are some who may claim to produce some of their best work at the last minute. That's not reliable because it's only sometimes, and such a tactic does not work for everyone.

CHAPTER 15

We Forced Ferguson . . .

If there was no ____, there'd be no ____.[1]

Gains from the activities of the Ferguson uprising, Tribe X, and concerned citizens forced the nation to wrestle with the Ferguson movement, resulting in shifts in capital and people. These areas cross political, social, and economic areas. Gains are reflected in policing, education, government, employment, culture, and health.

Right-wing perspectives on the question of gains flooded the halls of the academy around the question of which achievements were made by the uprising in Ferguson. This includes, and is not limited to, Manhattan Institute's Heather MacDonald. I felt that her work on the *Ferguson effect* slanders the good work with a broad brush of criminalization. I regularly reference Bill O'Reilly because he embodied a heinous effort to diminish the work being done.

In the area of policing, the Ferguson movement helped lead to several shifts due to the efforts of those on the ground. The changes range from, but are not limited to, reforms and resignations to reports. My people emphasized body cameras being implemented. According to *National Public Radio's* Brahm Sable-Smith, there's $130,000 invested, in addition to an annual $40,000, toward that technology through Taser International. The aim is to help document the activities of officers. My people forced municipal court revenue in Ferguson based on racist ticketing to decline tremendously. *St. Louis Post-Dispatch's* Stephen Deere wrote that in 2015, that revenue went from "$2.7 million in 2014 to roughly $500,000." In addition, my people caused leadership in Ferguson's police department to be in more alignment with community trust. *Riverfront Times*'s Lindsay Toler reported the resignation of acting police chief Thomas Jackson in March 2015. Since Jackson's resignation, there have been strong efforts to hire a qualified professional to

1. *The stated gains and wins around the Ferguson uprising are documented below, ranging from the time of the murder of Mike Brown Jr. to the near present (2024). While the timeline of the book's storytelling is nine months long, the results provided take shape over time.*

manage the role without the previous mistakes. This process has spiraled since the hiring of Andre Anderson in 2015 and, later, Delrish Moss in 2016. The lower ranks in the Ferguson Police Department also had turnovers. Moss's tenure faced the challenge of hiring nineteen officers.

Due to the Ferguson uprising, there have been efforts to analyze the complex conditions that precipitated its events. The actions of my people led to the release of the "Ferguson Commission Report," which *Saint Louis Public Radio's* Jason Rosenbaum shared in September 2015. This document contains a scathing report on the underlying racist issues that engulfed the city, tied to regional themes. The work of my people also resulted in a national call for investment in reforming policing practices. President Barack Obama made an entire committee aimed at addressing policing. *MSNBC* reporter Trymaine Lee and team told about the $75 million announced to reform policing structures since the Ferguson uprising in December 2014. My people led President Obama into establishing the Task Force on 21st Century Policing. Per the White House's Briefing Room website, it advised the commander-in-chief on addressing policing practices, community trust, and crime. Several efforts are still advancing.

My people helped put in place changes in higher education, which speak to the resilience of freedom fighters in the academy. My people put the importance of access front and center to area and national institutions of higher learning. This includes the efforts to hold Saint Louis University accountable through OccupySLU and the signing of the CTA. The attorney general, Eric Holder, affirmed our activities in a letter to both President Fred Pestello and Queen Mother Romona Taylor Williams. In addition, Mizzou's #ConcernedStudent1950 demands are being fought for toward improving the quality of education. This means improving the experience for Black prospective and current students, as well as alums of the institution. Several efforts are still advancing.

In the area of government, my people helped make differences in the conduct and mechanics of politics. This includes resignations, elections, and reports aimed at making the city accountable to its citizens. On a local level, there is the resignation of then city manager John Shaw following the release of findings on his collusion in racist policing practices. *CNN* correspondent Dana Ford captured the transition within the Ferguson Municipal Office in March 2015. In addition, a strong challenge was made to James Knowles's reign as mayor of Ferguson after derelict of duty in light of the problematic happenings of the local government. *St. Louis Magazine* contributor Alvin Reeds wrote about the goal of Black city councilmember Ella Jones's aim to unseat Mayor Knowles in April 2017.

My people led to the twenty-five-year incumbent Bob McCulloch being replaced in 2018 by Black prosecuting attorney Wesley Bell. *MSNBC* journalists Brittany Noble-Jones and Roy Allen shared about the latter's winning of a historic electoral race in August 2018. Sarah Fenske of the *Riverfront Times* wrote how Ferguson activist Rasheen Aldridge unseated Rodney Hubbard Sr. for committeeperson in November 2016. Tribe X activist Alisha Sonnier becomes elected as Saint Louis City Alderperson of the 7th ward and Committeeperson Rasheen Aldridge transitions from his later State Representative role to Alderperson of the 14th ward in April 2023. On a regional level, my people wrestled for local, state, and national seats. This looks like a couple of Ferguson activists winning and competing for political arenas. There were out-of-touch political dynasties (see Aldridge's win above) that ended following the activities of Ferguson activists. *St. Louis Public Radio* correspondent Jason Rosenbaum documented Bruce Franks's September 2016 unseating of State Representative Penny Hubbard, who had held her role since 2011. Similar to Hubbard's challenge, seventeen-year congressman Lacy Clay's seat was contested by Ferguson activist Cori Bush (and she later unseats Clay in August 2020). This effort was represented in *St. Louis Public Radio* journalist Caitlin Lally's profile of Bush's responses to questions tied to her platform.

Preceding several of the aforementioned electoral changes, the US Department of Justice issued a damning list of recommendations to the Ferguson Police Department. The report calls out leadership for the lack of attention to and care for the residents. This document, released in March 2015, lists findings such as the racist tactics utilized for generating revenue, violations of law enforcement practices, and solutions for rebuilding community trust. A month after a year following the Justice Department's report, Ferguson leadership and the federal government signed a consent decree that seeks to align community and policing strategies. Several efforts are still advancing.

In the arena of employment, my people helped usher in new institutions and means for job access. *St. Louis Public Radio* journalist Wayne

Pratt covered the additional efforts around jobs in an article looking at Centene, Monsanto, Emerson, and work-monitoring efforts in November 2016. The former Quick Trip that was located on Florissant and Northwinds is now the Salvation Army's Ferguson Community Empowerment Center. In partnership with the Urban League's *Save Our Sons* initiative, this location is a community-based asset. The site aims to invest in wraparound services to help Black residents gain footing in the often aggressive areas of employment. It has over thirty business sponsors and supporters that include but are not limited to AAA Missouri, Boeing, SLPS, Waffle House, Target, and the city of Saint Louis. Several efforts are still advancing.

Within the lens of culture, my people helped usher in aesthetic brilliance. Various art forms that illustrated the joy, truths, and pains of the Black freedom movement came to the fore. This was displayed in audio and visual forms experienced by millions. A high-schooler and Ferguson activist, David Pulphus, illustrated the lens through which he viewed the need for art to be central in the humanization of efforts on the ground. *National Public Radio* correspondent Susan Davis shared about this student, whose work reached Capitol Hill in an art contest in January 2017.

Following the higher-education trials of student activists at Mizzou, several participated in a documentary that raised awareness about the resilience of area scholars. Yale News journalist Susan Gonzalez wrote about Spike Lee's film *2 Fists Up: We Gon Be Alright*, which chronologizes the experiences of select activists in the efforts to hold Mizzou accountable to its mission in March 2016. There are also activities to bring to light the efforts of Ferguson activists in restoring joy following the murder of Mike Brown Jr. Local film directors Damon Davis and Sabaah Folyan successfully brought their work to the Sundance Film Festival, and it was released on August 11th, 2017. In addition, hip-hop artists Tef Poe, T-Dubb-O, and Darren Seals lyrically captured the rawness of residential pride in the face of state violence. Several other efforts are still advancing.

Within the perspective of health, my people made calls and demands around the effects of tear gas, trauma, and additional areas tied to mental health in light of state violence. There were several announcements and activities aimed at addressing the ways in which well-being and safety can be reimagined outside of the hands of law enforcement. The state's use of tear gas, banned in international use, was regularly encountered in the Ferguson uprising. It was a shameful tactic to deter the on-the-ground activities by activists pushing for justice. Ferguson activists and lawyers partnered together against this harmful practice in the courts. Journalists in the *Associated Press in St. Louis* listed the following legal restrictions in March 2015. In light of the harassment, attacks, and cruelty that demonstrators, families, and youths faced directly or vicariously in the form of state violence, there were regional efforts to treat the trauma and pain endured. Per the *Missouri Foundation for Health* website, the Alive and Well nonprofit organization made efforts to deal with the above toxic experiences. Through public awareness activities, experts on health called for the destigmatizing of Black pain and emphasized residential healing that later led to Alive and Well Communities stationing in 2017.

While none of the above results due to the strivings of the Ferguson uprising were captured by moderate or right-wing analysis, the work is still on. Let certain pundits have it their way—the movement left behind only damaged property and broken bottles of liquor. I felt relief knowing that my people did that. We did that.

CHAPTER 16

Near Present

Mind Games

"Born a dope boy, never wanted to go to college."—Young Dolph

Malcolm said Education is the passport to the future.
Many of my people are taught classrooms are for losers.
See celebrities on TV and think their path is smoother.
They are told to run up a check and get money sooner.

Fewer of us with a pension than in prison for a reason.
To be intelligent and black is like committing treason.
I'm not saying you need a degree to be decent.
What if the cure to cancer is in jail without freedom?

Thank Jesus but you ain't better because you have a bachelors.
Learned my ABCs in the Lou where we not a factor.
Where pain cries out loudly so it's hard to read a chapter.
Holding that piece of paper on stage felt like such a rapture.

The actors will act like getting that gown is an easy deal.
It's hard to chase a dream when your family need a meal.
It's hard to solve problems when you used to using steel.
The journey becomes too expensive and it loses its appeal.

The ideal situation is that college would be free.
Why does something so valuable come with such a fee?
They know access ain't available to people that look like me.
Rather lock us up in boxes and throw away the key.

On Monday, January 8, 2018, getting the position I had with the American Friends Service Committee (AFSC) was a dream come true.

At the time, I was working on two jobs: as a warehouse associate with Amazon and as a transcriber for Rev. Starsky Wilson at Deaconess Foundation. On the side, I was researching graduate school programs to further my knowledge of African American studies. I desired to teach and expand the curriculum to high schools because I recall growing up and never being exposed to this within an academic institution. The educational setting I navigated did not have courses or classes with a central focus on Black contributions to art, history, science, and law.

I remember receiving a call from Brother Joshua Saleem, my future supervisor, about being selected to move forward as the program associate. I was sitting in the car with Alisha Sonnier, and we both were gleeful about the offer. I immediately called my family, extended family, and mentors to make sense of the moment. This was my first time working for an organization that prioritized social justice and being paid full time. While I held several positions in the past, I never spent all hours of every week under one name toward a single goal.

I officially started working for the AFSC on January 8, 2018, a week after receiving the offer. I went to the local main office, which was located in a room on Skinker at the World Community Center (WCC), and connected with Brother Saleem. I remember going to the office. My eyes surveyed the space, desk, computer, huge posters with *Freedom School* in big letters on them, a file cabinet, and more. I felt like I was Robin in the Batcave. Brother Saleem told me to find a seat and let me know what I'd be doing for the coming weeks. Networking with previous as well as current partners and employees was the priority. The goal was to get a sense of the culture of AFSC beyond his perspective, which was already deep.

The conversations I had with those who've associated with AFSC brought great understanding to what I was getting myself into as a new member. I received some advice from Anna Ginsburg, a member of the AFSC Program Committee, on how to conduct one-on-one sessions. She taught me strategies on how to get the most substance out of whomever you are meeting with through AFSC. Using that help, I spoke with individuals like Jelani Brown, the former program associate, who shared about powerful and challenging times; Kristina Vidovic, an organizer with AFSC's Youth Undoing Institutional Racism, who gave input on her wisdom grounded in her experiences; and Program Director Amanda Gross, based in Pittsburgh, Pennsylvania, who spoke candidly about what could be better with the organization. Many others helped shape my mind around what it meant to join. I am deeply appreciative of their insights and vulnerability as they prepared me for the coming months.

One of the first efforts I learned about involving the Saint Louis office of AFSC was around the school-to-prison pipeline. The first event I would put on was also related to the issue. Before my joining, organizers with AFSC Saint Louis put together awareness and call-to-action campaigns. The aim was around keeping young people in school and eliminating suspensions. One of the efforts that emerged from that push was the *Pipe Dreams* documentary. This film peered into the pipeline, focusing on the perspectives of local students, lawyers, teachers, and more. I watched the film at the WCC on my assigned laptop and was touched by its message. My time in college focused on getting more Black students into a school like Saint Louis University. However, it didn't matter if they couldn't make it through high school. Ridiculous policies such as dress code violations, behavioral punishments, and other nonviolent insubordinations led to mostly Black students being kicked out of class. I had my personal experiences with suspensions coming up in Jennings and Patrick Henry, so this topic and issue hit home.

The first event I ended up helping to put together was the premiere screening of *Pipe Dreams*, followed by a panel discussion. I was to moderate a team of talented and impressive experts on the question of interest. I recruited my younger siblings David, T'Mya, and Chris to help out. Alisha also came through with the assist. The venue that hosted the event was the Landmark Theatres Tivoli. The first time I remember stepping foot there was to see *The Black Power Mixtape 1967–1975*, which featured the legendary Angela Davis on the movie poster. I attended this screening with my older sibling Ti. Hosting *Pipe Dreams* was a surreal experience. Once inside the theater, we had a table setup for attendees to sign in and give any contact information they wished to provide to stay connected with AFSC. The premiere had about 25–30 attendees.

For the panel, we had a host of different speakers. Rev. Deitra Baker, a powerful organizer with Metropolitan Congregation United (MCU), talked about MCU's work. This included eliminating the pipeline for elementary school students. Superintendent Terry Harris, within the Rockwood School District, led a conversation around trauma-informed staff. Jelani Brown, one of the directors and creatives behind the film, spoke on the connection among the prison industrial complex, education, and white supremacy. MenKhare Rawlins, a bright student and star in the film, incorporated his personal experiences with the pipeline. Aja McCoy, a former AFSC intern and cofounder of the Peer Mediation program (which I will cover later), also spoke. She graced the stage with her insights on the need for youth voices to be heard in the change process. Following my moderating the panel, I fielded questions from the audience. There were many, which pleased me because it showed that attendees were engaged and curious. Following the screening, we hosted about two more of them (one at the Friends Meeting House downtown on Park and another at Northwest Academy of Law High School in Walnut Park). Each time, I felt like I was doing my part to help educate and bring awareness to a critical issue.

The next effort I got involved in was helping plan Freedom School, which is also known as the Youth Undoing Institutional Racism Workshop. This push by AFSC came with a twist and a different taste. After graduating from Saint Louis University in 2017, I ended up reuniting with Brother Ted Gaitlin, as I was offered a summer position. This job was known as a servant leader intern with Deaconess Foundation's Freedom Schools. This program was different because it focused on younger ages. My assigned location was Saint John's United Church of Christ on Grand and Lee. The preacher at the time was Rev. Starsky Wilson, whom I first met during #OccupySLU back in 2014. He, alongside Rev. Osagyefo Sekou, was key in helping understand the possible roles Black churches played in transforming the community. Rev. Sekou is a storied activist preacher who worked and walked alongside civil rights luminaries such as Harlem freedom fighter Robert "Bob" Moses.

Looking into Rev. Wilson's eyes in the midst of the action at Saint Louis University, I knew he shared the uncelebrated principle of the mamas of Tribe X: care for youth on the margins. I remember my team of brilliant coworkers and bright-minded young people (who we referred to as *scholars*). Every weekday, from morning to evening, we filled the young people's day up just as my day had been filled up as a scholar at Jamison. We even sang Labi Siffre's "So Strong" to begin the day. Everything came full circle. Transitioning from Deaconess to AFSC, I got another perspective with the Freedom School workshop that we planned for young people. Before the workshop AFSC intended to plan, I went through an adult session. The brains behind this workshop was an organization from New Orleans, the People's Institute for Survival and Beyond (PISAB). This group is also the founder of Youth Undoing Institutional Racism, which is a national youth organizing project. After being exposed to the curriculum, I looked at organizing alongside the history of race and racism with a new language and analysis.

I remember meeting a group of talented and very skilled crusaders for social justice that would become the Saint Louis Undoing Racism Collective in association with PISAB. This happened following our hosting PISAB trainers and included such people as the brilliant Rachael Ibrahim, during our Freedom School with AFSC. Over time, I connected with Jessica Seratti, Angie Serwin, Keenan Morrison, Dr. Kim, Sarah Rose, Arissa Marniece, Barbara Stanford, and Chuck Smith. I also reconnected with Christopher Walter, my homeboy from SLU, through the work. Brother Saleem and I joined this team, knowing that the goals and values of the group connected to the work we were doing every week. There were many overlaps, and together, as a team, we put together an adult workshop (which I refer to above). Since that work, we organized additional sessions to educate the public. In addition, we made social spaces for relationship-building, and thinktank spaces to figure out how to capitalize on our individual and collective strengths.

Outside of the Saint Louis Undoing Racism Committee, I have worked with Brother Saleem in schools that are predominantly attended by Black students and located in Saint Louis City. The schools we worked out of included Northwest Academy of Law, Sumner High School, and Clay Elementary. We also worked with Roosevelt High School, Ritenour High School, and several organizations that cater to the uplift and empowerment of young people. The service that we have focused on primarily at schools was around peer mediation. Peer mediation is a strategy and program used to counter efforts aimed at kicking young people out of class or school. Rather than that, we encourage young people to solve their issues among themselves. Some may say we help young people squash the beef. The way the program works is that we train a team of mainly juniors and seniors in high school, sometimes freshmen and sophomores, around values and principles. These include skills related to public speaking, conflict resolution, empathy, and more. Using these skill sets, young people who complete training through our program become peer mediators. The role of a peer mediator is to provide intervention and help their classmates solve conflicts.

Schools that I attended coming up did not have a program like peer mediation in place. While AFSC's office had limited resources in terms of personnel, I prayed we'd get the resources needed to implement the program on a higher scale. The work we were doing was very impactful and offered the students involved a chance to use their voices for change. One of the larger benefits of my being involved in such a program was the ability to build with the future leaders of Saint Louis, Missouri, America, and the world. Each school we worked with has its own culture, mission, and values. Yet all of the institutions had Black young people who shared their own stories to de-escalate conflict and make a difference. We were reached out to by local organizations around social justice that sought young people and their opinions. They sought their voices on policy and issues impacting disadvantaged communities. Through our relationships, we were often able to refer them to opportunities. This also meant giving them even larger platforms to share their knowledge and experiences and learn from that process.

An example of this is when Metropolitan Congregation United reached out to AFSC Saint Louis seeking a young person to speak at their upcoming event. The program focused on addressing the school-to-prison pipeline and additional issues. We referred to MCU a young brother named Dominique for this effort. Dominique agreed to the event and wrote a powerful speech about why a program like mediation can serve as a tool to address issues happening in education that often lead to the criminal justice system. I shared about my witnessing this young brother's brilliance in an editorial I wrote for the *St. Louis American*. The title of that article was "What Will You Do about the State of Education?" Sharing a bit about Brother Dominique's speech, I wrote, "Dominic called for the institutionalization of more programs like peer mediation while condemning the mistreatment of [B] lack youth in schools. He received a standing ovation from audience members, including SLPS Superintendent Kelvin Adams. However, our youth deserve more than handclaps. They need increased levels of resources, support, care, alternatives to suspensions and a restorative, culturally sensitive learning environment."

Dominique's speech spoke to many themes and issues that adults, way beyond his age, wrestle with to this day. The fact that young people such as him have opinions, ideas, and solutions related to struggles they go through daily means that adults must humble themselves and listen. It is because of young people that I have hope for tomorrow. I thank Dominique and young people such as him for their courage. I have high hopes and expectations for them all.

In addition to the peer mediation programs that Brother Saleem and I promote in schools, we have opportunities to work with young people through tough conversations. An example of this is how we hosted a screening and discussion of the film *Fruitvale Station* by Ryan Coogler at Northwest and Sumner High Schools. This film covers the last moments prior to the police-involved murder of Oscar Grant Jr. We've also screened other films such as *The Hate U Give* by George Tillman Jr. This movie, based on Angie Thomas's book by the same name, follows the life of a young sister navigating community dysfunction and police brutality. The purpose of showing these films is so that youths have a creative outlet to express themselves and become more knowledgeable about relevant topics. Several young people from the schools cried during both movies for how relatable and tragic some scenes were. This reminded me that it's important to have space for healing when exposing young people to tough material. At the same time, screenings are an excellent way for the young people we work with to feel inspired to act in the service of building stronger communities grounded in justice.

EPILOGUE

The first lesson I sought to teach readers was that protesting *does* work. Massive civil rights campaigns and rebellions during the 1950s and 1960s resulted in changes. These are held up as advancing the quality of Black life in America. Whether the gains look like desegregation or voting rights, there were outcomes that could be pointed to as progress. However, there continues to be systemic racism in the United States.

In his 1964 "Ballot or the Bullet" speech, Malcolm X questioned the viability of any form of agitation in America. Before pews, he doubted overcoming structural racism within the "jurisdiction of Uncle Sam." There should be more literature looking into Ferguson protesters, their stories, and results of their involvement. While protests did not eliminate all injustice, they overcame many different issues. Knowledge about what happened, mistakes that were made, and the nature of the impact of participants help deepen one's understanding of the larger fight for freedom.

Historian and activist Vincent Harding, in his book *There Is a River*, describes Black freedom movements as a continuum. The rebellion of Ferguson is another wave in the larger ocean of efforts to make the United States live up to its promises. It re-radicalized the nation. Those involved during the Ferguson uprising are best positioned to describe the experience of swimming through this wave.

This current book covers nine months during an intense moment of my life that helped bring about varying levels of social change. None of my work was done in isolation or without the contributions of fellow soldiers. Due to #OccupySLU, we helped remind students at universities across the region and nation to radically push their institutions to address racist policies and practices. We forced municipal court revenue in Ferguson based on racist ticketing to decline tremendously. *St. Louis Post-Dispatch*'s Stephen Deere wrote in 2015 that revenue went from "$2.7 million in 2014 to roughly $500,000." Following months of various forms of collective direct action, soldiers in the streets made the US Department of Justice intervene. The problems of Ferguson could have been bogusly swept under the rug as an isolated local issue. This moment was significant because of the constant agitation from protests. The moment revealed the power of everyday people on the ground pushing the envelope forward. While none of these changes is the scale of justice we sought, they were all worthwhile.

The second lesson I sought to teach was cautionary. I aspire for this text to help advise youths and those involved in the work about what *not* to do after experiencing burnout. That advice is recapped below:

1. The movement is about wrestling with adversity. Courage demands pacing oneself and not falling for the illusion of immediate results. This was a mistake I made after being disappointed by the nonindictment decision. The example from the advisers of Tribe X throughout was about resilience. It truly is a virtue.
2. The movement is about distance, not a sprint. Character demands being open to growth rather than being static in the face of uncertain moments. This was a mistake I encountered in numbing my management of academics, jobs, and advocacy. The wisdom from veteran organizers at Washington Baptist Church in February was about patience. It truly is a virtue.
3. The movement is about devotion to community. Teachability demands appreciating that a plethora of tactics lead to gains. A mistake I made was focusing heavily on the misguided opinions of those in the media demeaning the movement. The outcome from the Ferguson uprising was about togetherness. It truly is a virtue.

As the old heads would say, I've made plenty of mistakes and wrong choices. However, I don't look like what I've been through. This book is complete with lessons I wish I had mastered when I was younger.

The story of those in the Ferguson uprising must be heard, as you heard mine. I hope this story helps reemphasize the significance of Michael Brown Jr. and the demonstrators involved in connection with the larger Black freedom movement. Ferguson re-radicalized the nation, sparking a divisive and necessary national conversation. The stories of those who risked everything in pursuit of transformation grounded in justice are critical. Having these perspectives will help influence the public's understanding of and reaction to history, discourse on social movement, policy, criminal justice reform, and policing.

Mike Brown Jr. was left outside for 4.5 hours, denied a career after getting a diploma, went without a headstone for nearly two years, and was slandered by clout chasers in the media. Through his family and the protest village, this child's honor was defended, and he undoubtedly became a vehicle for a national call to action. Brown's story revealed and continues to show the deep racial divisions in society. In his name, many everyday people answered a call to join forces and demand justice in the face of many risks. Decades later, when asked whom my community and I stood with, the answer is clear: *with my people.*

NOTES

FOREWORD BY REV. OSAGYEFO SEKOU

xiii ***"In the midst of an event":*** Alain Badiou, "Tunisie, Egypte : quand un vent d'est balaie l'arrogance de l'Occident," trans. Cristiana Petru-Stefanescu, Verso.com, accessed May 11, 2021, https://www.versobooks.com/blogs/394-alain-badiou-tunisie-egypte-quand-un-vent-d-est-balaie-l-arrogance-de-l-occident.

xiii ***"Every day I hear different stories":*** "Case: Grand Jury- Ferguson Police Shooting Transcript of: Grand Jury, Date: September 10, 2014," accessed February 26, 2025, https://www.voanews.com/MediaAssets2/projects/ferguson-documents/1_grand_jury/2014-09-10_-_181_pgs___grand-jury-volume-4.pdf, 60–61.

xiii ***"People are always giving you a warning":*** "Case: Grand Jury."

PROLOGUE

xvii ***"#BlackLivesMatter would not be recognized worldwide":*** Patrisse Khan-Cullors, "We Didn't Start a Movement. We Started a Network," February 23, 2016, https://medium.com/@patrissemariecullorsbrignac/we-didn-t-start-a-movement-we-started-a-network-90f9b5717668#.bviboogv5.

CHAPTER 1: DOES PROTESTING WORK?

5 ***The legal and social status of African Americans has been that of chattel:*** Cecar Pugh, "Buying One's Grandson," in *The Making of African American Identity: Vol. I, 1500–1865* (1841), http://nationalhumanitiescenter.org/pds/maai/community/text1/pughgrandson.pdf; M. A. McLaurin, *Celia, a Slave* (University of Georgia Press, 1991); J. R. Feagin, *Racist America: Roots, Current Realities, and Future Reparations* (Routledge, 2000).

5 ***The only thing that could happen to the perpetrator of the crime:*** See McLaurin, *Celia*; Wilma King, "'Mad' Enough to Kill: Enslaved Women, Murder, and Southern Courts," *Journal of African*

American History 92 (Winter 2007): 37–39, https://www.jstor.org/stable/20064153?seq=1#page_scan_tab_contents.

5 ***Historically, this has manifested into several forms of protest:*** Dessalines, Act of Independence, Marxists.org, 1804, https://www.marxists.org/history/haiti/1804/liberty-or-death.htm; Henry Garnet, "Address to the National Convention of Negro Men," in *The Making of African American Identity: Vol. I, 1500–1865* (1843), http://nationalhumanitiescenter.org/pds/maai/enslavement/text7/freeblacksaddress.pdf; Frederick Douglass, "Nelly's Noble Resistance," in *The Making of African American Identity: Vol. I, 1500–1865* (1855), http://nationalhumanitiescenter.org/pds/maai/enslavement/text7/douglassnellyresistance.pdf; J. P. Rodriguez, *Encyclopedia of Slave Resistance and Rebellion*, vol. 2 (Greenwood Press, 2007); Katrina D. Thompson, *Ring Shout, Wheel About: The Racial Politics of Music and Dance in North American Slavery* (University of Illinois Press, 2014), 7; Joseph Drexler-Dreis, "Nat Turner's Rebellion as a Process of Conversion: Towards a Deeper Understanding of the Christian Conversion Process," *Black Theology: An International Journal* 12, no. 3 (November 2014): 230–250, https://www.tandfonline.com/doi/abs/10.1179/1476994814Z.00000000037.

6 ***"for Blacks, performing constituted a way to gain agency":*** See Thompson, *Ring Shout, Wheel About*, 7.

6 ***there have been several direct revolutionary protests that occurred throughout Black history:*** See Drexler-Dreis, "Nat Turner's Rebellion."

6 ***there was a great struggle primarily for Black women to assert their rights over their bodies:*** Gwendolyn B. Bennett, "Hatred," in *The Making of African American Identity: Vol. III, 1917–1968* (1926), https://scalar.lehigh.edu/african-american-poetry-a-digital-anthology/gwendolyn-b-bennett-hatred-1926; W. E. B. Du Bois, "Criteria of Negro Art," *The Making of African American Identity: Vol. III, 1917–1968* (1926), http://www.webdubois.org/dbCriteriaNArt.html; J. L. Henry, "Letters of Protest to Lansburgh's Department Store," in *The Making of African American Identity: Vol. III, 1917–1968* (1945), http://nationalhumanitiescenter.org/pds/maai3/protest/text1/letterslansburghs.pdf; Student Nonviolent Coordinating Committee, "Statement of Purpose," in *The Making of African American Identity: Vol. III, 1917–1968* (1960), http://nationalhumanitiescenter.org/pds/maai3/protest/text2/sncestatementofpurpose.pdf; Robert Williams, "Negroes with Guns," in *The Making of African American Identity: Vol. III, 1917–1968* (1962), http://nationalhumanitiescenter.org/pds/maai3/protest/text6/williamsnegroeswithguns.pdf; Malcolm X, "The Ballot or the Bullet," in *The Making of African American Identity: Vol. III, 1917–1968* (1964), http://www.hartford-hwp.com/archives/45a/065.html; Reginald Gammon, "Freedom Now," in *The Making of African*

American Identity: Vol. III, 1917–1968 (1965), https://nationalhumanitiescenter.org/pds/maai3/protest/text4/text4read.htm; Bernice Johnson Reagon, "In Our Hands: Thoughts on Black Music," in *The Making of African American Identity: Vol. III, 1917–1968* (1976), http://nationalhumanitiescenter.org/pds/maai3/protest/text3/inourhands.pdf; Jo Ann Robinson, "The Montgomery Bus Boycott and the Women Who Started It," in *The Making of African American Identity: Vol. III, 1917–1968* (1987), http://nationalhumanitiescenter.org/pds/maai3/protest/text5/robinsonbusboycott.pdf; Jacquelyn Dowd Hall, "The Long Civil Rights Movement and the Political Uses of the Past," *Journal of American History* (2005), http://nationalhumanitiescenter.org/ows/seminars/tcentury/movinglr/longcivilrights.pdf; D. L. McGuire, *At the Dark End of the Street: Black Women, Rape, and Resistance—A New History of the Civil Rights Movement from Rosa Parks to the Rise of Black Power* (Vintage, 2011).

6 ***Rosa Parks is often looked at as someone who was "just tired":*** See McGuire, *At the Dark End of the Street.*

6 ***there have been several iterations of the Black freedom struggle:*** Richard Jones, "Thousands Protest Arrests of 6 Blacks in Jena, La," *New York Times*, September 21, 2007, https://www.nytimes.com/2007/09/21/us/21cnd-jena.html; Uhuru Hotep, "Protest Politics and the Jena Generation: Lessons for 21st-Century Black Leaders," *Harvard Journal of African American Public Policy* (2008), https://go.gale.com/ps/i.do?id=GALE%7CA192367910&sid=googleScholar&v=2.1&it=r&linkaccess=abs&issn=10810463&p=AONE&sw=w&userGroupName=anon%7E14acbd26&aty=open-web-entry; Joseph Channing and Ravi Somaiya, "Demonstrations Across the Country Commemorate Trayvon Martin," *New York Times*, July 20, 2014, https://www.nytimes.com/2013/07/21/us/demonstrations-across-the-country-commemorate-trayvon-martin.html; Monica Davey and Alan Blinder, "Ferguson Protests Take New Edge, Months After Killing," *New York Times*, October 13, 2014, https://www.nytimes.com/2014/10/14/us/st-louis-protests.html; Taylor Keeanga-Yamahtta, *From #BlackLivesMatter to Black Liberation* (Haymarket Books, 2016); Angela Davis, *Freedom Is a Constant Struggle: Ferguson, Palestine, and the Foundations of a Movement* (Haymarket Books, 2016); Sarah Jackson, "(Re)Imagining Intersectional Democracy from Black Feminism to Hashtag Activism," *Women's Studies in Communication* 39, no. 4 (2016): 375–379, https://doi.org/10.1080/07491409.2016.1226654.

6 ***the Jena Six became widely known, in part, after the uproar and uprisings:*** See Richard Jones, "Thousands Protest Arrests of 6 Blacks in Jena, La," *New York Times*, September 21 2007, http://www.cnn.com/2007/US/law/09/20/jena.six/?iref=nextin.

6 ***The same can be said of the responses from the freedom fighters:*** See Keeanga-Yamahtta, *From #BlackLivesMatter to Black Liberation.*

7 ***We must remember the suspicious 2013–2014 firing of Art McCoy:*** See Tim Lloyd and Dale Singer, "McCoy Resigns as Ferguson-Florissant Superintendent," March 12, 2014, https://www.stlpr.org/education/2014-03-12/mccoy-resigns-as-ferguson-florissant-superintendent.

7 ***The Department of Justice's probe into the Ferguson Police Department also shows findings of several racist horrors:*** See Department of Justice, "Ferguson Findings Report," p. 4, https://www.justice.gov/sites/default/files/opa/press-releases/attachments/2015/03/04/ferguson_police_department_report.pdf.

8 ***scholar Keeanga Taylor and activist Angela Davis characterize Ferguson as a "catalyst":*** See Keeanga-Yamahtta, *From #BlackLivesMatter to Black Liberation*; Davis, *Freedom Is a Constant Struggle.*

CHAPTER 2: WE OUTSIDE

23 ***"This could have been my son":*** Barack Obama, "Remarks by the President on Trayvon Martin," White House Office of the Press Secretary, 2013, https://obamawhitehouse.archives.gov/the-press-office/2013/07/19/remarks-PRESIDENT-TRAYVON-MARTIN.

23 ***"Law enforcement has got a very tough job":*** Obama, "Remarks by the President."

26 ***"Ferguson Police Just Executed My Unarmed Son":*** "Ferguson, Missouri, Community Furious After Teen Shot Dead by Police," *Huffington Post*, August 9, 2014, https://www.huffpost.com/entry/ferguson-teen-police-shooting_n_5665305.

26 ***citizens should "begin to make race-free judgments on who should lead them":*** Daniel Schorr, "A New, 'Post-Racial' Political Era in America," NPR, January 8, 2008, https://www.npr.org/2008/01/28/18489466/a-new-post-racial-political-era-in-america.

26 ***it is "used to describe a time in which racial prejudice and discrimination no longer exist":*** National Education Association for Social Justice, "Racial Justice in Education: Key Terms and Definitions," 2021, https://www.nea.org/professional-excellence/student-engagement/tools-tips/racial-justice-education-key-terms-and-definitions.

27 ***"Black students accounting for 15% of enrollment . . . made up 38% of expulsions":*** April Duncan, *Black Students Matter: Play Therapy Techniques to Support Black Students Experiencing Racial Trauma* (Oxford University Press, 2024).

27 ***"Black boys were nearly two times":*** From 2020 to 2021 published in 2023: https://www.ed.gov/media/document/crdc-discipline-school-cli mate-reportpdf, p. 7.

28 **"Brown v. Board of Education *was meant to be a turning point":*** Jasmine Harris, *Black Women, Ivory Tower* (Broadleaf Books, 2024), https://www.broadleafbooks.com/store/product/9781506489834 /Black-Women-Ivory-Tower.

28 ***"Willpower and grit may improve achievement":*** Harris, *Black Women, Ivory Tower.*

28 ***"Black youth experience an average of five incidents of discrimination a day":*** Duncan, *Black Students Matter.*

29 ***"Culturally incongruent curricula, discipline disparities and bias":*** Marcene Robinson, "To Help Black Students Feel Safer, Schools Must Embrace Their Cultural Identity," *Learn Magazine*, Spring 2022, https:// ed.buffalo.edu/content/dam/ed/magazine/2022/spring/gse-magazine -spring-2022.pdf.

29 ***teachers should "discuss White fragility, race and racism:*** Edith Lewis, "How to Create a Sense of Belonging for Black Students in a Majority White Academy," *Times Higher Education*, February 15, 2022, https://www.timeshighereducation.com/campus/how-create -sense-belonging-black-students-majority-white-academy.

30 ***"How actively does your university seek":*** Lewis, "How to Create a Sense of Belonging for Black Students in a Majority White Academy."

31 ***"the unconscious assumption of the inherently superior qualities of White people and White culture":*** Mary Green et al., "Achieving Racial Equity Through Social Work: Internalized Racial Oppression," *New Social Worker*, June 2016.

31 ***"Today, most whites greatly underestimate the degree to which the United States remains a very racist society":*** Joe Fegain, *Racist America: Roots, Current Realities, and Future Reparations* (Routledge, 2001).

31 ***"Virtually any representation of human is based on white people's norms":*** Robin DiAngelo, *White Fragility: Why It's So Hard for White People to Talk About Racism* (Beacon Press, 2018).

32 ***"If nothing else, they have found a sense of community":*** Greta Anderson, "The Emotional Toll of Racism," *Inside Higher Ed*, October 22, 2020.

32 ***"a sense of agency":*** Anderson, "The Emotional Toll of Racism."

33 ***"Outside our classrooms, students began organizing silent processions":*** Ty-Ron Douglas, *Campus Uprisings: How Student Activists and Collegiate Leaders Resist Racism and Create Hope* (Teachers College Press, 2020), 5.

34 ***"Black students employed 'equalization strategies'":*** Erica Morales, "Black Boundary Lines: Race, Class and Gender Among Black Undergraduate Students" (PhD diss., UCLA, 2012), iii.

CHAPTER 3: ELBOWS, FAST FEET, AND BUTT CHEEKS

42 ***"The more students work at storing the deposits entrusted to them":*** Paulo Freire, *Pedagogy of the Oppressed* (The Continuum International Publishing Group, 2005), 73.

42 ***"transformers of that world":*** Frier, *Pedagogy of the Oppressed*, 73.

43 ***"great teaching is about knowing that community":*** bell hooks, *Teaching Community: A Pedagogy of Hope* (Routledge, 2003).

43 ***"Teachers who have a vision of democratic education":*** hooks, *Teaching Community*, 41.

44 ***"the community provides the foundation of the curriculum":*** Bertram C. Bruce, *Beyond the Classroom Walls: Imagining the Future of Education, from Community Schools to Communiversities* (Rowman & Littlefield Publishers, 2022), 137.

44 ***"Through adult guidance in the process of youth transformation":*** Kong Wah Cora Chan and Gloria B. K. So, "Cultivating Servant Leaders in Secondary Schooling," *Servant Leadership: Theory and Practice* 4, no. 1 (Spring 2017): 12–31.

44 ***students "develop an awareness of how they might change oppressive power structures":*** Chan and So, "Cultivating Servant Leaders," 18.

46 ***"As a servant leader to students, the effective teacher":*** Joe Nichols, *Teachers as Servant Leaders* (Rowman & Littlefield Publishers, 2011), 38.

46 ***"As servant leaders in the teaching profession, we serve the needs of the children":*** Nichols, *Teachers as Servant Leaders*, 50.

47 ***"Greenleaf marked the difference between 'servant-first' and 'leader-first'":*** Mary Culver, *Applying Servant Leadership in Today's Schools* (Taylor & Francis, 2013), 4.

47 ***"Servant leaders are not about quick fixes":*** Daniel Wheeler, *Servant Leadership for Higher Education Principles and Practices* (Wiley, 2012), 19.

47 ***"servant leaders relish time with those who encourage growth":*** Wheeler, *Servant Leadership for Higher Education*, 158.

CHAPTER 4: THE SAME SHEET OF MUSIC

50 ***Robert Cohen captured her experience:*** Robert Cohen, "Woman Gassed Helped by Strangers," Photo #1, *St. Louis Post-Dispatch*, August 17, 2014.

51 ***Dr. Bradley coordinated an interview between Chris Hayes:*** Chris Hayes, "All In with Chris Hayes, Tuesday, August 19th, 2014," August 20, 2014, https://www.nbcnews.com/id/wbna55905061.

55 ***I feel compelled to speak:*** Jonathan Pulphus, "SLU: Moving Slowly and Taking Credit," *University News*, September 4, 2014.

57 ***"education is the passport to the future":*** Malcolm X, *By Any Means Necessary: Speeches, Interviews, and a Letter by Malcolm X* (Pathfinder Press, 1970), 43.

57 ***Currently, there are efforts from descendants:*** Travis Cummings, "'We're Asking for That Debt to Be Paid': Descendants of Slaves Who Built Saint Louis University Demand Recognition and Compensation," February 9, 2024, https://www.ksdk.com/article/news/local/black-history/descendants-of-slaves-who-built-saint-louis-university-demand-compensation/63-d52f559a-83da-47b3-a5d2-219f33edafc8.

57 ***"two in three Americans (68%) say the Supreme Court's June 2023 ruling":*** Justin McCarthy, "Post-Affirmative Action, Views on Admissions Differ by Race," Gallup, January 16, 2024, https://news.gallup.com/poll/548528/post-affirmative-action-views-admissions-differ-race.aspx#:~:text=Among%20racial%20groups%2C%2063%25%20of,25th%20to%20November%209th%2C%202023.

57 ***"about half of Black adults say the ruling":*** McCarthy, "Post-Affirmative Action."

58 ***"many Americans who believe that the vestiges":*** Linda Darling-Hammond, "Unequal Opportunity: Race and Education," Brookings Institute, March 1, 1998, https://www.brookings.edu/articles/unequal-opportunity-race-and-education/.

58 ***"Affirmative action is needed to protect opportunities":*** See Darling-Hammond, "Unequal Opportunity."

58 ***SLU, which is situated in a city that's nearly half Black:*** Sarah Fenske, "Protest Targets SLU Plan to Tear Down Former Mill Creek Valley Buildings," *Riverfront Times*, September 12, 2023, https://www.riverfronttimes.com/news/protest-targets-slu-plan-to-tear-down-former-mill-creek-valley-buildings-40841634.

59 ***universities have conducted "extractive research relationships:*** Sharon Stein, "Confronting the Racial-Colonial Foundations of US Higher Education," *Journal for the Study of Postsecondary and Tertiary Education* 3 (2018): 89.

59 ***"violence is foundational to US higher education's structure":*** Sharon Stein, *Unsettling the University: Confronting the Colonial Foundations of US Higher Education* (Johns Hopkins University Press, 2022).

59 ***"all schools built prior to the Civil War":*** See Stein, *Unsettling the University*, 115.

59 ***"wealth that was expropriated from Black and Indigenous peoples":*** See Stein, *Unsettling the University*, 54.

60 ***"Universities all throughout the nation supported the economy of slavery":*** Oriel María Siu, "On the Colonial Legacy of U.S. Universities and the Transcendence of Your Resistance," Mujeres Talk, Ohio State University Libraries, October 13, 2015, https://kb.osu.edu/server/api/core/bitstreams/00439746-cacf-4338-992f-ac0fd0002ca1/content.

61 ***"Black students are more than the manner in which they cope":*** Antar A. Tichavakunda, *Black Campus Life: The Worlds Black Students Make at a Historically White Institution* (State University of New York Press, 2021).

61 ***"Black students are people leading normal lives":*** See Tichavakunda, *Black Campus Life*, 14.

61 ***"students across the nation protested inequitable campus experiences":*** Tichavakunda, *Black Campus Life*, 21.

61 ***"demanding more Black representation of students, staff, and faculty":*** Tichavakunda, *Black Campus Life*, 21.

62 ***"I have come to see white privilege":*** Peggy McIntosh, "White Privilege: Unpacking the Invisible Knapsack," *Peace and Freedom Magazine*, July/August 1989, 10–12, a publication of the Women's International League for Peace and Freedom, Philadelphia.

62 ***"compensated in part by a sort of public and psychological wage":*** Stein, *Unsettling the University*.

62 ***"By the early 1970s, it fell out of favor":*** Nolan Cabrera, *White Guys on Campus: Racism, White Immunity, and the Myth of "Post-Racial" Higher Education (The American Campus)* (Rutgers University Press, 2018).

63 ***"the lack of access to higher education for People of Color":*** See Cabrera, *White Guys on Campus*, 10.

63 ***"research has found that even when students of color":*** Kira Banks, "African American College Students' Experience of Racial Discrimination and the Role of College Hassles," *Journal of College Student Development* 51 (2010): 23–34, https://doi.org/10.1353/csd.0.0115.

CHAPTER 5: I HAVE MY ID AND A LOT OF GUESTS

66 **New York Times *correspondents Monica Davey and Alan Blinder:*** Monica Davey and Alan Blinder, "Ferguson Protests Take New Edge, Months After Killing," *New York Times*, October 13, 2014.

68 ***Saint Louis American reporter Rebecca Rivas:*** Rebecca Rivas, "Black Students Make Demands of SLU After Campus Hate Crimes," *St. Louis American*, May 7, 2014, https://www.stlamerican.com/news/local-news/black-students-make-demands-of-slu-after-campus-hate-crimes/.

71 ***"Youth have played vital roles in the abolition":*** Jerusha O. Conner, *The New Student Activists: The Rise of Neoactivism on College Campuses* (John Hopkins University Press, 2020).

71 ***"The college environment presents students":*** See Conner, *The New Student Activists*, 2.

72 ***"I did come here to be a student":*** Gari De Ramos, "Clark University's Black Student Union Demands Admin Do More for Black Students," *Worcester Magazine*, November 4, 2020.

72 ***"intend to continue their encampment":*** Noreen Nasir, James Pollard, and Nick Perry, "Columbia Protesters Say They're at an Impasse with Administrators and Will Continue Anti-War Camp," AP News, April 26, 2024.

73 ***Rev. Dr. Martin Luther King talked about the urgency of now:*** Randolph Walters, "MLK Day Reflection: The Fierce Urgency of Now," Eastern University, January 15, 2021.

73 ***"activism tends to emerge when conventional processes":*** Joseph L. DeVitis and Pietro A. Sasso, *Student Activism in the Academy: Its Struggles and Promise* (Myers Education Press, 2019), 9.

74 ***"it is evident that the formation of a committee":*** DeVitis and Sasso, *Student Activism in the Academy*, 15.

74 ***"The strategy was to make exorbitant demands":*** Stefan Bradley, *Harlem vs. Columbia University: Black Student Power in the Late 1960s* (University of Illinois Press, 2009), 150.

CHAPTER 6: AN OUNCE OF THE GAME

80 ***the Delmar Loop die-in:*** Rebecca Rivas, "Protesters Demonstrate with Mass 'Die-in' Near Delmar and Skinker," *St. Louis American*, November 16, 2014, https://www.stlamerican.com/news/local-news/protesters-demonstrate-with-mass-die-in-near-delmar-and-skinker/.

86 ***"The university is not your friend":*** Phil Agnew, panelist, "Sustaining Student Activism," Children's Defense Fund, Ella Baker Child Policy Training Institute National Training, Panel Discussion, Wednesday, May 29, 2024, Nashville.

86 ***"this is a long distance run":*** Erin B. Logan, "Advice for Student Activists: It's a Marathon, Not a Sprint," NPR, March 23, 2018.

87 ***"I was told many years ago":*** "John and Jamala—#STL2039," Forward Through Ferguson, n.d., accessed December 26, 2024, https://forwardthroughferguson.org/stories/john-and-jamala-stl2039/.

87 ***"Effective activists need to be strong":*** Marie Cieri and Claire Peeps, *Activists Speak Out: Reflections on the Pursuit of Change in America* (Palgrave Macmillan, 2000).

88 ***"Conflict is an opportunity":*** Aidan Ricketts, *The Activists' Handbook: A Step-by-Step Guide to Participatory Democracy* (Zed Books, 2012).

89 ***"Conflict transformation is a process":*** Randy Janzen, *Conflict Analysis and Transformation: An Introduction for Students, Activists and Communities* (Cambridge Scholars Publishing, 2018).

90 ***"The first thing to remember is that rest and joy":*** Andee Tagle and Mansee Khurana, "How to Find Joy in Activism," NPR, June 10, 2022.

90 ***"Joy is how we gather the energy":*** Tagle and Khurana, "How to Find Joy in Activism."

90 ***"Caring for myself is not self-indulgence":*** Audre Lorde, *A Burst of Light and Other Essays* (Dover Publications, 2017).

CHAPTER 7: IF IT'S BIGGER THAN YOU OR ME, IT AIN'T BIGGER THAN US

99 ***New York Times correspondent John Eligon:*** John Eligon, "Protesters United Against Ferguson Decision, but Challenged in Unity," *New York Times*, November 28, 2014, https://www.nytimes.com/2014/11/29/us/protesters-united-against-ferguson-decision-but-challenged-in-building-movement.html.

99 ***for at least thirty minutes by "1,000 protesters":*** Rebecca Rivas, "Protesters 'Black Out' Black Friday," *St. Louis American*, November 28, 2014, https://www.stlamerican.com/business/protesters-black-out-black-friday/.

100 ***"More than 400 Arrested as Ferguson Protests Spread":*** Ellen Wulfhorst, Daniel Wallis, and Edward McAllister, "More Than 400 Arrested as Ferguson Protests Spread Across the Country," Reuters (Reposted with Huff Post), November 26, 2024, https://www.huffpost.com/entry/ferguson-protests-arrests_n_6228672.

100 ***"Ferguson Decision Triggers Nationwide Protests":*** John Bacon and Gary Strauss, "Ferguson Decision Triggers Nationwide Protests," *USA Today*, November 25, 2014, https://www.usatoday.com/story/news/nation/2014/11/25/ferguson-michael-brown-darren-wilson-nationwide-protests/70080116/.

CHAPTER 8: AIN'T FATTENING NO FROGS FOR NO SNAKES

106 ***Lawrence Bryant got a legendary close-up of:*** Rebecca Rivas, "Protest Movement Goes Global," *St. Louis American*, December 11,

2014, https://www.stlamerican.com/remembering-michael-brown/protest-movement-goes-global/.

106 ***Lawrence Bryant got a legendary close-up of:*** "Small Group Conducts Theatrical Demonstration Outside the Fox," St. Louis Public Radio, December 7, 2014, https://www.stlpr.org/government-politics-issues/2014-12-07/small-group-conducts-theatrical-demonstration-outside-the-fox.

106 ***"Protesters Gather at the Fox":*** Jacob Barker, "Protesters Gather at the Fox, Hoping to Send Message to Annie Patrons," December 7, 2014, https://www.stltoday.com/news/local/protesters-gather-at-the-fox-hoping-to-send-message-to-annie-patrons/article_7f32dbe7-3b37-572c-8463-f94e894f8438.html.

107 ***Bill O'Reilly did a segment:*** Fox News or Bill O'Reilly, "Bill O'Reilly: What the Ferguson Protesters Accomplished," December 2, 2014, https://www.foxnews.com/transcript/bill-oreilly-what-the-ferguson-protesters-accomplished.

110 ***"Protesters 'Reclaim' STL City Police Headquarters":*** Rebecca Rivas, "Protesters 'Reclaim' STL City Police Headquarters," *St. Louis American*, December 31, 2014, https://www.stlamerican.com/remembering-michael-brown/protesters-reclaim-stl-city-police-headquarters/.

114 ***"Depending on the magnitude of the action":*** Christopher J. Broadhurst and Georgianna L. Martin, *"Radical Academia"? Understanding the Climates for Campus Activists New Directions for Higher Education* (Wiley, 2014).

115 ***"What happens when we rely on conceptually constrained or narrow accounts":*** Judith Bessant, Analicia Mejia Mesinas, Sarah Pickard, eds., *When Students Protest: Universities in the Global North* (Rowman & Littlefield Publishers, 2021).

115 ***A student's school losing against another school:*** Nate Schweber, "Penn State Students Clash with Police in Unrest After Announcement," November 10, 2011, https://www.npr.org/sections/thetwo-way/2014/03/30/296714665/arizona-fans-riot-after-close-march-madness-loss.

115 ***A student's university dismissing their beloved football coach:*** Nate Schweber, "Penn State Students Clash with Police in Unrest After Announcement," *New York Times*, November 10, 2011, https://www.nytimes.com/2011/11/11/sports/ncaafootball/penn-state-students-in-clashes-after-joe-paterno-is-ousted.html.

116 ***"Activists have not been passive":*** Micah White, *The End of Protest* (Knopf Canada, 2016).

116 ***"'Slacktivism' is the ideal type of activism":*** Evgeny Morozov, "The Brave New World of Slacktivism," *Foreign Policy*, May 19, 2009.

117 ***"Negotiation, which is about 'getting to yes'":*** Amy C. Finnegan and Susan G. Hackley, "Negotiation and Nonviolent Action: Interacting in the World of Conflict," *Negotiation Journal* 24 (January 2008): 7–24, https://doi.org/10.1111/j.1571-9979.2007.00164.x.

118 ***"Not negotiating with an enemy on moral grounds":*** Katie Shonk, "Negotiation Strategies and Techniques for Activists: Lessons from Mandela," Harvard Law School Program on Negotiation, July 6, 2020, https://www.pon.harvard.edu/daily/negotiation-skills-daily/negotiation-strategies-and-techniques-for-activists-lessons-from-mandela/.

119 ***"Most commonly, the impact is conceptualized":*** Victoria Canning, Greg Martin, and Steve Tombs, *The Emerald International Handbook of Activist Criminology* (Emerald Publishing Limited, 2023).

CHAPTER 9: DON'T HOP FENCES—THE GATES ARE WIDE OPEN

122 ***"[We] inspired an entire generation":*** Mike Lillis, "MLK Receives Congressional Gold Medal," The Hill, June 24, 2014, https://thehill.com/homenews/house/210442-mlk-receives-congressional-gold-medal/.

123 ***A piece by Nancy Fowler of* St. Louis Public Radio*:*** Nancy Fowler, "'NODhouse' Challenges a Divide," St. Louis Public Radio, January 20, 2012, https://www.stlpr.org/arts/2012-01-20/nodhouse-challenges-a-divide.

124 ***"Friendly Crowd Gathers in St. Louis to Support Police":*** Tim O'Neil, "Friendly Crowd Gathers in St. Louis to Support Police, Who Return the Favor," *St. Louis Post Dispatch*, January 1, 2015, https://www.stltoday.com/news/local/metro/friendly-crowd-gathers-in-st-louis-to-support-police-who-return-the-favor/article_875d0333-d56a-5b35–9443-d4cd036b2e46.html.

125 ***"What's the price for a black man's life?":*** J. Cole, "January 28th (Live)," accessed December 20, 2024, https://genius.com/J-cole-january-28th-live-lyrics.

127 ***"There can be a range of different consequences":*** Leila Fadel, "What Are College Students Potentially Risking When They Engage in Protests?," NPR, May 3, 2024.

128 ***"Activism is how we change the world":*** David "Dirk" Smith, "Maintaining Balance in the Stress and Life of an Active Activist," *Compete Sports Diversity*, July 6, 2022.

129 ***"As the number of racial incidents increase":*** Lauren Lumpkin and Devan Cole, "The Costs of Campus Activism," *Nation*, May 23, 2018.

130 ***"Today, jail support includes legal observers":*** Rebecca Nathanson, "Jail Support: What Is It and How Does It Support Social Movements?," *Teen Vogue*, June 15, 2020.

131 ***"Several organizations trained us for copwatch":*** Derecka Purnell, *Becoming Abolitionist* (Astra House, 2022).

132 ***Despite the success of our digital media campaign:*** Charles H. F. Davis, *Student Activism, Politics, and Campus Climate in Higher Education* (Taylor & Francis, 2019).

133 ***Instead of defending Khan's rights:*** John Wilson, *Patriotic Correctness Academic Freedom and Its Enemies* (Taylor & Francis, 2015), Print.

CHAPTER 10: YOU KNOW KING; I KNOW LIL MIKE

138 ***"Protests Create Moments of Chaos":*** Kenya Vaughn and Rebecca Rivas, "Protests Create Moments of Chaos During STL City Dr. King Celebration," *St. Louis American*, January 19, 2015, https://www.stlamerican.com/news/local-news/protests-create-moments-of-chaos-during-stl-city-dr-king-celebration/.

138 ***Ti and peers protesting for Ferguson:*** Alex Zivkovic, "Students Protest at Circle of Death for Ferguson," *The Stanford Daily*, October 28, 2014, https://stanforddaily.com/2014/10/28/students-fill-circle-of-death-for-ferguson-awareness/.

139 ***Caleb Smith interviewed participants in the protest:*** Caleb Smith, "Students Shut Down San Mateo-Hayward Bridge; 68 People Arrested, 11 Jailed," *The Stanford Daily*, January 19, 2015, https://stanforddaily.com/2015/01/19/students-shut-down-san-mateo-hayward-bridge-reclaim-mlk-day/.

140 ***Through his affiliation with Karen House:*** Paulna "Ajala" Valbrun, "Ferguson and Mike Brown: A Wider Lens," 2014, 11–14, https://newsite.karenhousecw.org/wp-content/uploads/2013/12/FergusonVoicesRT.pdf.

CHAPTER 11: DUE TO #OCCUPYSLU

143 ***The expectation that others will fulfill:*** Ming-sho Ho, "Relational Tactics and Trust in High-Risk Activism: Anonymity, Preexisting Ties, and Bonding in Hong Kong's 2019–2020 Protest," *International Journal of Comparative Sociology* 65 (December 2023), https://doi.org/10.1177002071522312220524.

144 ***"Interpersonal trust increases both an individual's odds":*** Michelle Benson and Thomas Rochon, "Interpersonal Trust and the Magnitude of Protest: A Micro and Macro Level Approach," *Comparative Political Studies* 37, no. 4 (May 2004): 435–457.

145 ***"We all play different roles in life":*** William Moyer, *Doing Democracy: The MAP Model for Organizing Social Movements* (New Society Publishers, 2001).

146 ***"Bill's advice was to recognize":*** George Lakey, *How We Win: A Guide to Nonviolent Direct Action Campaigning* (Melville House, 2018).

147 ***"People struggle, learn, educate, and theorize":*** Aziz Choudry, *Learning Activism: The Intellectual Life of Contemporary Social Movements* (University of Toronto Press, 2015).

147 ***"I don't care how much theory you got":*** Fred Hampton, "Power Anywhere Where There's People!" speech, 1969, https://www.marxists.org/archive/hampton/1969/misc/power-anywhere-where-theres-people.htm.

CHAPTER 12: KEEP CAMPAIGNING, YOU GON' GET ELECTED

150 ***"captures the spirit and importance of the demonstration":*** Jacob Kirn, "SLU Plans Sculpture Commemorating Ferguson Protest on Campus," *St. Louis Business Journal*, February 4, 2015, https://www.bizjournals.com/stlouis/morning_call/2015/02/slu-plans-sculpture-commemorating-ferguson-protest.html.

156 ***"Networking and coalition building emerged as common strategies":*** Jerusha O. Conner, *The New Student Activists: The Rise of Neoactivism on College Campuses* (John Hopkins University Press, 2020).

158 ***Undeterred by Columbia University's sanctioning:*** Julia Conley, "US College Students Demonstrate in Solidarity with Palestinians, Columbia Protesters," *Common Dreams*, April 19, 2024.

159 ***"activism demands participation in events":*** Sandra Jeppesen and Paola Sartoretto, *Media Activist Research Ethics: Global Approaches to Negotiating Power in Social Justice Research* (Springer International Publishing, 2020).

CHAPTER 13: THIS A MARATHON, NOT A SPRINT

162 ***"Justice Department's Report on the Ferguson Police Department":*** "Malcolm X: On Racist Violence," Lecture, London School of Economics, February 11, 1965, http://www.hartford-hwp.com/archives/45a/461.html.

163 ***"Justice Department's Report on the Ferguson Police Department":*** Wilson Andrews, Alicia Desantis, and Josh Keller, "Justice

Department's Report on the Ferguson Police Department," *New York Times,* March 4, 2015, https://www.nytimes.com/interactive/2015/03/04/us/ferguson-police-racial-discrimination.html.

165 ***"In many societies, young people are looked down on":*** Emmaline Soken-Huberty, "11 Student Protests That Changed the World," Human Rights Careers, n.d., accessed December 26, 2024, https://www.humanrightscareers.com/issues/student-protests-that-changed-the-world/.

166 ***Soken-Huberty cites the following eleven movements:*** Soken-Huberty, "11 Student Protests That Changed the World.".

167 ***"Students have adopted the building takeovers":*** Kiara Alfonseca, "How Campus Protests of the Past May Inform Pro-Palestinian Student Demonstrations," ABC News, May 6, 2024.

167 ***"Of all our studies, history is best qualified":*** George Breitman, ed., *Malcolm X Speaks: Selected Speeches and Statements* (Pathfinder, 1990).

CHAPTER 14: EARLY BIRD GETS THE WORM

170 ***"Protesters Pay Early Morning Visit":*** Steve Giegerich, "Protesters Pay Early Morning Visit to Stenger's Home," *St. Louis Post-Dispatch,* February 23, 2015, https://www.stltoday.com/news/local/metro/protesters-pay-early-morning-visit-to-stengers-home/article_100fc81b-c2f7–5a22-a0ea-f23e590f0f36.html.

171 ***Mama Lola went to Mayor Francis Slay's house:*** Rebecca Rivas, "Protesters Leave Coffin, Demands on Mayor Slay's Doorstep," *St. Louis American,* February 9, 2015, https://www.stlamerican.com/news/local-news/protesters-leave-coffin-demands-on-mayor-slays-doorstep/.

171 ***"MLK Scholarship Needs 'Magis'":*** Jonathan Pulphus, "MLK Scholarship Needs 'Magis'," University News, April 15, 2015, https://unewsonline.com/2015/04/mlk-scholarship-needs-magis/.

175 ***"Our Demand Is Simple: Stop Killing Us":*** Jay Caspian Kang, "Our Demand Is Simple: Stop Killing Us," *New York Times,* May 4, 2015, https://www.nytimes.com/2015/05/10/magazine/our-demand-is-simple-stop-killing-us.html.

176 ***most Americans did not approve of King:*** Beatrice Dupuy, "Most Americans Didn't Approve of Martin Luther King Jr. Before His Death, Polls Show," *Newsweek,* January 15, 2018, https://www.newsweek.com/martin-luther-king-jr-was-not-always-popular-back-day-780387.

CHAPTER 15: WE FORCED FERGUSON . . .

179 ***her work on the Ferguson effect slanders the good work:*** Heather Mac Donald, "The Ferguson Effect," Manhatten Institute, July 21, 2016, https://manhattan.institute/article/the-ferguson-effect.

179 ***According to*** **National Public Radio's** ***Brahm Sable-Smith:*** Bram Sable-Smith, "After Ferguson, Police Body Cameras Catching On," NPR, November 12, 2024, https://www.npr.org/2014/11/12/363547611/after-ferguson-police-body-cameras-catching-on.

179 ***that revenue went from "$2.7 million in 2014 to roughly $500,000":*** Stephen Deere, "2 Years Later, Ferguson Protests Have Produced Some Change," *St. Louis Post-Dispatch*, August 7, 2016, https://www.stltoday.com/news/local/metro/2-years-later-ferguson-protests-have-produced-some-change/article_7cd4d141-e912–5893–83d8-fecee2d6922d.html.

179 ***the resignation of acting police chief Thomas Jackson:*** Lindsay Toler, "5 Reasons We Won't Miss Ferguson Police Chief Tom Jackson," *Riverfront Times*, March 14, 2014, https://www.riverfronttimes.com/news/5-reasons-we-wont-miss-ferguson-police-chief-tom-jackson-2612821.

180 ***The actions of my people led to the release of the "Ferguson Commission Report":*** Jason Rosenbaum, "'We Have Not Moved Beyond Race': Ferguson Commission Report Details Course for a Divided St. Louis," St. Louis Public Radio, September 14, 2015, https://www.stlpr.org/government-politics-issues/2015-09-14/we-have-not-moved-beyond-race-ferguson-commission-report-details-course-for-a-divided-st-louis.

180 ***the $75 million announced to reform policing structures:*** Trymaine Lee, Zachary Roth, and Jane Timm, "Obama to Announce $75 Million for Body Cameras," MSNBC, December 1, 2014, http://www.msnbc.com/msnbc/obama-announce-75-million-body-cameras.

181 ***captured the transition within the Ferguson Municipal Office:*** Dana Ford, "Injustice in Ferguson: Who Will Be Held Accountable?," CNN, March 4, 2015, https://www.cnn.com/2015/03/04/us/ferguson-justice-report-accountability/index.html.

181 ***Ella Jones's aim to unseat Mayor Knowles:*** Alvin Reid, "City Council Member Ella Jones Seeks to Unseat Incumbent Mayor James Knowles III in Ferguson," *St. Louis Magazine*, April 3, 2017, 2024, https://www.stlmag.com/news/politics/ella-jones-seeks-to-unseat-incumbent-mayor-james-knowles-in-/.

181 ***winning of a historic electoral race:*** Roy Allen and Brittany Noble Jones, "Game Changer: Wesley Bell Ousts Bob McCulloch for Prosecutor in St. Louis County," MSNBC, August 10, 2018, https://www.nbcnews.com/news/nbcblk/game-changer-wesley-bell-ousts-bob-mcculloch-prosecuting-attorney-stl-n899671.

181 ***Ferguson activist Rasheen Aldridge unseated Rodney Hubbard Sr.:*** Sarah Fenske, "Rasheen Aldridge Crushes Rodney Hubbard Sr.

in Central Committee Revote," *Riverfront Times*, November 8, 2016, https://www.riverfronttimes.com/news/rasheen-aldridge-crushes-rodney-hubbard-in-central-committee-revote-3128241.

181 ***Bruce Franks's September 2016 unseating of State Representative Penny Hubbard:*** Jason Rosenbaum, "On the Trail: Lessons Learned from Bruce Franks' Thunderous Victory," St. Louis Public Radio, September 21, 2016, https://www.stlpr.org/government-politics-issues/2016-09-21/on-the-trail-lessons-learned-from-bruce-franks-thunderous-victory.

181 ***Bush's responses to questions tied to her platform:*** Caitlin Lally and Evie Hemphill, "10 Questions for Cori Bush, Primary Challenger in 1st Congressional District Race—And Her Answers," St. Louis Public Radio, August 1, 2018, https://www.stlpr.org/show/st-louis-on-the-air/2018–08–01/10-questions-for-cori-bush-primary-challenger-in-1st-congressional-district-race-and-her-answers.

181 ***the US Department of Justice issued a damning list:*** "Investigation of the Ferguson Police Department," United States Department of Justice Civil Rights Division, March 4, 2015, https://www.justice.gov/sites/default/files/opa/press-releases/attachments/2015/03/04/ferguson_police_department_report.pdf.

182 ***Wayne Pratt covered the additional efforts around jobs:*** Wayne Pratt, "After 2 Years: Are Commitments Turning into Action in Ferguson?," St. Louis Public Radio, November 1, 2016, https://www.stlpr.org/economy-business/2016-11-01/after-2-years-are-commitments-turning-into-action-in-ferguson.

182 ***The former Quick Trip that was located on Florissant:*** Rachel Lippmann, "Ferguson Community Center Opens at Site of QuikTrip Burned During 2014 Protests," St. Louis Public Radio, July 26, 2017, https://www.stlpr.org/government-politics-issues/2017-07-26/ferguson-community-center-opens-at-site-of-quiktrip-burned-during-2014-protests.

182 ***this student, whose work reached Capitol Hill:*** Susan Davis, "Student Painting Depicting Cops as Animals Sparks Tensions on Capitol Hill," NPR, January 10, 2017, https://www.npr.org/2017/01/10/509168850/student-painting-depicting-cops-as-animals-sparks-tensions-on-capitol-hill.

182 ***Yale News journalist Susan Gonzalez wrote about Spike Lee's film:*** Susan Gonzalez, "Director Spike Lee Shows '2 Fists Up' and Talks About Student Protest Movement," YaleNews, May 2, 2016, https://news.yale.edu/2016/05/02/director-spike-lee-shows-2-fists-and-talks-about-student-protest-movement.

182 ***Local film directors Damon Davis and Sabaah Folyan:*** Adam Gabbatt, "Whose Streets? Powerful Ferguson Film

Focuses on 'Flashpoint Moment'," *The Guardian*, August 11, 2017, https://www.theguardian.com/film/2017/aug/11/ferguson-documentary-whose-streets-michael-brown-race-protests.

182 ***hip-hop artists Tef Poe, T-Dubb-O, and Darren Seals:*** "Nato Caliph—Even Feat. Ackurate, T-Dubb-O, and Tef Poe," YouTube, accessed December 20, 2024, https://www.youtube.com/watch?v=44mWnM1u-ws.

182 ***hip-hop artists Tef Poe, T-Dubb-O, and Darren Seals:*** "D.O.A Ft. Young Noble—Born Targets (Rip Darren Seals)," YouTube, accessed December 20, 2024, https://www.youtube.com/watch?v=fR5l5wdiw1w.

183 ***listed the following legal restrictions:*** Jim Suhr, "Charges Dropped Against 2 Reporters Covering Ferguson Unrest," *AP News*, May 19 2016, https://apnews.com/general-news-86c69 15184414734a28896ce77a3273a.

183 ***the Alive and Well nonprofit organization:*** "Confronting Health Issues Highlighted in Forward Through Ferguson Report," Missouri Foundation for Health, June 1, 2016, https://mffh.org/news/confronting-health-issues-highlighted-in-forward-through-ferguson-report/.

CHAPTER 16: NEAR PRESENT

190 ***"Dominic called for the institutionalization":*** Jonathan Pulphus, "What Will You Do About the State of Education?," *St. Louis American*, December 26, 2018, https://www.stlamerican.com/news/columnists/guest-columnists/what-will-you-do-about-the-state-of-education/.

EPILOGUE

193 ***revenue went from "$2.7 million in 2014":*** Stephen Deere, "2 Years Later, Ferguson Protests Have Produced Some Change," *St. Louis Post-Dispatch*, August 7, 2016, https://www.stltoday.com/news/local/metro/2-years-later-ferguson-protests-have-produced-some-change/article_7cd4d141-e912–5893–83d8-fecee2d6922d.html.